D0549784

# New Directions in Contemporary Architecture:

Evolutions and Revolutions in Building Design Since 1988

## Luigi Prestinenza Puglisi

John Wiley & Sons, Ltd

| Milton Keynes Council | |
|---|---|
| 2083214 | |
| Askews | May-2008 |
| 724.7 PRE | £19.99 |
| | |

Published in Great Britain in 2008 by John Wiley & Sons Ltd

Copyright © 2008   John Wiley & Sons Ltd, The Atrium, Southern G[ate], West Sussex PO19 8SQ, England

Telephone +44 (0)1243 779777

Email (for orders and customer service enquiries): cs-books@wiley[.co.uk]

Visit our Home Page on www.wiley.com

All Rights Reserved.  No part of this publication may be reproduced, stored in a retrieval system or transmitted in any form or by any means, electronic, mechanical, photocopying, recording, scanning or otherwise, except under the terms of the Copyright, Designs and Patents Act 1988 or under the terms of a licence issued by the Copyright Licensing Agency Ltd, 90 Tottenham Court Road, London W1T 4LP, UK, without the permission in writing of the Publisher.  Requests to the Publisher should be addressed to the Permissions Department, John Wiley & Sons Ltd, The Atrium, Southern Gate, Chichester, West Sussex PO19 8SQ, England, or emailed to permreq@wiley.co.uk, or faxed to +44 (0)1243 770620.

Designations used by companies to distinguish their products are often claimed as trademarks.  All brand names and product names used in this book are trade names, service marks, trademarks or registered trademarks of their respective owners. The Publisher is not associated with any product or vendor mentioned in this book.

This publication is designed to provide accurate and authoritative information in regard to the subject matter covered.  It is sold on the understanding that the Publisher is not engaged in rendering professional services.  If professional advice or other expert assistance is required, the services of a competent professional should be sought.

**Other Wiley Editorial Offices**

John Wiley & Sons Inc., 111 River Street, Hoboken, NJ 07030, USA

Jossey-Bass, 989 Market Street, San Francisco, CA 94103-1741, USA

Wiley-VCH Verlag GmbH, Boschstr. 12, D-69469 Weinheim, Germany

John Wiley & Sons Australia Ltd, 42 McDougall Street, Milton, Queensland 4064, Australia

John Wiley & Sons (Asia) Pte Ltd, 2 Clementi Loop #02-01, Jin Xing Distripark, Singapore 129809

John Wiley & Sons Canada Ltd, 5353 Dundas Street West, Suite 400, Etobicoke, Ontario M9B 6H8, Canada

Wiley also publishes its books in a variety of electronic formats.  Some content that appears in print may not be available in electronic books.

Executive Commissioning Editor: Helen Castle
Project Editor: Miriam Swift
Publishing Assistant: Calver Lezama

ISBN  978-0-470-51889-2 (hb)
         978-0-470-51890-8 (pb)

Cover design, page design and layouts by aleatoria.com
Printed and bound by Printer Trento S.r.l., Italy

# Photocredits

The author and the publisher gratefully acknowledge the people who gave their permission to reproduce material in the book. While every effort has been made to contact copyright holders for their permission to reprint material the publishers would be grateful to hear from any copyright holder who is not acknowledged here and will undertake to rectify any errors or omissions in future editions.

Front and back covers: © Paola Veronica dell'Aira; © Aldo Aymonino; © Anna Cornaro; © Caterina Frazzoni; © Cesare Querci; © Giampiero Sanguigni; p 9 © 2007. Digital image, The Museum of Modern Art, New York/Scala, Florence; pp 10, 22, 23, 56, 58(l), 58(cl), 69(l), 88(t&b), 98(t), 99(b), 100(c), 142, 143, 144, 163, 202(br) © Aldo Aymonino; pp 11, 29, 30, 70(b), 71(b) © Zaha Hadid; p 12 © Bernard Tschumi Architects; pp 13, 32, 33, 35, 66, 92(b), 93 © Hans Werlemann; pp 15, 72, 145(t&c), 155(b), 156(tr), 202(t), 214(t), 215(tl), 218(b) © Anna Cornaro; pp 17, 45, 164, 184 © Courtesy of Eisenman Architects; pp 18, 44, 73(b) © Gerald Zugmann; pp 19, 129, 130, 131, 181, 182 © Courtesy Studio Daniel Libeskind; p 24 © Toyo Ito & Associates, Architects, photo Tomio Ohashi; p 25 © Toyo Ito & Associates, Architects, photo Naoya Hatakeyama; pp 34, 92(t), 113, 125, 126, 127, 203(b) © Images courtesy of the Office for Metropolitan Architecture (OMA); pp 36, 37, 67, 104, 105(b), 106(t), 107(b), 108, 143(r), 153(tr), 157(t), 165, 213(b), 222(b) © Giampiero Sanguigni; pp 38, 173 © Michael Moran; pp 39, 63(r) © Scott Frances/ESTO/VIEW; pp 40, 110, 132, 154(b), 156(b), 157(b) © Cesare Querci; p 43 © Bernard Tschumi, photos Peter Mauss/ESTO; p 47 @ Archivo Fuksas, photo Aki Furudate; p 48 © Steven Holl Architects; pp 49, 50, 80, 83, 84, 157(c) © Margherita Spiluttini; p 52(t) © Peter Cook/VIEW; p 52(b) © Dominique Perrault, photo Michel Denancé; p 53 © Dominique Perrault, photo Georges Fessy; pp 54(t), 90(b) © Tadao Ando Architect & Associates, photos Mitsuo Matsuoka; p 54(b) © Bernard Tschumi, photos Pinkster & Tahl; pp 55, 86, 221 © Shinkenchiku-sha; p 57 © Mattia Morgavi – HSL; p 58(b) © James Morris; p 58(tr) © RPBW, photo Berengo Gardin Gianni; p 59(t) © Fernando Alda/CORBIS; pp 059(b), 153(b) © Rogers Stirk Harbour + Partners; p 60 © Courtesy Venturi, Scott Brown and Associates, Inc, photo Matt Wardo; pp 61(l), 76, 91, 150(t), 160(b), 170(b), 172 © Duccio Malagamba; p 61(r), 87(b) © Hisao Suzuki; p 62 © Photograph courtesy of Pei Cobb Freed/John Nye; p 63(l) © Harald A Jahn/CORBIS; p 68 © Jeff Goldberg/ESTO/VIEW; pp 69(b), 70(t), 71(t), 160(t) © Hélène Binet; p 73(t) © Odile Decq Benoît Cornette, photo Georges Fessy and Xavier Testelin; p 74 © Young Il-Kim; p 75 ©

Christian Kandzia; pp 77, 78 © Gaetano Pesce Studio New York; p 79 © Atelier Mendini; pp 81, 90(t), 133, 134, 186, 202(bl), 203(t), 210(b), 211, 212(t) © Philippe Ruault; pp 85(t), 105(t), 106(b), 107(t), 151(t), 200(bl), 205(t), 220 © Christian Richters; p 85(b) © Heinrich Helfenstein, Atelier für Architektur fotografie GmbH; pp 87(t), 207 © Richard Bryant (arcaid@arcaid.co.uk); pp 88(c), 100(b) © Paola Veronica dell'Aira; p 89 © Hufton+Crow/VIEW; p 96 © Jakob + Macfarlane; p 98(b) © Werner Huthmacher/Artur/VIEW; p 99(t) © Peter Cook/VIEW; p 100(t) © Akio Kawasumi; p 101 © RPBW, photo Kawatetsu; p 102 © SMC Alsop; p 103 © RPBW, photo Michel Denancé; pp 109, 147, 216(t) © NOX/Lars Spuybroek; p 114 © 2005. Digital Image, Timothy Hursley/The Museum of Modern Art, New York/Scala, Florence; pp 115, 201 © Toyo Ito & Associates, Architects; pp 118, 119 © Yann Arthus-Bertrand/CORBIS; p 120 © Jose Fuste Raga/CORBIS; pp 121, 122, 123 © Gehry Partners LLP; pp 135, 136 © Hariri & Hariri – Architecture; p 137 © Preston Scott Cohen; pp 139, 141 © UNStudio; pp 140, 223(b), 224(br) © UNStudio, photos Christian Richters; p 145(b) © Satoru Mishima; p 150(b) © Eduard Hueber/archphoto.com; pp 151(b), 152 © Nigel Young/Foster + Partners; pp 153 (tl), 213(t) Richard Davies; pp 154(t), 216(cr) © Edmund Sumner/VIEW; p 155(t) © RPBW, photo John Gollings; p 156(tl) © Toyo Ito & Associates, Architects, photo Nacasa & Partners; p 158 © Emilio Ambasz, photo Hiromi Watanabe; p 159 © Claudio Lucchesi; pp 161, 204 © Roland Halbe; p 166 © Paul Warchol; p 167(t) © Greg Lynn FORM; p 167(b) © Asymptote, photos Eduard Hueber; p 168(t) © Courtesy RUR Architecture; p 168(b) © Greg Lynn FORM, photo Jan Staller; p 169(t) © SMC Alsop, photo Roderick Coyne; p 169(b) © SHoP Architects; p 170(t) © Karl Chu; p 183 © Rafael Viñoly Architects, PC; pp 187, 209 © Diller Scofidio + Renfro; p 189 © RPBW, photo Serge Drouin; pp 190, 192 © Michel Denancé; pp 199, 200(t) © Caterina Frazzoni; p 200(br) © Gerhard Hagen/Artur/VIEW; p 205(b) © Paolo Riolzi ; p 206(t) © Archivo Fuksas; p 206(b) © Maurizio Marcato Photographer; p 208 © Werner Huthmacher; p 210(t) © Albert Verceka/ESTO/VIEW; p 212(b) © Acconci Studio; p 214(b) © SMC Alsop, photo Richard Johnson; p 215(tr) © Roland Halbe/Artur/VIEW; p 215(b) © Mansilla y Tuñón Arquitectos, photo Luis Asin; pp 216(cl), 222(t) © Paul Raftery/VIEW; p 217(t) © Art on File/CORBIS; p 217(c) © Mathias Klotz; p 217(b) © AEDS Ammar Eloueini Digit-all Studio; p 218(t) © Exposure Architects; p 219(t) © Courtesy David Chipperfield Architects and Des Moines Public Library, photo Farshid Assassi; p 219(b) © Paul Smoothy; p 223(t) © JDS Architects, photo Paolo Rosselli; p 224(t&bl) © Mario Cucinella

009 1    After Deconstructivism 1988–92

009 1.1 Precedents
016 1.2 Deconstructivist Architecture
022 1.3 A New Paradigm
028 1.4 Zaha and the Game of Opposites
031 1.5 Rem Koolhaas: Method and its Paradoxes
037 1.6 Frank O Gehry: New Compositions
041 1.7 Disjunction and Dis-location
046 1.8 Between Gesture and Perception:
      Fuksas and Holl
048 1.9 The Minimalist Approach:
      Herzog & de Meuron
051 1.10 Minimalism in England, France and Japan
055 1.11 The Development of High Tech
060 1.12 Post-Modernism and Modernism Continued
063 1.13 The Inheritance of Deconstructivism

065 2    New Directions: 1993–7

065 2.1 The Turning Point
068 2.2 Explosive Buildings
072 2.3 Los Angeles, Graz and Barcelona
077 2.4 The Radicals and Coop Himmelb(l)au
079 2.5 Nouvel: Beyond Transparency
082 2.6 Herzog & de Meuron and the
      Skin of the Building
085 2.7 Minimalisms
087 2.8 Questions of Perception
091 2.9 Koolhaas: Euralille
094 2.10 The Poetics of the Electronic:
      Between the Blob and the Metaphor
098 2.11 Eco-Tech
101 2.12 Renzo Piano's Soft-Tech
104 2.13 PAYS-BAS_perspectives
109 2.14 Pro and Versus a New Architecture
112 2.15 The MoMA Extension
115 2.16 The Beginnings of a New Season

**117 3    A Season of Masterpieces: 1998–2001**

117  3.1  The Guggenheim in Bilbao by Frank O Gehry

124  3.2  The House in Floriac by Rem Koolhaas

129  3.3  The Jewish Museum in Berlin
          by Daniel Libeskind

133  3.4  The KKL in Lucerne by Jean Nouvel

135  3.5  The Un-Private House

139  3.6  The Möbius House

142  3.7  A Dutchness in the State of Architecture

147  3.8  New Landscapes, New Languages

162  3.9  New Landscape: The West and East Coast

166  3.10 A New Avant-Garde

170  3.11 Landscapes or Aesthetic Objects?

174  3.12 Aesthetics, Ethics and Mutations

177  3.13 The Eleventh of September
          Two Thousand and One

179  3.14 Starting Over

**181 4    Trends: 2002–7**

181  4.1  The World Trade Center

185  4.2  Clouds and Monoliths

187  4.3  The Star System

192  4.4  The Crisis of the Star System

195  4.5  The Crisis of Architectural Criticism

198  4.6  The End of the Star System?

199  4.7  Ten Projects

212  4.8  Super-Creativity and Ultra-Minimalism

217  4.9  Back to Basics

222  4.10 The Next Stop

**225      Timeline**

**232      Bibliography**

**236      Index**

# Acknowledgements

Special thanks to Helen Castle, the Commissioning Editor on the UK architecture list at John Wiley & Sons, for her intelligent, tenacious and competent assistance in making this book a reality. I would also like to thank the rest of the staff at Wiley for their assistance in producing and editing this book, particularly Project Editor Miriam Swift; freelance editor Caroline Ellerby for her invaluable assistance in researching the images; and freelance designer Karen Willcox (aleatoria.com) for her innovative design.

My heartfelt thanks to Paul Blackmore, with whom I have been working for many years who, as always, has translated the original Italian text with care, competence and skill.

I must also thank the various photographers, architects and foundations who have allowed me to use their images, especially my friends: Aldo Aymonino, Anna Cornaro, Paola Dell´Aira, Alessandro D´Onofrio, Caterina Frazzoni, Nicolas Nebiolo, Cesare Querci and Giampiero Sanguigni.

This book is dedicated to Antonella, luce dei miei occhi.

1 Coop Himmelb(l)au, founded in 1968 by Wolf D Prix (born 1942), Helmut Swiczinsky (born 1944) and Rainer Michael Holzer (who left the group in 1971), have been characterised since the outset by their radical ideas, such as rendered concrete in their proposals for spatial constructions made from lightweight and plastic materials or installations based on the presupposition that architecture should represent, through works that are capable of generating immediate emotive feedback, the tensions and contradictions of the context within which the work is located. Peter Eisenman (born 1932) is an architect who, since his earliest works, has proposed a theoretical approach that leads him to consider architecture as a construction which is articulated through the rigorous assembly of abstract forms, beginning with a set of arbitrarily chosen rules. The author of numerous theoretical texts, he was the director of the Institute for Architecture and Urban Studies (IAUS), which he helped to found, from 1967 to 1982, and from 1973 to 1981 he was one of the directors of *Oppositions*, a magazine that actively promoted architectural debate, publishing articles by, amongst others, Koolhaas and Tschumi. Frank O Gehry (born 1929), unlike Eisenman, avoids any confrontation with abstract theoretical issues. During the 1970s he completed projects that became known for their articulated and playful forms and, at the same time, their unfinished appearance, obtained using poor and unusual materials and exposed wooden structures. Zaha Hadid (born 1950) studied at the Architectural Association and later, between 1977 and 1980, worked for the Office for Metropolitan Architecture (OMA), with Elia Zenghelis and Rem Koolhaas. Prior to the exhibition, her projects were known for their powerful expressive force and dynamic presentation. Rem Koolhaas (born 1944) founded OMA in 1975, quickly becoming its singular point of reference. In 1978 he published *Deliri-ous New York*, a highly idiosyncratic book, in which he re-evaluates the metropolis and the aesthetic of congestion. Daniel Libeskind (born 1946) was a professor at Cooper Union in New York, the Architectural Association in London and the Cranbrook Academy of Art in Bloomfield Hills, Michigan. Prior to 1988 he had already been designing projects composed of fragmented and disarticulated forms that made reference to obscure theoretical texts and are not without references to structuralist and post-structuralist philosophies. Also influenced by these themes is Bernard Tschumi (born 1944) who, at the time of the 'Deconstructivist Architecture' exhibition, was known for his teaching activities at the Architectural Association in London and his theoretical writings in which he proposed an architecture that went beyond its own limits to emotionally and intellectually stimulate its users.

# AFTER DECONSTRUCTIVISM: 1988–92

## 1.1 Precedents

'Deconstructivist Architecture' opened on 23 June 1988 at the Museum of Modern Art (MoMA) in New York. The exhibition presented the work of seven offices which at the time were not particularly well known internationally. They were: Coop Himmelb(l)au, Peter Eisenman, Frank O Gehry, Zaha Hadid, Rem Koolhaas, Daniel Libeskind and Bernard Tschumi.[1]

The show, as we will see later, was successful enough to launch a new style: Deconstructivism. Deconstruction can be characterised by its captivating spatial experimentation: the invention of complex and articulated forms with a highly sculptural impact; by the use of new building materials; by references to the poetics of the incomplete; and by a preoccupation with the imbalanced and the precarious. Furthermore, Decon-

structivism defined the end of the Post-Modern period in architecture. Unlike the direct spatial involvement of Deconstructivism, the Post-Modern favoured a more contemplative and cerebral approach. It frequently featured consolidated images and simple, stereometric forms, which were enriched by decorative and figurative elements – such as pediments, column capitals, arches – that were more often than not historical.[2]

The 'Deconstructivist Architecture' show did no more than group together a variety of formal investigations in design under a single label. Initially periodic, these explorations intensified during the 1980s. In fact, even by 1978 Gehry had already completed the addition to his own home in Santa Monica, California, which was to become synonymous with the 'Deconstructivist Architecture' exhibition and the style it advocated. Using sheet metal and chain-link fencing, the house's construction played with the contrast between interior and exterior, old and new, and finished and unfinished. The year 1983 had witnessed the competition designs

**Catalogue cover of 'Deconstructivist Architecture' exhibition, Museum of Modern Art, New York, USA, 1988.**

The exhibition, curated by Philip Johnson and Mark Wigley, opened on 23 June 1998 at the MoMA, launching a new style that took the place of Post-Modernism: Deconstructivism. Seven offices were invited: Coop Himmelb(l)au, Peter Eisenman, Frank O Gehry, Zaha Hadid, Rem Koolhaas, Daniel Libeskind and Bernard Tschumi.

2 The Post-Modern trend in architecture was theorised by Charles Jencks in his famous book entitled *The Language of Post-Modern Architecture*, Academy Editions (London) and Rizzoli International Publications Inc (New York), 1977. In this book the American-born, English-based critic introduces the notion of 'double coding' – that is, a language with two levels of meaning: a deeper one for a more sophisticated public, and another, more immediate, for the average person. It is structured around the recovery of architectural ⋯⋯⋯⋯

**Frank O Gehry, House in Santa Monica, California, USA, 1978–9: exterior view.**

The addition to Gehry's house, completed in 1978, in the midst of the Post-Modern period, anticipated Deconstructivism in the use of its unusual forms, poor materials and the choice to highlight, instead of hiding, the contrast between the new and the old. It was one of the works presented at the MoMA in 1988.

for The Peak in Hong Kong and the new Parc de la Villette in Paris. The first was won, to everyone's surprise, by a 33-year-old Zaha Hadid, whose project appeared to skim across the surface of its hilly site; in contrast the Parc de la Villette was characterised by the juxtaposition of order and chaos, generated by the overlapping of internally coherent but unrelated functional layers. It was a design strategy proposed both in the winning project by Tschumi and in the competition entry by Koolhaas. Once again, at the beginning of the 1980s, Coop Himmelb(l)au had produced a series of highly expressive projects, including a fragmented apartment complex in Vienna[3] and a manifesto entitled *Capturing Architecture in Words* that, amongst other things, stated: 'We do not believe in the architectural dogmas which try to put us back in the nineteenth century and – not coincidentally – always speak of closing down... We do not want any closed, confined square, any closed, confined house, any closed, confined street, any closed, confined minds, any closed, confined philosophy.'[4]

Furthermore, back in August 1986 the *Architectural Review* had already sensed the new cultural climate, publishing a monographic number emblematically entitled 'The New Spirit'.[5] The introduction by Elizabeth M Farrelly read: 'Post-Modernism is dead. Some have

elements that, over the course of history, have become part of the collective imagination and thus, at an elementary level, can be deciphered by anyone – although, under further analysis, they reveal themselves to be rich and complex with meaning. However, this also generates the negative consequence of an excessive recourse to references to the past and the 'Disneyland' effect of so many works of Post-Modern architecture. It should be noted that the term 'postmodern' was also used in a broader

sense to indicate an approach that, in the field of art, culture and theory, created a situation of crisis for the presuppositions of modern culture, without entirely overcoming them with a new one. One text that seeks to define postmodernism from this point of view is Fredric Jameson's *Postmodernism: Or, The Cultural Logic of Late Capitalism*, Verso (London), 1991.
3 The project, designed in 1983 and known as Vienna2, is a complex of 50 low-cost apartments that were to have been co-operatively owned and built by

their inhabitants.
4 Coop Himmelb(l)au, 'A Manifesto: Capturing Architecture in Words' (1984), in *The Architectural Review*, no 1074 (August 1986), p 19.
5 *The Architectural Review*, no 1074 (August 1986).

**Zaha Hadid, The Peak, Hong Kong, competition, 1982–3: axonometric site plan.**

With this project, organised by volumes that seem to float freely in space, the 33-year-old Zaha Hadid won the competition for a new recreational centre on the mountain that overlooks the Hong Kong Harbour. Though it was never built, it contributed to Hadid's international fame.

6 EM Farrelly, 'The New Spirit', in *The Architectural Review*, no 1074 (August 1986), pp 7–8.

known from the start that it was no more than a painted corpse, but for others it has taken a little longer... Now, however something else is happening. Something new. After the relentless ossification of the Post-Modern era things are beginning to stir again. Like the first breath of spring after a long and stultifying winter, these first stirrings are signs of hope.'[6]

For Farrelly, Post-Modernism, even while produced by a real need for innovation,[7] had quickly been transformed into a 'meaningless mannerist charade', if not an annoyingly static, symmetric, heavy and stylistically confused academia. In opposition to this classical and conservative attitude, the renaissance taking place appeared to be related to a vigorous, vital and romantic approach, an attempt to translate, into a language of forms, the complexity and contradictions of the world, rather than hiding behind a system of pre-established rules. This was similar to what the most interesting protagonists of the Modern Movement had been able to do at the beginning of the 1900s, and unlike what those who followed them had done after the Second World War in the name of the canons of the International Style,[8] translating the research of their masters in exclusively formal and stylistic terms.

Another important figure to have defined this phenomenon was Peter Cook, in his article entitled 'At last! Architecture is on the wing again'.[9]

7 In truth Post-Modernism is the result of a desperate reaction, in the name of complexity and the recovery of the values of tradition, against the coldness and uniformity of the works of Modernist architecture built during the 1950s and '60s in the so-called International Style. In this sense Robert Venturi's *Complexity and Contradiction in Architecture*, MoMA (New York), 1966 and *Learning From Las Vegas*, The MIT Press (Cambridge, MA and London), 1972, written with Denise Scott Brown and Steven Izenour, are worthy for their ability to propose a complex and contradictory language that can be compared with the average person's taste. What is more, books such as Aldo Rossi's *L'architettura della città*, Marsilio (Venice), 1966, translated as *The Architecture of the City*, Opposition Books, The MIT Press (Cambridge, MA and London), 1984, refocus the attention of the design process on the theme of the relationship with history and the insertion of architecture within its urban context. The aforementioned text by Charles Jencks, *The Language of Post-Modern Architecture*, proposes a more sophisticated attitude that was later employed by many Post-Modern architects and – as is the case with the 1980 Venice Biennale, entitled 'La Presenza del Passato' and curated by Paolo Portoghesi – often reduced to a confused mishmash of historical references.

8 The term Modern Movement is used to refer to that vast phenomenon of architectural renewal that began during the first decade of the 1900s and which, according to some critics (for example, Nikolaus Pevsner in *Pioneers of Modern Design: From William Morris to Walter Gropius*, first published as *Pioneers of the Modern Movement: From William Morris to Walter Gropius*, Faber & Faber (London), 1936) has its origins at the end of the 1800s in the Arts & Crafts movement. The term International Style is used as a simplification of the principles of the Modern Movement, theorised in the exhibition held at the MoMA in New York in 1932 entitled 'The International Style' – an exhibition that was criticised by many for having rendered banal, through stylistic indications, what was otherwise a new, highly articulated, motivated and differentiated approach.

9 Peter Cook, 'At last! Architecture is on the wing again', in *The Architectural Review*, no 1074 (August 1986), pp 34–9.

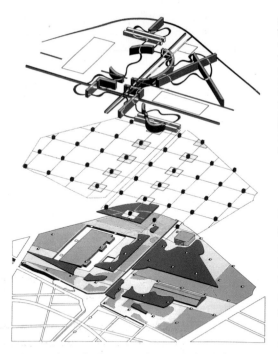

**Bernard Tschumi, Parc de la Villette, Paris, France, 1982–6: site plan.**

The plan of the park is the result of superimposed layers, each of which expresses a specific design strategy. Thus the project, rather than generating a synthesis, produces an overlapping of functions and events that respond, nonetheless, to a principle, even pluralist, order.

hour. What had captured the interest of these young students? Surely it was the return to a heroic tradition of architecture – the same that had been embodied by Bruno Taut[11] and the Constructivists[12] in the 1920s; the CIAM[13] in the 1930s; the Smithsons[14] in the 1950s; Archigram[15] in the 1960s. This is the tradition of the avant-garde who saw architecture as hand-to-hand combat with things and not with semantics, semiotics of the rhetorical syllogisms that, instead, represented one of the central aspects of the Post-Modern period. Coop Himmelb(l)au , it would appear, was not an isolated phenomenon. In reference to Zaha Hadid's victory in The Peak competition and that of Tschumi at Parc de la Villette, Cook affirms: 'Both [produced] schemes of great verve and thrust, great confidence and a reaching

Cook speaks of the two lectures held by Coop Himmelb(l)au in 1984, in Frankfurt and at the Architectural Association in London, that he attended together with attentive and enraptured students – the opposite of what took place during the lecture by Michael Graves,[10] who watched the room empty after only an

........................................................................................................

10 Michael Graves (born 1934) is one of the primary architects of the Post-Modern period. His Portland Building in Portland, Oregon (1980–3) is considered to be one of the most important and emblematic examples of this movement: see Charles Jencks, *Kings of Infinite Space: Frank Lloyd Wright and Michael Graves*, Academy Editions (London) and St Martin's Press (New York), 1983.

11 Throughout the 1920s and '30s Bruno Taut was the undisputed guide of the utopian wing of the German Expressionist movement. Obsessed by the idea of lightness and transparency, his was the glass pavilion at the 1914 Werkbund Exhibition, in addition to numerous essays, including *Alpine Architektur*, which prefigured the dream of an architecture that was

closely related to nature. His skills as an organiser were clearly demonstrated in the magazine *Frülicht* and numerous low-cost social building programmes.

12 The Constructivist movement was born in Russia at the time of the Revolution (1917) and lasted until the 1930s, when Stalin prohibited avant-garde research. The movement's primary figure was Vladimir Tatlin (1885–1953), author of a futuristic project for the Monument to the Third International, a 400-metre-high steel sculpture.

13 The Congrès International d'Architecture Moderne (CIAM) was an international organisation whose aim was the promotion and diffusion of contemporary architecture. Its members included the leading architects

and critics of the Modern Movement, such as Le Corbusier (1887–1965), Ludwig Mies van der Rohe (1886–1969), Walter Gropius (1883–1969), Alvar Aalto (1898–1976), Josep Lluís Sert (1902–1983) and Siegfried Giedion (1888–1968). The first congress was held in La Sarraz, Switzerland, in 1928 and the last in Otterlo, The Netherlands in 1959.

14 Alison (1928–93) and Peter (1923–2003) Smithson attempted to update the principles of the Modern Movement to meet the demands of post-war society, rendering it compatible with the new conditions of life. The protagonists of New Brutalism, an attitude that preferred the useful and the functional to the graceful, they were amongst the promoters of Team X, a group of architects from differ-············

ent countries who, after the CIAM, sought to bring architecture closer to the needs of man without, however, renouncing a Modernist language.

15 Archigram was a group of six architects, one of whom was Peter Cook (born 1936). The other members were Warren Chalk (1927–88), Dennis Crompton (born 1935), David Greene (born 1937), Ron Herron (1930–94) and Michael Webb (born 1937). The authors of innovative projects, they proposed the use of advanced technologies to build contemporary habitats. This led to the proposal for a macrostructure that contained industrial dwelling capsules, and others that could be removed and moved, flexible spaces that could be organised in dif-

ferent ways, throughout the course of the day. Archigram are considered to be amongst the forefathers of the High Tech movement.

16 Peter Cook, 'At last! Architecture is on the wing again', p 34.

17 In particular, on page 35, Cook mentions Raimund Abraham (born 1933), Günter Domenig (born 1934) and Eilfried Huth (born 1930) amongst the primary exponents of the first generation, and Heidulf Gerngross (born 1939), Helmut Richter (born 1941), Michael Szyszkowitz (born 1944), Karla Kowalski (born 1941) and Volker Giencke (born 1947) of the second.

18 Cook mentions Glenn Murcutt (born 1936).

19 In the 1970s John Hejduk (1929–2000), together with Peter Eisenman, was one of the New York Five. His work, primarily theoretical, involved a re-elaboration, in poetic and nostalgic terms, of the forms of Le Corbusier's Purist period. From 1965 onwards he was a professor and later Dean at Cooper Union in New York, making it one of the centres of American architectural research.

20 Other than Frank O Gehry, Cook (p 35) mentions Thom Mayne (born 1944), Eric Owen Moss (born 1943), Coy Howard (born 1943) and Craig Hodgetts (born 1937).

out into space. The subsequent history of architecture – both built and unbuilt – could never be the same. An immediate spin-off was the feeling of elation amongst their friends and some students, who knew that these schemes were no flashes in the pan, but a recognition point in years of increasingly dynamic work.'[16]

Continuing his examination, Cook underlines the interesting nature of the work of OMA, in particular the results of the collaboration between Rem Koolhaas and Zaha Hadid for the competition for an addition to the Dutch Parliament. He also recalls how the two generations of the school of Graz,[17] whose architecture has a decidedly expressive impact – the new Australian designers who managed to establish a beneficial dialogue between nature and contemporary forms;[18] and the New Yorkers from Cooper Union, under the direction of John Hejduk[19] – were all investigating the relationships that unite signs and space. Finally, he speaks of the architects of Los Angeles, distinguished by their particularly inventive approach.[20] These groups were the result of

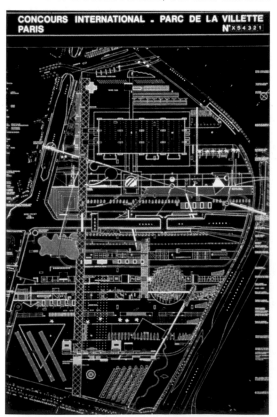

**Rem Koolhaas, Parc de la Villette, Paris, France, competition, 1982: site plan.**

Rem Koolhaas' project for the Parc de la Villette, like Tschumi's winning entry, uses the technique of overlapping layers. The idea is based on the logic of addition, balanced between chaos and order, a theme that was widely developed at the Architectural Association, where both architects taught at the time.

21 Cook (p 35) writes that the West Coast was also home to architects of such calibre as Frank Lloyd Wright (1867–1959), Rudolf Schindler (1887–1953), Bruce Goff (1904–82), Paolo Soleri (born 1919) and John Lautner (1911–94).

22 The Bauhaus school (1919–1933), run by Walter Gropius (until 1928), Hannes Meyer (until 1930) and Mies van der Rohe (until 1933), had a significant impact upon the diffusion of the Modernist language in the fields of applied arts and architecture.
23 High Tech was born in the 1970s with the works of Norman Foster and the Centre Pompidou (1971–7) designed by Renzo Piano, Richard Rogers and Gianfranco Franchini. These were the first projects to have

clearly exposed technological materials, exalting them in figurative terms – in particular glass and steel – and to avoid any attempts to conceal the building systems such as piping and air conditioning ducts. The precursors of High Tech, who worked on a more utopian and poetic level, included Buckminster Fuller (1895–1983), Cedric Price (1934–2003), Jean Prouvé (1901–84) and the aforementioned Archigram.

the arrival, in 1968, of Archigram and students from the Architectural Association and later exponents of the school of Graz. This grafting exploded in the fertile climate of the West Coast, where innovation and avant-garde approaches have always attracted interest.[21]

What were the references of this new generation? Peter Cook mentions at least three:

One: the recovery of the anti-institutional values of the Modern Movement. Not the classicist elements of much of the Bauhaus,[22] but phenomena that were lateral to it. In particular, Constructivism, with its airships, agit-trains, theatre sets, paintings, towers and huge creaking abstractions.

Two: the progressive traditions of English High Tech,[23] derived from Buckminster Fuller and Cedric Price; not the stylistically attractive typology adopted by large international corporations and, as a result, focused on a more conservative approach.

Three: the mastery of the Brazilian architect Oscar Niemeyer,[24] an authentic and reckless modern artist, the inventor of sensual and attractive forms and, perhaps for this reason, ostracised by contemporary culture.

In short: the creation of a network of men and ideas, founded on a common tradition, allowing us to look with hope towards the future. Cook concludes: 'The present messages being sent out are just the first few hops from branch to branch, but those with good hearing can discern a fantastic rustling and the healthy sound of twigs breaking.'[25]

Cook's forecast proved to be both timely and exact. In fact, from 1986 onwards there was a flowering of projects and built works that oriented architecture in a new direction.

In 1986 Zaha Hadid designed the residential and shop complex for the IBA (completed in 1993), which has an

24 From his earliest years Oscar Niemeyer (born 1907) was influenced by the poetics of Le Corbusier and attracted to the plastic organisation of architectural volumes. His projects, including the public structures in the city of Brasilia, for which he is best known, are notable for their widespread use of voluptuous curves

juxtaposed against more abstract and rational grids. Accused of being baroque, in reality Niemeyer seeks to render desirable and sensual a language, in this case Modernism, that otherwise risked becoming cold and abstract.
25 Peter Cook, 'At last! Architecture is on the wing again', p 39.

**26** Le Corbusier hypothesised that architecture – like music, which is articulated based on a succession of rhythms – unfolds through a succession of spaces, each with its own precise qualities, and that the role of architecture is that of tying them together along a path: the *promenade architecturale*. Le Corbusier is also responsible for the definition of architecture as an intelligent play of volumes under light, a definition that intends that they must be connected by a *promenade architecturale*.

**Frank O Gehry, Chiat/Day Building, Venice, California, USA, 1986–91: view of the entrance.**

The entrance to the building, designed in collaboration with the artist Claes Oldenburg, has the form of a pair of binoculars. Blown up to the scale of the building, it is both a sculptural element and an effective piece of publicity for the Advertising Agency Chiat/Day.

articulated profile that contradicts the requirement laid down in the rigid Berlin building codes to maintain a single eaves line, in order to give movement to the building mass and greater expressive importance to the resolution of the corner. She also designed a cantilevered office building on the Kurfürstendamm in Berlin, located on a strip of land that was only 2.7 x 1.6 metres, demonstrating that it is possible to create excellent architecture, with an extremely dynamic visual impact, even under almost impossible conditions.

Meanwhile Rem Koolhaas was designing the Villa Dall'Ava in Paris (completed in 1991), a single-family residence that represents a clash between Le Corbusier's *promenade architecturale*[26] and the poetics of the almost nothing of Mies van der Rohe,[27] and creating a paradigmatic house that is simultaneously as introverted as a sequence of volumes under light and as

extroverted as a glass house. In 1987, while completing the new IJ Plein neighbourhood in Amsterdam, which controversially recalls the principles of settlement proposed by the Modern Movement,[28] Koolhaas also completed the neo-Constructivist dance theatre in The Hague (begun in 1980) and, the following year, two patio houses of a vaguely Miesian flavour in the periphery of Rotterdam.

In 1986 Frank O Gehry commenced the Chiat/Day Building in Venice, California, whose entrance is marked by a pair of binoculars, designed in collaboration with the artist Claes Oldenburg.[29] The result is a gigantic pop insertion that caused a discussion of the distinction between sculpture and architecture. In the same year he inaugurated the retrospective exhibition dedicated to him by the Walker Art Center in Minneapolis.[30] In 1987 he began the design for the Vitra museum and

**27** A recurring theme in the work of Mies van der Rohe is the dematerialisation of space. This might be obtained using walls that, conceived of like planes, more than enclosing a volume, delimit it in virtual terms; or, as with the Farnsworth House in Plano, Illinois (1945–51), through the extensive use of glass walls. This in turn led to the hypothesis that architecture can be reduced to 'almost nothing'.
**28** The controversy involved those Post-Modern architects who, instead, were oriented towards the rediscovery of 18th-century urban planning and the road-corridor: for example we can look at the Strada Novissima, built by

Paolo Portoghesi for the 1980 Venice Biennale, with the explicit intention of a recovery through the re-proposal of the forms of the traditional city. Due to a series of strange coincidences that are too involved to explain here, Koolhaas also participated in the Strada Novissima. However, his was a decidedly provocative and controversial piece that deliberately avoided the creation of a traditional street facade.
**29** Claes Oldenburg (born 1929) is an American sculptor and one of the protagonists of the Pop Art movement. He is known for his giant sculptures of banal objects from everyday life. He is attributed with the joke that the difference between sculpture and archi-

tecture lies in the fact that sculptures contain no washrooms.
**30** The exhibition caused significant reverberations. This is how it was presented by the critic Paul Goldemberg, when it arrived at the Whitney Museum, published in the *New York Times* on August 16, 1988: 'When "The Architecture of Frank Gehry" opened at the Walker Art Center in Minneapolis in the fall of 1986, it seemed to make the definitive statement on the work of this brilliant, iconoclastic architect, increasingly one of the critical figures in contemporary American architecture.'

factory in Weil am Rhein, an attempt to juxtapose, in a single building, the exuberant volumes that, in previous buildings, appeared as separate elements. He returned to this form of experimentation the next year for the American Center in Paris.

Coop Himmelb(l)au continued to work on the design of fragmentary and highly gestural buildings, often based on a sketch produced in an 'altered' state of mind: in 1987 they designed the Ronacher Theatre in Vienna and won the international competition for the Melun-Sénart museum in southern Paris.

Bernard Tschumi and Peter Eisenman were working with Jacques Derrida on the Parc de la Villette, attempting to find a correspondence between Deconstructivism in architecture and in philosophy.

In 1986, Eisenman began a series of experiments – including the Wexner Center for the Arts in Columbus, Ohio, and, in the following year, the Biocentre for the University of Frankfurt, seeking to import the formal principles that guided the design process of other disciplines.

In 1987 Libeskind won the City Edge award in Berlin with a project whose lines and volumes, rather than coming together, appear to crash into one another, generating dynamic and exhilarating elements.

## 1.2 Deconstructivist Architecture

What made the 'Deconstructivist Architecture' exhibition a true event was the choice of its Guest Curator: Philip Johnson.[31]

At 82 years of age Philip Johnson was a famous figure and one of the principal protagonists of the entire history of contemporary architecture: together with Henry-Russell Hitchcock he was responsible, through the 1932 International Style exhibition, for the importation of

31 'Deconstructivist Architecture' opened to the public on 23 June 1988 and closed two months later, on 30 August. The Guest Curator of the show was Philip Johnson (1906–2005), and the Associate Curator was Mark Wigley.

**Peter Eisenman, Biocentre for the University of Frankfurt, Frankfurt, Germany, project, 1987.**

Eisenman's projects from this period represent the movement of nature, caught in a moment of transition between two states. The objective is that of questioning the classical systems that place man at the centre of the composition and tend to create an architecture of stability, which is functional, harmonious and hierarchical.

modern European architecture to the United States. He was the former director of the architectural department at the MoMA, responsible for a Miesian fashion of the almost nothing after the completion of his Glass House (1947–9), which he had built for himself in New Canaan, Connecticut, and had worked with Mies van der Rohe on the Seagram Building in New York (1954–8). Finally, after a sudden shift, he had become the champion of Post-Modern architecture, the anti-Miesian style *par excellence*, after completing – amongst other projects – the AT&T Tower in New York (1979–84),[32] together with his partner John Burgee.

Johnson, who abandoned Post-Modernism after this exhibition in order to embrace Deconstructivism, was returning to the world of curating after over 30 years, that is since 1954, when he left the direction of the architectural department at the MoMA.

In the preface to the catalogue,[33] Johnson presents two images: a ball bearing, from the cover of the catalogue of the 1934 MoMA exhibition entitled 'Machine Art', and a partially underground refuge (the Spring House), built during the 1860s in the Nevada desert, that was little more than a hole in the ground, the entrance to which is marked by a canopy made of found materials, photographed by Michael Heizer. Nothing, he states, could better present these two eras than the crude difference between these images. On the one hand the platonic ideal of the Modern Movement, represented by the perfection of a steel mechanism with its pure geo-

32 The AT&T Tower has become one of the icons of Post-Modernism, so much so that it was shown, together with its designer, on the cover of the weekly *Time* magazine (8 January 1979). The title of the piece, which also appeared on the cover, was: 'US Architects: Doing Their Own Thing'.

33 Philip Johnson, 'Preface', in Philip Johnson and Mark Wigley, *Deconstructivist Architecture*, Museum of Modern Art (New York), 1988, pp 7–9.

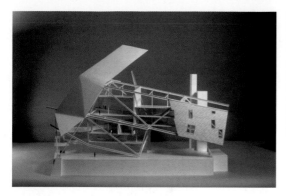

**Coop Himmelb(l)au, Residential Building, Vienna, Austria, project, 1983–5: model.**

The objective pursued by Coop Himmelb(l)au was that of creating structures capable of generating strong emotional reactions on the part of their inhabitants by using complex geometries and unbalanced and spatially involving forms.

metric form. On the other, an unsettling construction, dislocated, mysterious, made of rough-hewn wooden boards and sheet steel.

While both objects were designed by unknown hands for utilitarian purposes, today – Johnson continues – we feel closer to the sensibility of the second, rather than the abstract rationality of the first. It is the same sensibility that we find in the work of the seven architects invited to reflect upon the theme of 'violated perfection' – a theme that, even if unconsciously, inspired artists such as Frank Stella, Michael Heizer and Ken Price.[34]

A further development of Johnson's theses is provided in the essay by the Associate Curator of the exhibition, Mark Wigley,[35] according to whom the 1970s were witness to the birth of a culture of disharmony, as demonstrated by the martyred Best supermarkets built by SITE[36] and the programmed lacerations of Gordon Matta-Clark.[37] Today, nonetheless, deconstruction no

longer implies the refusal of architecture – this took place through non-architecture (SITE) or an-architecture (Matta-Clark) – but the awareness that imperfections (flaws) are inherent to the making of architecture, are part of its very structure, and cannot be removed without destroying it. For this reason the work of these contemporary architects recalls the inheritance of the historical avant-garde and, in particular, the Russians.[38] Both make use of pure forms to produce impure compositions, and both step back from the elegant aesthetic of functionalism, which did not go beyond the perfection of the envelope, without investigating the contradictory dynamic of function in and of itself. Obviously, as Wigley affirms, it is not important that all the architects presented are aware of their references to the Constructivist tradition. What counts is that they create an architecture of tension, distorting the structure, without willing its destruction.

Deconstructivist architecture, on par with that of the Russians, has a dialectic approach to context: it neither

**34** Frank Stella (born 1936), Michael Heizer (born 1944) and Ken Price (born 1935) are the authors of large-scale sculptures that interact with their context and the landscape to the point that – as with Heizer – they become part of it.
**35** Mark Wigley, 'Deconstructivist Architecture', in Philip Johnson and Mark Wigley, *Deconstructivist Architecture*, pp 10–20.
**36** SITE, founded in 1969, is a group of designers whose major exponent is James Wines (born 1932). During

the 1970s they completed a number of buildings, including the Best supermarkets, that were ruptured, peeled or ruined as if by natural processes of erosion. SITE later became interested primarily in issues of sustainability and Green Architecture.
**37** Gordon Matta-Clark (1943–78) graduated with a degree in Architecture, although he works primarily as an artist, proposing structures or architectural fragments that are marked by cuts and lacerations, with the objective of

placing the observer in a condition to look at the space in which he lives from a different point of view, which is normally not allowed.
**38** One of the elements that led many architects to focus their attention on Constructivism was undoubtedly the research and writings of Catherine Cook. It is probably no coincidence that she was teaching at the Architectural Association at the same time as Hadid and Koolhaas. Cook's writings include *Russian Avant-Garde*, Academy Editions (London), 1995.

imitates nor ignores it, but uses it as an instrument of dislocation. In the same way it uses traditional dialectic categories – inside/outside, above/below, open/closed. It is perhaps precisely for this stylistic interest – Wigley concludes – that Deconstructivism cannot be defined as avant-garde. It is not a means of announcing the new, a rhetoric of the new, but rather displays the unfamiliar concept that is hidden behind what is known. It is, in the end, the surprise of the old.

Let us look at the projects that were presented. Many of them were not new. For example the work of Gehry was precisely the aforementioned addition to his house in Santa Monica, California (completed primarily between 1978 and 1979, with a third phase in 1988) and his project for the Familian House, from 1979. Koolhaas presented his Apartment Building and Observation Tower in Rotterdam (1982), Hadid The Peak (1983) and Tschumi the drawings for the 1985 version of the Parc de la Villette in Paris. The three Coop Himmelb(l)au projects were from 1985 to 1986: the Rooftop Remodelling in Vienna (1985), an Apartment Building in Vienna (1986) and the Hamburg Skyline (1985). The most recent projects were Eisenman's Biocentre for the University of Frankfurt (1987) and the City Edge in Berlin (1987) by Libeskind.

Thus, if we exclude Gehry's Santa Monica house, we are dealing with a collection of works that were still under construction or destined to remain on paper. The exhibition and the catalogue featured only drawings and models, rendering the projects homogenous and, where possible, underlying the common formal qualities. There were no photographs or images of construction sites, which would have shifted attention from an abstract formal reflection to the more concrete issues of construction.

**Daniel Libeskind, City Edge, Berlin, Germany, competition, 1987.**

In this project lines and volumes generate dynamic and powerful tensions.

39 The mania for Deconstructivism and Derrida was so fashionable during the 1980s on university campuses that David Lodge made it the protagonist of his highly successful novel *Small World*, Penguin Books (New York), 1984.

The 'Deconstructivist Architecture' exhibition, as mentioned at the beginning of the text, had an immediate and unexpected echo, presenting a new sensibility and focusing international attention on the seven invited architects together with others who were not asked to present their work but who shared the same sensibilities.

Nonetheless, with respect to the impassioned article by Peter Cook for *The Architectural Review* published in August 1986, the exhibition was a step backwards, reducing to a common stylistic detail poetics that were, in reality, very different. This is demonstrated by the exaggerated references made by Johnson and Wigley to the formal analogies with Russian Constructivism, whose over-evaluation disqualifies the novelty of the research. Thus, in an era of rapid formal consumption,

Deconstructivism is nothing other than a style like any other: similar to strict classicism and strict Modernism.

On the other hand, the very word Deconstructivism generates a misunderstanding given that it represents both an attitude of surpassing the Russian avant-garde (de-Constructivism) and the parallel philosophical trend founded on the writings of Jacques Derrida (philosophical deconstructivism), particularly in vogue at the time.[39]

What is more – as demonstrated by the failed 1985–6 experiment begun when Tschumi asked Eisenman and Derrida to work together on a garden in the Parc de la Villette – philosophical deconstruction has little or nothing to do with its architectural cousin.[40] In fact, the first is applied to concepts and used to identify,

40 The history of this failed encounter between philosophical and architectural deconstruction is narrated by Derrida and Eisenman in the book *Choral Works*, edited by Jeffrey Kipnis and Thomas Leeser, The Monacelli Press (New York), 1997. The collaboration began with Derrida's suggestion to propose a theme for a garden in La Villette based on a passage from Plato's *Timaeus*, which speaks of *Chora*, the space used by the demiurge to transform ideas into worldly objects. This passage is one of the most obscure in all of Greek philosophy. Despite the efforts of translators, Derrida included, no one has ever been able to properly understand exactly what qualities were possessed by this site that contained no sites, both limited and limitless, homogenous and not homogenous. However, the intent was not to clarify the theme, but to work with it, taking advantage of the contradictions and, together, creating new interpretations. Eisenman enthusiastically accepted and, a lover of titles composed of plays on words, baptised the project *Choral Works*, alluding to a shared project, the word *Chora* and choral music. The project was founded on a grid that recalls that used by Tschumi for the park. However, it recalls above all the grid used by Eisenman for his previous project in Cannaregio (1978) – a composition that was developed based on entirely arbitrary hypotheses, taken from a reading of signs that were literally, virtually or even hypothetically superimposed upon the landscape, including, for example, the grid proposed by Le Corbusier for his Venice hospital (designed in 1965 but never built). It is a complex and perverse game of references and signs of spatial measurement and their history – a game that was ambiguous even for Tschumi regarding the originality of the choice (was it Tschumi who was copying Eisenman when he used the grid in Cannaregio or Eisenman who was copying the grid used by Tschumi for the plan of the park?). The project, after a few meetings with Derrida,

within a rational discourse, the presuppositions, even terminological, that are taken for granted and that instead, once revealed, place the structure of reasoning in a state of crisis, opening it up towards new and unexpected interpretations. The second, on the other hand, is a technique for increasing the interest of a project through a series of conceptual references and, as a result, organising it according to formal logics that can no longer be related to any previous canons. All the same, the idea of uniting philosophical and architectural research, as is the case in all these examples, attracted a great number of scholars and led to a flowering of theoretical books and essays that attempted to unite architectural and philosophical deconstructivism, seeking to overcome the conceptual problems encountered by Derrida and Eisenman.[41]

Other lines of research focused on the rediscovery of Russian Constructivism, explicitly referenced in the work of Koolhaas and Hadid. Yet, as can be easily observed, this category, already ambiguous, is not so easy to apply to the work of Libeskind, Coop Himmelb(l)au and, above all, Gehry. However, at least at the outset, this was of little importance.

Despite this collection of ambiguities, or perhaps because of this openness to differing and contradictory interpretations, the term Deconstructivism was wildly successful. It synthesised the optimism of the late 1980s and early 1990s. By proposing an experimental approach focused on creating a new relationship with the world, it ran contrary to the conformist traditionalism of the 1980s – embodied by Post-Modern architecture – that, on the other hand, was unable to consider the future if not in terms of a re-proposal, more or less nostalgic, of the past.

What is more, in 1989, only one year after the 'Deconstructivist Architecture' exhibition, the world was witness to the fall of the Berlin Wall, one of the most profound processes of de-structuring the world had ever known. It was the collapse of an empire, the USSR, that

was complicated by other signs – the remains of an old slaughterhouse, a sieve/lyre – creating a project that was overflowing with intellectual references, of quotations that were confirmed and quickly denied, of sudden shifts in scale. Derrida began to object when he realised that Eisenman was beginning to take over, ending the collaboration with a letter that, hidden behind a succession of allusions – confirmed, denied and then reconfirmed – to the relationship between Nietzsche and Wagner, accused Eisenman of Wagnerism, that is the rhetoric founded upon the primacy, what is more the absolutist nature of the Id, from which the architect sought to escape. An embittered Eisenman responded by saying: 'Perhaps what I do in architecture, in its aspirations and in its fabric, is not what could properly be called deconstruction. But things are not quite so simple: if my work is not something, then it raises questions as to what it is not' (*Choral Works*, p 187).

41 One of these was Mark Wigley: *The Architecture of Deconstruction: Derrida's Haunt*, The MIT Press (Cambridge, MA), 1995.

**Jean Nouvel, Institut du Monde Arabe, Paris, France, 1981–7: detail of the steel oculus.**

The steel oculus of the Institut du Monde Arabe creates a suggestive and contradictory image, somewhere between high technology and the memory of Arabian shutters and screens.

no one had even come close to forecasting. It was the collapse of cultural and ideological barriers and the freeing of energies that, in previous years, had been mortified and compressed. Above all it represented the delineation, amongst the younger generation, of an awareness of the possibility of living in a better world, where creativity is not constricted to the confines of conformism and clichés.

The universities and magazines were filled, in an extraordinarily rapid manner, with more courageous ideas. Those greatest contributors to the debate, with their projects and theoretical positions, assumed a charismatic role. In architecture this led to the creation of the phenomenon of the Star System.[42] The greatest benefits went to the aforementioned seven architects who, even while seeking to capitalise on the notoriety gained with the Deconstructivist trend, were very careful to not be labelled as the exponents of a movement characterised by shared objectives.

## 1.3 A New Paradigm

Beyond the attempt to express the tensions and energies of a new era through a dislocated and fragmented architecture, the theme that became the yardstick for the next decade was that of the IT revolution.

In the 1980s new products spread in a capillary manner: first entering the world of production, later professional offices and finally the everyday. From the 1990s onwards, computers, new media, real-time television, Internet, faxes and video games created an ethereal and artificial world that was both parallel to and superimposed upon real space. It could be examined and dominated by products whose ultimate expression is found in the 'smart bombs' so successfully employed by the Americans during the Gulf War (1991), guided by flows of information produced by the enemy and capable of targeting, with surgical precision, even what is hidden to the naked eye.

42 Koolhaas, for example, begins his book *S,M,L,XL* (p xiii) with a chart that illustrates the number of kilometres he has travelled by air and the number of nights passed in hotel rooms (in 1993: 360,000 kilometres and 305 out of 365 nights). OMA, Rem Koolhaas and Bruce Mau, *S,M,L,XL*, The Monacelli Press (New York) and 010 Publishers (Rotterdam), 1995.

**Jean Nouvel, Institut du Monde Arabe, Paris, France, 1981–7: night view of the entrance facade.**

The interactive facade of the Institut du Monde Arabe changes its appearance in relation to the amount of light it receives. Here Nouvel demonstrates the potential of digital technologies, transforming a cladding into a light-sensitive skin.

Immersed in the universe of information – infospace – contemporary architecture needed to redefine itself. This problem was intuited by Jean-François Lyotard back in 1985, when he organised an exhibition at the Centre Pompidou entitled 'Les Immatériaux':[43] how does one render visible the concept of flows of information that, by its very nature, is invisible?

This theme had already been anticipated by the French architect Jean Nouvel,[44] who demonstrated an extraordinary ability to take advantage of new instances and situations. His Institut du Monde Arabe was completed in 1987 (the design is from 1981). The project was one of the *Grands Travaux* that were changing the face of Paris during those years under the presidency of François Mitterrand (1981–95).[45] The building is notable for its continuous glazed facade, behind which are positioned a series of metal oculi that, like the lens of a camera, open and close based on the quantity of light perceived. These are controlled by electronic sensors programmed to guarantee constant values of internal illumination, independent of the variations in the intensity of the sunlight outside the building. The result is a building whose appearance is in constant mutation, behaving like a living organism that activates strategies of change which are both functional and formal.

The same line of research also motivated the Japanese architect Toyo Ito[46] who completed his Tower of the

43 'Les Immatériaux', the exhibition curated by Jean-François Lyotard at the Centre Pompidou in Paris, ran from 28 March to 15 July 1985.
44 Jean Nouvel (born 1945) theorised a 'critical architecture', structured on the basis of images and metaphors. His first works – for example the Val-Notre-Dame general surgery hospital in Bezons (1976–80), which is reminiscent of transatlantic ships and offers patients the impression of being on a short trip – brought him immediate recognition as one of France's most

interesting architects.
45 The other projects were the Grand Louvre by Pei Cobb Freed & Partners (two phases, 1989 and 1993), the Grande Arche at La Défense by Johann Otto von Spreckelsen and Paul Andreu (1982–9), the Finance Ministry Building by Paul Chemetov and Borja Huidobro (1981–9), the Opéra de la Bastille by Carlos Ott (1983–9) and the Parc de la Villette by Bernard Tschumi.
46 Toyo Ito (born 1941) is a disciple of Kiyonori Kikutake (born 1928), one of the founders of Metabolism. His first

works, including the U House (1976) designed for his sister, have a strong metaphorical and symbolic presence (the U form of the house represents the owner's suffering folded back on itself – she had recently been left a widow).

**48** Marshall McLuhan (1911–80) was a contemporary media researcher and creator of the widely accepted image of the 'global village'. His ideas, particularly innovative, were wildly popular in the 1970s, though later forgotten. At the end of the 1980s they were rediscovered by architects, thanks in part to their divulgation and elaboration by one of his most talented disciples, Derrick de Kerckhove who, in 1991, published *Brainframes: Technology, Mind and Business*, BSO/Origin (Utrecht), 1991. In the following years de Kerckhove would have important contacts with the community of architects, an activity that led to a collaboration with *Domus* magazine and the publication of essays on the relationship between media and architecture: *The Architecture of Intelligence*, Birkhäuser (Basel), 2001.

Winds in Yokohama in 1986, a structure that, once again using electronic sensors, transforms the air, sounds and noises of the city into shifting patterns of light.

Between 1985 and 1986, with his installations *Pao 1* and *Pao 2: Dwelling for Tokyo Nomad Woman*,[47] Ito used highly suggestive images to represent the new electronic house. He designed an oval tent, made up of transparent curtains. The interior was occupied by three almost evanescent furnishings: a make-up table, a dining table and a table for intellectual activities. The differences between this and a traditional house are evident: the latter is rooted to the ground and, overburdened with symbolic and functional objects, constitutes a world apart, almost a microcosm, whilst the contemporary house is the exact opposite, by its very nature unstable and not self-sufficient. In fact, new technologies stimulate nomadism, the willingness to be uprooted, to travel continuously, both in material terms (car, train, aeroplane) and via instruments of communication (radio, television, Internet, telephone,

teleconferencing). Furthermore, it does not imply closed and introverted spaces because it ties us together, as if we lived inside a single nervous system. Finally the ease of transferring information accelerates the exchange of goods and, by rendering them available anywhere, renders their conservation unnecessary.

It is from Marshall McLuhan,[48] the genial Canadian media researcher, that Ito takes his reflection on the centrality, in a society based on both electronics

**47** Toyo Ito, *Pao 1*: 'Pao: Dwelling of Tokyo Nomad Woman', installation in the Seibu Department Stores, Tokyo, 1985. *Pao II*: 'Pao: a Dwelling for Tokyo Nomad Woman', installation in Brussels, Belgium, 1989.

**Toyo Ito, Tower of the Winds, Yokohama, Japan, 1986: exterior view.**

With the Tower of the Winds, Ito creates an evanescent building, the appearance of which varies in relation to the conditions of its context, based on the diktats of a new poetics founded on transformation and lightness.

49 'Visions of Japan', Victoria and Albert Museum, London, 1991.

50 This story is told in Toyo Ito, 'Architecture in a Simulated City', in *El Croquis*, no 71 (1995), pp 6–8.

and information, of the meaning of the tactile and the importance of the skin: a sensible epidermis that wraps buildings and allows for interaction between the domestic environment and urban space, absorbing lights, sounds and flows and returning them as images and vital tensions.

In 1991 Ito took part in the London exhibition 'Visions of Japan', creating a room that he initially wanted to call *Simulation* but to which, based on the advice of Arata Isozaki, he finally gave the more popular name of *Dreams*.[49] This 10 x 28 metre space featured a raised floor made of opaque acrylic panels onto which 26 projectors, suspended from the ceiling, cast images of Tokyo. The short wall featured an LCD display. Along the long side, a slightly undulating wall covered with aluminium panels and hidden behind a curtain displayed images of life in the Japanese capital from 44 projectors. A battery of speakers filled the space with music, processed by a synthesiser and based on the sounds of the metropolis.

Ito was amused by the fact that the Prince of Japan, while inaugurating the exhibition, had to drink a few glasses of saké before entering such a chaotic and evanescent space and that Prince Charles – a well-known enemy of the metropolis – asked what messages were hidden behind the image. When Ito responded that there were no hidden messages, the Prince asked if he was not perhaps an incurable optimist.[50]

Ito often works with an image that is devoid of any meaning, left in an almost impressionistic state, at a point that has reached the senses but is not yet formalised in the intellect – like the *Egg of Winds* (1988–91) in Okawabata River City, a sculpture-kaleidoscope clad with perforated aluminium panels that reflect images of the city projected onto its surface and allow for a glimpse of other images screened on televisions inside the sculpture. The images, exactly like those on a television with no sound, lose any meaning, becoming purely sensorial phenomena: colours and forms that vibrate and fluctuate in space.

**Toyo Ito, 'Visions of Japan' exhibition, London, England, 1991: exterior view.**

The exhibition 'Visions of Japan' highlighted the dynamic and changing nature of the contemporary city, suggesting that in these contexts it is necessary to use instruments other than those of traditional architecture.

Space, seen in this light, no longer appears as the void that is home to solid bodies, but as the medium through which to propagate information. 'The object differs in character from TV sets installed on street posts or a large Jumbotron colour display which decorates the wall of a building in downtown. It is the object of video images which can be seen through the information-filled air in the surroundings. It is the object of images which come with the wind and which are gone with the wind.'[51]

Let us return to Ito's comment to Prince Charles that the images did not conceal any meaning. This could easily have been said by Andy Warhol,[52] with whom Ito certainly shares a fascination for reality, independently of any contextualisation or conceptual mediation.

While Warhol freezes the image in easily recognisable figures (whether it is the box of Campbell's soup cans or his portraits of Marilyn, Jackie or Mao Tse-tung), Ito captures it at the moment when it is still a flow of energy. Electronics, we will see later on when we look at the Sendai Mediatheque, is like a vital breath that can be metaphorically associated with the waves of the ocean. It is precisely this immateriality, which privileges the intelligence and flexibility of software over the materiality of hardware, that has made it possible to surpass the mechanical society that preceded us.

However, if this process was taking place in the most advanced industries, it had not yet appeared in the world of construction, where there had been no changes to a rigidly functionalist — and in the end mechanised — organisation of residential space: 'We have not yet found,' Ito affirms, 'a space suitable for the ideal life in the computer age.'[53]

Yet new technologies have overturned the formal coordinates of the environment in which we live. All we have to do, Ito tells us, is to look at the design of the automobile. The Citroën 2CV and the Volkswagen Beetle were replaced by more modern Japanese models

026

51 ibid, p 9.

52 Andy Warhol (1928–87), painter and protagonist of the Pop Art movement. His paintings were inspired by advertisements of mass-consumerism products or by images, often of famous people, taken from glossy magazines and television.

53 Toyo Ito, 'Architecture in a Simulated City', p 11.

by Toyota and Nissan, whose forms no longer reflected internal mechanics, but more abstract processes: comfort and ease of driving, the recognition and management of instrumentation, automated location control, radio and telephone communications, climatic comfort, ergonomics, energy savings and manageable and automated safety functions. In other sectors the changes were even more profound: we need only look at the field of bioengineering, where biology and microelectronics work together.

In 1992 Ito participated in the competition for the new University Library in Paris. He designed a Minimalist box: a plate created by the union of two-storey longitudinal volumes that overlook other longitudinal and double-height volumes. The scheme is interrupted at two points by two elliptical volumes that act as points of encounter; the external surfaces are clad with transparent materials that allow for a glimpse of the shelving and furnishings.

Ito refuses any concessions to expression: there are no references or alluring connections with history, allusions to consolidated languages, plays of chiaroscuro, chromatic tones or harmonic traces or modulations. What he pursues, as noted by Iñaki Ábalos and Juan Herreros, is the search for an almost absolute simplicity: 'a sort of new ease, a new simplicity that believes that complexity is no longer expressible in geometric terms, or to be more exact, that geometric complexity and its deformations have ceased to be pertinent resources in relation to architectural expression.'[54]

The ideal of this architecture is thus the search for a space that is neutral, homogenous, a-perspectival and transparent, in the end becoming ephemeral, the antithesis of the principles of the monumental architecture of the classical tradition, expressed in buildings intended to last for eternity.

The precariousness and lack of expression of the envelope shift the observer's attention from the container

54 Iñaki Ábalos and Juan Herreros, 'Toyo Ito: Light Time', in *El Croquis*, no 71 (1995), p 39.

55 Koji Taki, 'A Conversation with Toyo
Ito', in *El Croquis*, no 71 (1995), p 29.

to the content. The result is that the Library resembles a chip in a calculator: both are aseptic spaces that offer interconnections which facilitate the passage of information and both are marked by a grid of paths, preferably orthogonal and, in any case, structured on the logic of the shortest possible connection.

What is more, the two elliptical volumes, even while not finding any immediate resonance in the architecture of information, in this case the microchip, suggest the movement of energy flows: 'The oval – Ito notes – contrasts with the classical square court configuration formed by the inner walls of a group of buildings. I am creating a new kind of square to express the dissemination of information in more or less dense areas. It is the oval, rather than the circle, which embodies the sense of flowing.'[55]

# 1.4 Zaha and the Game of Opposites

Without a doubt Zaha Hadid is amongst those who most benefited from the 'Deconstructivist Architecture' exhibition, obtaining two important commissions: the Monsoon Restaurant in Sapporo, Japan, and the Vitra Fire Station in Weil am Rhein, Germany.

The latter suffered a number of setbacks, the result of a budget that 'constantly changed',[56] and was completed only in 1994.[57]

The Monsoon Restaurant (1989–90) in Sapporo[58] can be interpreted in two ways, the first being metaphorical: the restaurant represents the contrast between cold and hot, between fire and ice. The furnishings on the first floor are sharp and cutting like crystal, while those

56 The story is mentioned briefly in Ziva Freiman, 'The Concrete Evidence', in *Progressive Architecture* (August 1993), pp 48–59.
57 The Vitra Fire Station will be examined in paragraph 2.2, 'Explosive Buildings'.

58 It is interesting to note that this design for a bar-restaurant that occupies two floors of the Kita Club, a nightclub in the Suskino district along the Sapporo River, was commissioned in 1989 by JASMAC's Michihiro Kuzawa, the builder who, during the same period, commissioned the Post-Modernist Aldo Rossi to design the Kyushu Palazzo Hotel.

Zaha Hadid, Monsoon
Restaurant, Sapporo, Japan,
1989–90: interior view.

In this project Zaha Hadid uses
interior furnishings to create
a highly dynamic composition.
The orange structure, which runs
from the ground floor to the ceiling, brings warmth to the space
by introducing a strong element
of colour.

on the second floor are warm and soft, references to Sapporo, a winter city famous for its ice sculptures, and the fire of the hearth and warmth of interior spaces. The second interpretation is formal and founded on a technique that Hadid learned at the Architectural Association in London from Rem Koolhaas, who uses it often in his projects. It consists of playing with opposites – hot and cold, solid and void, opaque and transparent, light and heavy, spiral and box. What is more, in this case, the recovery of the contrast between the acute nature of cold and the softness of hot allows her to bring together, in one project, the penetrating experimental geometries of the Hong Kong Peak project and the wrapping elements of other projects, for example the renovation of the apartment building at 24 Cathcart Road in London (1985–6).

The Music Video Pavilion in Groningen, Netherlands (1990) – like the Monsoon Restaurant, though different from the Vitra Fire Station – is a multicoloured object, fragmented by a plurality of signs, chaotic to the point of confusion. It is also split into two halves: a closed space, clad in metal and delineated by a window from which protrude off-kilter ribbons with triangular forms; and an open space, resolved with a thread-like structure of slender columns and beams, allowing for glimpses of plastic volumes.

It is useless, Hadid suggests, to opt for one or the other of the countless couplings of opposites inherent to the dynamics of form; it is necessary, on the other hand, to accept their coexistence, exalting contrasts. This

Zaha Hadid, The Hague Villas,
The Hague, The Netherlands,
project, 1991: study model.

The project is based on the
opposition of two geometries, the
static box of the parallelepiped
and the wrapping dynamic of
the spiral. Their meeting-clash
creates unusual and visually
stimulating spaces.

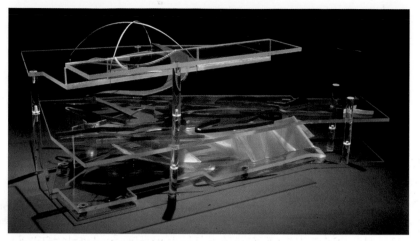

**Zaha Hadid, Monsoon Restaurant, Sapporo, Japan, 1989–90: study model.**

The model exposes the design strategy used by Hadid. It consists of structuring space based on lines of force. There is also a clear difference between the cool colours of the lower floor and the warm colours of the upper floor.

irreducible dualism is taken to the extreme at the most private scale of existence: the single-family dwelling, a field dominated by conventional ideas and the rarity of radically innovative proposals. This is the case with The Hague Villas (1991), a study for the construction of eight single-family units to be located in the Dutch capital.

Hadid proposed two typologies: the 'cross house', derived from a linear generating principle, and the 'spiral house', founded on the opposing matrix of the curve.

The 'cross house' is based around the intersection of two rectangles, one negative and one positive. The first, at ground level, is a parallelepiped subtracted from the volume of the surrounding dwelling: a void. The second, on the first floor, is the same parallelepiped, this time a solid, though almost perpendicular to the void below

and completely carved out to contain the living spaces. The result is a dwelling that wraps around an internal courtyard at ground level, while the first floor opens towards the landscape: simultaneously introverted and extroverted, it is part of a dualism that synthetically expresses the dilemma of contemporary architecture, in a constant balance between the 'brick house', with its perimeter wall to defend the interior spaces, and the 'glass house', whose glazed surfaces project the interior into its natural surroundings.

The 'spiral house', instead, is the result of the opposition between the cube of the envelope and the spiral of the ramp that passes through the spaces. The coming together of these two geometries creates surprising internal views and unexpected channels of communication and interaction. There is also a vertical progression from heavy to light, from enclosed to transparent.[59]

**59** It is not difficult, even in these projects, to observe a correspondence with the work of Rem Koolhaas. The theme of the house, simultaneously introverted and extroverted, is investigated by Koolhaas in the Villa Dall'Ava in Paris (1985–91) and the Nexus World Housing complex in Fukuoka, Japan (1988–91), and developed in numerous later projects. The theme of the contrast between the box and the spiral is confronted, in particular, in the Rotterdam Kunsthal (1987–92).

60 The exhibition 'The Great Utopia:
The Russian and Soviet Avant-Garde,
1915–1932' ran from 25 September
1992 to 3 January 1993 at the Solomon
R Guggenheim Museum in New York.

61 Suprematism was an artistic movement initiated by Kasimir Malevich
(1878–1935) around 1913. It shares
with Constructivism the need for
abstraction, though with a stronger
vein of mysticism and poetics,
which brings it to represent a world
composed of pure spaces, freed of the
needs of matter.

In 1992 the Guggenheim Museum inaugurated the exhibition entitled 'The Great Utopia',[60] dedicated to the masters of Suprematism[61] and Constructivism. This was the occasion – Hadid confessed – to verify the three-dimensional force of Malevich's abstraction and range of influence.[62]

The installation is a direct response to this idea: the reconstruction of the tower designed by Tatlin as the Monument to the Third International at the centre of the museum, and a series of parallel episodes, each dedicated to a spatial theme. They can be described as the opposition between the constructions of the *Red Square* by Malevich and the *Corner Relief* by Tatlin; the extrusion of one of Malevich's compositions, laid out on the ground; paintings hung in the form of a flow of energy, a geometric storm; apparently 'floating' paint-ings, displayed in transparent Perspex supports; and the gravitational placement of Suprematist sculptures that follow an orbit which emerges from the floor and moves upwards to the ceiling. What was important in this show, beyond the single inventions, was a decla-ration of principle: that architecture is not a neutral support of walls to be used for the orderly display of a sequence of works. On the contrary, it is a spatial con-struction that, precisely because of its qualities of in-volvement, offers interpretations and becomes a text. It is the result of a form of artistic research which, in order to verify its assumptions, can and must enter into conflict with the current system of expectations.

## 1.5 Rem Koolhaas: Method and its Paradoxes

Is architecture able to respond to the needs of contemporary society? Is it possible to design based on rational principles? If we admit that it is possible, what results can we hope to obtain? To respond to these demands in 1989 Rem

62 'The design for an exhibition
on Russian Suprematism and
Constructivism offered the
opportunity to revisit my student
explorations of the three-dimensional
qualities of Malevich's tektonik... For
the first time Malevich's tektonik was
habitable: visitors had to pass through
it to reach the upper galleries.'
Quoted by Aaron Betsky in his essay
in *Zaha Hadid: The Complete Buildings
and Projects*, Thames and Hudson
(London), 1998, p 82.

63 For some critics, in this case Bruno Zevi (1918–2000), the novelty of Deconstructivism consisted precisely of the desire to refocus the architect's attention on the theme of space: the void. It was considered relevant enough to move formal excesses into the background, leading other critics, for example Hans Ibelings, to see Deconstructivism as a stylistic derivation that remains within the aestheticising logic of Post-Modernism: Hans Ibelings, *Supermodernism: Architecture in the Age of Globalization*, NAi Publishers (Rotterdam), 2002, p 24.

## Koolhaas participated in three important competitions: the Bibliothèque Nationale de France in Paris, the Zentrum für Kunst und Medientechnologie in Karlsruhe and the Sea Trade Centre in Zeebrugge.

In each proposal the Dutch architect defines a strategy that, when coherently applied, in the end produces paradoxical results. The first strategy, refined in the competition for the Bibliothèque Nationale de France, focuses on voids and their interconnection. In fact, this project consists of a compact parallelepiped – the built volume filled by the book deposits – inside of which a system of interconnected spaces is carved out by excavation and subtraction: the reading rooms, the auditorium, the conference rooms and horizontal and vertical circulation located in a continuum of tunnels and underground spaces. Designed by focusing primarily on the void and not, as was the case with Post-Modernism, the solid, it shifts interest from the container to the content, that is the space in which activities take place and thus, in the end, to the events themselves.[63] However, the fact that the voids contain the events makes it difficult to design the exterior envelope of the building – that is unless the architect chooses, as Koolhaas has, to execute it in the form of a piece of 'Swiss cheese', perforated by holes created by the intersection of the facade with the volumes of the voids.

The second strategy was created in order to respond to a no less embarrassing question: if movement is the generating principle of the contemporary metropolis, does this not lead to the dissolution of architecture that, instead, is founded on the principles of solidity and permanence?

In the project for the Zentrum für Kunst und Medientechnologie in Karlsruhe, Koolhaas designed a building conceived of as a 'Darwinian arena' that was to have involved its urban surroundings and hosted temporary and permanent exhibitions, events and performances

**Rem Koolhaas, Bibliothèque Nationale de France, Paris, France, competition, 1989: two study models.**

The model in the foreground highlights the voids of the building and their interconnections as if they were solids. The intent is that of showing that architecture, more than solids, is composed of voids, the spaces that house events. The model in the background shows the appearance of the building.

**Rem Koolhaas, Zentrum für Kunst und Medientechnologie, Karlsruhe, Germany, competition, 1989: model.**

The building interacts with the surrounding city using a large facade, designed like a giant projection screen, visible from the sloping plaza created above the entrance to the railway station.

of various types. Located near Karlsruhe Station, the Centre was to have connected with the historical city via the railway underpass, partially occupying it. In this manner, passengers who daily passed through the station could observe the works of art and artistic events through a glass wall. A similar function of diffusion and attraction was to have been played by the large projection screen located on the facade facing the public square. After entering the building, the visitor found himself in an *espace piranesien*,[64] with escalators and ramping floors that would have allowed for a sequential sampling of the various programmes contained in the building, culminating in the roof garden. During his vertical ascent, the visitor would have been offered an aerial view of the station, the movement of the trains and, finally, a panoramic view of the historical centre of Karlsruhe. Observed from the point of view of the architectural drawing the result is, however, paradoxical: the building tends to dematerialise and exist in a situation of precarious equilibrium between form and non-form.

The third strategy, represented in the project for the Sea Trade Centre in Zeebrugge, Belgium,[65] deals with the symbolic dimension.

Already in *Delirious New York*[66] Koolhaas had identified two urban archetypes: the needle and the globe. The needle is a building with no interior, occupying the minimum volume and projecting upwards. The globe, on the other hand, has the maximum internal volume with the minimum surface area. What is more, it has a notable ability to absorb objects, people, iconographies and symbolisms thanks to its ability to make them coexist within it. The history of the Modern metropolis is, for Koolhaas, the attempt to make these two archetypes live together, 'with the needle wanting to become a globe and the globe trying, from time to time, to turn into a needle – a cross-fertilisation that results in a series of successful hybrids in which the needle's capacity for attracting attention and its territorial modesty are matched with the consummate receptivity of the sphere'.[67]

64 By using this term, Koolhaas intended a space similar to that shown in the drawings of the *Carceri* by the Italian engraver and architect Giovanni Battista Piranesi (1720–78), considered by the Italian critic Manfredo Tafuri (1935–94) as emblematic of the Modern condition: Manfredo Tafuri, *Progetto e utopia: Architettura e sviluppo capitalistico*, Laterza (Bari), 1973, English translation by Barbara Luigia La Penta, *Architecture and Utopia, Design and Capitalist Development*, The MIT Press (Cambridge, MA), 1976.

65 The competition was a response to the desire to build a terminal to support ferry traffic between the Continent and Great Britain, in order to stimulate an activity that, at the time of the construction of the Eurotunnel beneath the English Channel, appeared to be seriously threatened.

66 Rem Koolhaas, *Delirious New York: A Retroactive Manifesto for Manhattan*, Oxford University Press (New York), 1978; new edition, The Monacelli Press (New York) and 010 Editions (Rotterdam), 1994.
67 Rem Koolhaas, *Delirious New York: A Retroactive Manifesto for Manhattan*, new edition, p 27.

**Rem Koolhaas, Sea Trade Centre, Zeebrugge, Belgium, competition, 1989: model.**

The Sea Trade Centre, accessed from below, spirals upwards in a manner that is reminiscent of Wright's Guggenheim Museum in New York. The top floor features a panoramic dome that overlooks the surrounding landscape.

68 On more than one occasion Koolhaas has written that this method derives from the Surrealist approach of the Spanish painter Salvador Dalí (1904–89).

The prototype of the needle is the New York skyscraper and the prototype of the globe the geodesic dome by Buckminster Fuller. Koolhaas, in a shocking move, seeks to synthesise them in a single object: the resulting form is a volume that opens up like a spiral and is crowned by a dome. The centrifugal expansion is suggested by the movement of automobiles that run along the heliocoidal ramps inside the building, and along which parking spaces are located. On the upper levels, restaurants, offices, hotels and casinos alternate with one another all the way to the top of the building, with its panoramic dome.

Though these three projects were never built, thanks to the paranoiac clarity of their conceptual structure[68] they had a considerable influence on theoretical debate. What is more, they helped Koolhaas to define the ideas that he would theorise in his 1994 article entitled 'Bigness or the Problem of Large', in which he proposes the investigation of a dimension that lies somewhere between that of the building and that of urban planning[69] becoming, from this moment onwards, the subject of growing theoretical interest.[70]

The same lucid, ironic and paradoxical method is applied by Koolhaas to his smaller projects from this

69 Rem Koolhaas, 'Bigness or the Problem of Large', in *Domus*, no 764 (October 1994), pp 87–90. The essay appears under the same title in OMA, Rem Koolhaas, Bruce Mau, *S,M,L,XL*, The Monacelli Press (New York) and 010 Publishers (Rotterdam), 1995, pp 494–516. In the essay Koolhaas reassumes the prerogatives of the large scale in five points:
1. That of being composed of multiple components, with the consequent break with the traditional idea of unity.
2. The superimposition of levels obtained by mechanical juxtapositions of overlapping layers.
3. The break with the relationship between interior and exterior. While traditional architecture, with its 'transparency' between interior and exterior, offered certainty, the *large scale* causes doubts, results in mysteries.

4. The predomination of the quantitative dimension: the impact of the large building is independent of its architectural quality.
5. Extraneousness to one's surroundings: the *large scale* is no longer part of the built structure, it is a self-sufficient island that is not integrated with its surroundings, but at best coexists with it. Furthermore, Koolhaas delineates the advantages that a reflection on bigness may have on the discipline:
1. It would mark a new beginning because whilst it is true that the *large scale* destroys, it is also true that it recomposes what it interrupts.
2. It would favour the reinsertion of the architect within a team effort, supported by new technologies, engineers, builders, contractors, politicians and many others.

3. It would contribute to creating a new type of city, overcoming the current difficulties faced by urban planning. Large buildings, by cancelling the perennially frustrated desires of planning, could be dropped like UFOs onto the current urban tabula rasa, becoming the city themselves, self-sufficient islands within a context that, otherwise, is destined to offer progressively fewer answers to emerging needs for quality.

70 Together with the reflections made by Koolhaas, there was another book, written by an anthropologist, that had a significant impact on this discussion: Marc Augé's *Non-Places: Introduction to an Anthropology of Supermodernity*, Verso (London), 1995, translated by John Howe from: *Non-lieux. Introduction à une anthropologie de la surmodernité*, Seuil, (Paris), 1992.

**Rem Koolhaas, Villa Dall'Ava, Paris, France, 1985–91: rear elevation.**

The two transversal volumes of the Villa Dall'Ava recall the work of Le Corbusier, while the longitudinal volume is inspired by Mies van der Rohe's glass houses. Koolhaas does not hesitate to slope the pilotis, and mix poor and sophisticated materials with a studied inattention to detailing, in particular that of alignments.

period, which demonstrate an approach to construction that joins a paratactic[71] logic with fragments of famous works of architecture. It is a method that recalls the Post-Modern approach to composition, with the difference being that while the latter did not hesitate to build works by copying – or as one said at the time, citing – the architecture of a pre-modern past, in most cases with classical roots, Koolhaas' works used examples from the Modern Movement, precisely the innovative and experimental tradition that Post-Modernism attempted to abolish. The objective was to create a contemporary language that displayed, through the plurality and fragmentariness of references, the tensions and contrasts of our contemporary era.

For example, in the Villa Dall'Ava, a project begun in 1985 though only completed in 1991, Koolhaas, inspired by Mies van der Rohe and Le Corbusier, attempted to unite the opposing needs of two clients, one of whom wanted a glass house, and the other a pool on the roof. He thus created a longitudinal volume that ends in two transversal volumes. The longitudinal volume is a glass house, surrounded on four sides by glazing reminiscent of the work of Mies. The two transversal volumes, on the other hand, recall the work of Le Corbusier: like his Villa Savoye in Poissy, France (1928–31) they are tripartite spatial organisms – pilotis, inhabited space and roof garden – with strip windows. Through the use of these two references, Koolhaas resolves a professional dilemma and, simultaneously, guarantees the coexist-

........................................................................................................................

**71** Koolhaas, like many of his contemporaries, refuses the syntactic logic typical of traditional composition, where each part is tied to the others by a logic structured on principles of unity, harmony and proportion. His approach, instead, is towards techniques of paratactic composition, founded on the placement and juxtaposition of elements that conserve their individuality and differences. The objective is that of questioning the traditional and academic concept of beauty, something that has proven itself to be totalising and, in the end, suffocating and unsuitable to expressing the multiplicity and contradictions of contemporary society.

**Rem Koolhaas, Kunsthal, Rotterdam, The Netherlands, 1987–92: exterior view.**

The Kunsthal is a box cut by a street and a pedestrian crossing, located at different levels that are perpendicular to one another. Inside a spiral ties together the various activities separated by the two paths. This image shows the road that passes beneath the building.

ence of two different languages by placing one beside the other. The result is an aesthetic of the fragment that is typically Deconstructivist in flavour, in which the sum of the pieces that come together could not be harsher, or less organic. No alignments are respected and there is no well-resolved corner condition. When a window meets a transversal wall, it is rudely interrupted and the passage from one material to the next is brusque and unforgiving.

Koolhaas' most important work from this period is the Kunsthal in Rotterdam, Netherlands (1987–92). The project resulted from a desire to construct a square building, the volume of which is cut by two streets: an existing east–west road and a pedestrian ramp that runs north–south, used to identify the entrance to the park and the Kunsthal. Reconnecting the box, cut into four parts, is a spiral created by the placement of the

sloping planes of the ramps, the raked seating in the auditorium and the horizontal planes of the display spaces, offsetting them in order to create a spatial continuum that begins on the ground floor and, passing through all of the spaces, culminates in the open area of the roof garden. The display spaces and the auditorium thus become elements of a single path that, when followed, allows for an informal meandering from one exhibition to the next, and from the latter to a conference.

The motivation behind this strategy is primarily formal: the encounter between opposing principles. It is not, however, without functional merit: if the spaces articulate a chain of events, then free circulation between them undoubtedly moves towards the culture of multiplication of stimuli, or what Koolhaas calls the culture of congestion.

If we look at the exterior volume of the Kunsthal and its four facades what we see is a banal rectangle of an alarming linearity. However, if we look at the building from an angle we note, at all four corners, that the two converging facades use different materials and are not visually or formally connected with one another: there is no alignment or juxtaposition that is resolved in a pleasurable or harmonious architectural composition, despite the fact that each elevation honestly declares the functions behind it. It is thus a strange paradox typical of the Deconstructivist aesthetic: the application of canonical rules (such as the correspondence between interior and exterior), though within a complex and paradoxical context that creates non-canonical buildings, with a de-structured appearance.

## 1.6 Frank O Gehry: New Compositions

At the time of the 'Deconstructivist Architecture' show, Frank O Gehry was undoubtedly the most well known of the architects involved. By 1988 he could already boast a lengthy and brilliant professional career[72] and, only the year before, he had been the subject of a personal exhibition in Minneapolis, later shown in Houston, Toronto,

72 The office of Frank O Gehry and Associates was founded in 1962. Prior to this he had worked with Victor Gruen (in 1953–4), Hideo Sasaki (1957) and Pereira & Luckman (1957–8).

**Rem Koolhaas, Kunsthal, Rotterdam, The Netherlands, 1987–92: corner detail.**

The facades reveal the functions inside the building, resulting in entirely unresolved corner conditions.

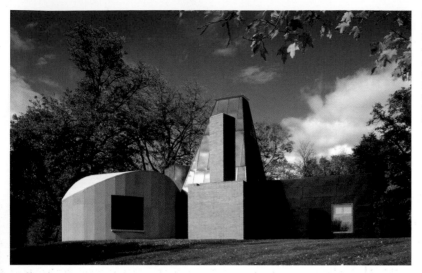

Frank O Gehry, Winton Guest House, Wayzata, Minnesota, USA, 1983–7: exterior view.

The house is composed of elementary volumes, each with a different form. The composition has been compared to the metaphysical and/or still life paintings of the Italian artist Giorgio Morandi.

Atlanta, Los Angeles, Boston and New York. This show foreshadowed the awarding of the Pritzker Prize, one of the most sought after in the field of architecture,[73] which he received in 1989.

As highlighted by Alejandro Zaera Polo in an article on Gehry published in *El Croquis*,[74] the primary fascination with this figure consisted of his solid popular roots, which allowed him to escape from annoying debates between other architects.[75] In fact, Gehry, unlike Eisenman, Koolhaas, Tschumi or Libeskind, lost no time with complicated theoretical questions. His work focused directly on the imagination, involving the senses rather than the intellect, presenting a decisively iconic impact, a highly plastic and sculptural appearance and the creative use of the 'poor' materials of industrial production.

Gehry had been working on his home in Santa Monica, California (1978–9) in previous years, attempting to define a progressively more convincing design strategy. To this end he did not hesitate to experiment with numerous types of research, of which three appear to be the most convincing.

The first focuses on the de-composition of the building into distinct, elementary volumes, each of which is characterised by a form and a material: stucco, stone, copper and zinc. This is the case with the Winton Guest House in Wayzata, Minnesota (1983–7), where four

73 The Pritzker Architecture Prize was established in 1979 by the Hyatt Foundation in Japan to honour 'significant contributions to humanity and the built environment through the art of architecture'.

74 Alejandro Zaera Polo, 'Frank O Gehry, Still Life', in *El Croquis*, no 45 (November 1990), pp 6–21.

75 'The extraordinary success of Frank Gehry in the last few years has perhaps been due to his capacity to attend to the object and the detail without falling into the merely disciplinary discussions that have monopolized cultivated architectural debate since the mid-1970s.' Alejandro Zaera Polo, 'Frank O Gehry, Still Life', p 6.

76 'Winton Guest House', in *El Croquis,*
no 45 (November 1990), p 23.

volumes 'are placed together in a tight complex, like a still life, like a Morandi';[76] the Schnabel Residence in Brentwood, California (1986–9); the psychiatric centre in New Haven, Connecticut (1985–9); and the Edgemar Development in Santa Monica, California (1984–8).

The second focuses on creating unitary buildings, obtained by uniting different elements, or elements that appear to have been subjected to forces of deformation, placing the overall composition in a state of crisis. This can be observed in the American Center in Paris (1988–93), played out entirely on the dialectic between the monolithic nature of the building and the fragmentary aspect of its multiple parts, some of which, surprisingly, appear to slip and pop out of the building itself. Later – the design is from 1992, though

the building was only completed in 1997 – Gehry used the formal strategy with the ING Bank headquarters in Prague, a building better known as 'Fred & Ginger' because it recalls the two famous dancers as they move in a close embrace. What strikes us about this building is the particular solution of the corner, where the glass volume narrows at the midpoint and flares at the base, resembling the hips and dress of a female dancer. In reality, beyond the iconic references, it is a brilliant way of ensuring unexpected views of the building and creating a dialogue with the Baroque forms of the city of Prague.

The third approach focuses on objects with complex forms and highly sculptural impact such as the Vitra Design Museum in Weil am Rhein, Germany (1987–9).

**Frank O Gehry, American Center, Paris, France, 1988–93: view of the main facade.**

In the American Center, Gehry works with the contrast between compact volumes and specific elements, which tend to emerge with their own individual qualities. The effect is rendered more dramatic by steel and glass elements that seem to slip out of the building.

**77** The museum, for example, is mentioned as a precursor in the 'Folding in Architecture' issue of *Architectural Design*, guest-edited by Greg Lynn (1993; revised edition 2003). According to Kenneth Powell's opening essay entitled 'Unfolding Folding': 'The Vitra Museum was an harbinger of things to come' (p 23).

In this work, greatly admired by a generation of young architects who, from the early 1990s, sought to propose a new aesthetic founded on morphogenesis and digital calculation,[77] Gehry sought to subtract architecture from the traditional aspect that marked it, up to this point, in order to make it a purely plastic event.[78] Gehry later pursued this latter direction with great perseverance, resulting in the completion of his two masterpieces: the Walt Disney Concert Hall in Los Angeles (1988–2003) and the Guggenheim Museum in Bilbao (1991–7). More will be said about both of these projects later.

····· **78** This can be seen in the scarcity of the openings along the walls, substituted by skylights on the roof. In the Walt Disney Concert Hall in Los Angeles and the Guggenheim Museum in Bilbao, even the difference between wall and roof disappears, thanks to the use of metal cladding.

## 1.7 Disjunction and Dis-location

In 1992, ten years after the competition for the Parc de la Villette and four years after the 'Deconstructivist Architecture' show, Bernard Tschumi won another important international competition for the Le Fresnoy art school in Tourcoing, northeast of Lille, France.

The site is a piece of land with a few buildings that Tschumi, as per the competition brief, maintained, making only a few modest changes. He occupied the open space with a cinema, recording spaces and administrative offices, covering the entire complex with a steel roof of approximately 100 x 80 metres, composed of opaque and transparent elements. He thus gave the entire complex a coherence of image and simultaneously exalted the different morphologies of the buildings he covered. Between the tops of the

buildings and the underside of the roof he created new covered spaces, connected by a complex system of stairs and walkways, capable of hosting educational activities, lessons and exhibitions and of offering havens of tranquillity and for study.

The resulting space is neither unitary nor fragmentary, neither interior nor exterior. It would probably have found favour with Guy Debord and the Situationists[79] due to its characteristic of not falling into the banality and mechanical nature of the Modernist style, but emerging, almost unexpectedly, from the interaction between structures belonging to different eras and styles. It is precisely for this reason that it represents an example of disjunction, an architectural praxis theorised by Tschumi for some time.[80]

Disjunction is founded on the assumption that, after the crisis of the Modern Movement and its concrete certainties, it no longer makes sense to propose syntheses of resolution, whether they are functional,

**Frank O Gehry, Vitra Design Museum, Weil am Rhein, Germany, 1987–9: exterior view.**

The Vitra Museum is the result of the union and integration of volumes. It anticipates the compositional approach used in more important projects, such as the Guggenheim in Bilbao, and the neo-Baroque research of a new generation of digital architects.

**79** Situationism was founded in 1957 and Guy Debord (1931–94) was one of its leaders. The International Situationist Programme was the creation of situations, defined as 'moments of life concretely and deliberately constructed through the collective organisation of a unitary environment and a play of events'. These situations were to be created through Unitary Urban Planning, a new spatial environment to be realised.

**80** Bernard Tschumi, 'Disjunctions', in *Perspecta 23: The Yale Architectural Journal* (January 1987). This is also found in Bernard Tschumi, *Architecture and Disjunction*, The MIT Press (Cambridge, MA), 1996, pp 207–13. It should be mentioned that Tschumi's education took place in a Situationist environment.

82 Peter Eisenman, "Visions" Unfolding', pp 24–5.

organic or rationalist. Instead, it may be more productive for architecture to become the expression of a lack of something, of a tension. This lack transforms into an opening (this is the meaning of the word dis-junction), into a desire, a stimulus for discovery, and an invitation to exceed limits.

The same year that Tschumi won the competition for the Fresnoy school, Peter Eisenman wrote an article for *Domus* entitled *"Visions"* Unfolding: Architecture in the Age of Electronic Media'[81] in which he proposed theoretical questions based on his recent architectural work, oriented towards complex geometries, vibrant spaces and precarious points of view. The architecture that has been handed down to us – Eisenman states – has, up to now, been responsible for overcoming gravity, monumentalising this action and translating it into visual relationships. This has two consequences: firstly it has established, through the opposing categories of inside and outside, above and below, in front and behind, left and right, a precise relationship between itself and the

user; secondly, it is structured in such a way that 'any position occupied by a subject provides the means for understanding that position in relation to a particular spatial typology, such as a rotunda, a transept crossing, an axis, an entry'.[82]

At the base of this architecture, stable, functional, conceptually harmonious and hierarchical, there is a perspectival conception of space that, as much as it was criticised by 19th-century avant-garde art, for example Cubism and Constructivism, still survives in architecture. However – Eisenman continues – if electronic society is discarding the traditional way of understanding vision, transforming it from an intellectual activity (perspective) into an emotional fact (pure image), then architecture must also take this into account in some way.

This leads to the proposal of introducing a new operative category – 'dis-location' – that, for various reasons, resembles the 'dis-junction' proposed by

81 Peter Eisenman, "Visions" Un-
folding: Architecture in the Age of
Electronic Media', in *Domus*, no 734
(January 1993), pp 17–25.

Tschumi. Dislocation is an attempt to separate the subject of the work of rationalisation from the space that it instinctively attempts to create within a given site. We are thus speaking primarily of 'separating the eye from the mind'. Dis-location allows one to glimpse the existence of different spaces, 'other', with respect to those that we are used to experiencing and, above all – as hermetically affirmed by Eisenman – to understand that there exists 'an affective space, a dimension in the space that dislocates the discursive function of the human subject and thus vision, and at the same moment, creates a condition of time, of an event in

**Bernard Tschumi, Le Fresnoy art school, Tourcoing, France, 1992–7: interior view.**

The roof that Tschumi designed for the Le Fresnoy project reinserts the existing architectural elements, giving them new meanings. In this way Tschumi demonstrates the possibility of using a strategy that goes beyond the rigid autonomy that opposes conservation to new construction. He also demonstrates the potential of an in-between space that is neither interior nor exterior.

**Coop Himmelb(l)au, rooftop remodelling, Falkestrasse 6, Vienna, Austria, 1983–9: exterior and interior views.**

Seen from the exterior, this addition appears to be strident and out of context, almost a steel insect resting on the roof of a 19th-century building. From the interior it offers unexpected views of the sky.

84 A similar direction was pursued by Lebbeus Woods (born 1940), one of the poets of Deconstructivist fragmentation, who tied his activities to the design of a world that moved outside of the logic of functionalism and profit. See Lebbeus Woods, *Anarchitecture: Architecture Is a Political Act,* Academy Editions (London), 1992.

83 Peter Eisenman, "Visions" Unfolding', p 25.

which there is the possibility on the environment to look back at the subject, the possibility of the *gaze*'.[83]

If the dis-location proposed by Eisenman aims primarily at criticising the conceptual references through which the intellect appropriates space, the work of Coop Himmelb(l)au aims at involving the senses and the body. This leads to the construction of strident and anti-ergonomic spatial creations that are simultaneously curious and involving. An example of this is the rooftop remodelling at Falkestrasse 6 in Vienna (1983–9), where the new construction appears like some mechanical and parasitic monster that sits atop the 19th-century building. However, once we overcome our initial reaction, we notice that it is an object that creates unexpected relationships with

the sky, dis-locating the observer towards a sublime dimension that boxes, on the other hand, preclude. We can also mention the Funder 3 factory in St Veit/Glan in Austria (1988–9), where the dis-articulation of the building volumes into planes and lines in an apparent state of precariousness and imbalance creates a sense of discomfort that observers can overcome only when they free themselves of the academic idea of order, allowing for the enjoyment of an explosive landscape that is rich with surprises.[84]

Another architect who moves along the lines of dis-location is Daniel Libeskind, though in a metaphorical, analogical and poetic way. For Libeskind, in fact, architectural signs are understood only in relation to another reality: that of history, music and poetry. Vice

versa, history, music and poetry can only be understood if they are translated into signs that define the spaces of our existence: architecture. All of these signs, which together create a vortex of references,[85] weave the pattern of the world, constituting its meaning (meaning is in fact the translation of a system of signs into another system of signs). However, it is a meaning whose ultimate aspects escape us because, as hard as we try to organise a matrix of meaning and identify its roots, in the end the framework that we manage to reveal is always incomplete, temporary, fragmentary and dis-articulated.[86]

Inspired by Hebrew mysticism, the work of Libeskind has a cryptic and esoteric aspect. There is also a fascination with a metaphysical vision that he matured with the Jewish Museum in Berlin, a work that he began in 1989, though it was only inaugurated in 1998.

During the same years in which the poetics of Deconstructivism were being developed, there were also other lines of research that were less disarticulated and more unitary. Some were aimed at the rediscovery of the concrete qualities and materiality of space, others at a more Minimalist approach – which we will discuss later – and others still were more focused on the technological dimension.

**Peter Eisenman, Rebstock Park, Frankfurt, Germany, 1990–1: perspective.**

The design of the residential blocks is the result of the deformation imposed by the surrounding landscape. Rebstock Park had a notable influence on younger architects, in particular Greg Lynn, who saw the blocks as the anticipation of the techniques of digital architecture.

85 This also results in the original means of presenting his work, which makes use of the overlapping of different media: architectural drawings, writing, musical annotations.
86 The pattern is the root and matrix of the world. This can be intuited in his book that is, in many ways, intentionally obscure: Daniel Libeskind, *Radix-Matrix*, Prestel (Munich and New York), 1997.

## 1.8 Between Gesture and Perception: Fuksas and Holl

After moving to Paris in 1985, motivated by the search for new professional opportunities,[87] Massimiliano Fuksas[88] abandoned the style that had marked his previous work, characterised by elementary geometric figures that, due to their iconic aspect, are a Post-Modern derivation. The definitive break from these forms took place in 1986 when, after being invited by François Geindre, the Mayor of Hérouville-Saint-Clair, he called upon Otto Steidle,[89] Will Alsop[90] and Jean Nouvel to work together on the construction of the Europe Tower. The designers avoided the production of a unitary organism, opting to casually pile their four different projects on top of one another, developing the logic of overlapping that, in 1983, led Tschumi and Koolhaas to their proposals for the Parc de la Villette.

In later projects, such as the Culture Centre and Media Library in Rezé, France (1986–91), the Îlot Candie Saint-Bernard in Paris (1987–96), the Saint-Exupéry College in Noisy-le-Grand, France (1989–93) and the Faculty of Law and Economic Sciences in Limoges, France (1989–96), Fuksas returned to the creation of a more unitary image generated by a unifying design gesture. At the same time, by using different materials for each project – from glass to metal mesh, from corten steel to copper and wood – he experimented with a sensual architecture, rich with material and chromatic values. The apex of this approach is the Musée des Graffiti at Niaux, France (1988–93). The entrance to the grotto that contains a series of famous prehistoric

.......................................................................................................................

87 At the end of the 1980s, France was witness to an extraordinary period. Competitions were held, in addition to the large projects called for by Mitterrand, for numerous public buildings and schemes in and around Paris and other cities. In 1988 Fuksas participated in six competitions, followed by 16 in 1989, 18 in 1990 and 10 in 1991, of which he won a total of 11. See Luca Molinari, *Massimiliano Fuksas: Works and Projects, 1970–2005* Skira International Corporation (Milan), 2005, p 47.

88 Massimiliano Fuksas (born 1944) studied in Rome, where he played a primary role in student protests in the 1960s, graduating in 1969. His first projects include a gymnasium in Paliano, Italy (1979–85) and the new Town Hall in Cassino, Italy (1980–90). 89 Otto Steidle (born 1943) is a German architect born in Monaco and active as a university professor. His works display a balanced relationship between the formal motifs of current construction and the use of lightweight technologies, glass and steel.

90 William Allen Alsop (born 1947), while studying at the Architectural Association, participated in the competition for the Centre Pompidou, coming second. After an apprenticeship with Maxwell Fry (1899–1987) and Cedric Price, he opened his own office, Alsop & Lyall, which became Alsop & Störmer in 1991. His work features colourful and playful forms and elements of High Tech, and is permeated by a pop and surreal vein.

**Massimiliano Fuksas, Musée des Graffiti, Niaux, France, 1988–93.**

The entrance to the painted cave recalls the profile of a prehistoric animal and the gestures of Neanderthal man as he drew. The rusted surface of the cor-ten steel recalls the ferrous layers visible in the stratification of the rock face.

cave paintings is defined by a walkway sandwiched between two angled walls of cor-ten steel, which recall an abstract representation of a prehistoric animal or an ancestral force that emerges from the cave. As the layer of patina covers the steel, it gives the object a strong tactile component and favours its insertion within its natural context.

The American architect Steven Holl[91] was also of the opinion that it was necessary to move beyond Deconstruction.

'Deconstruction' – Holl states, in the words of Mark Taylor – 'has finally run its course. We have tried to deconstruct, to fragment everything ad infinitum.

What we need now is a philosophy of how to put things together. My insistence is on the value of the whole, especially for architecture.' To achieve this, Holl implements a strategy that combines phenomenology with a conceptual approach.[92]

The phenomenological approach that Holl attributes to the philosophy of Maurice Merleau-Ponty[93] results in his valorisation of materials, sites, colours and light. The conceptual aspect is derived from the search for a theory that guides each project, bringing unity to the composition and avoiding a chaotic and disordered design in which various effects follow one another without a precise guiding line. For example, in the Stretto House in Dallas, Texas (1990–2) the concept is

91 Steven Holl (born 1947) graduated from the University of Washington and continued his architectural studies in Rome in 1970 and later at the Architectural Association in 1976, the same year he founded Steven Holl Architects in New York City.
92 For Alejandro Zaera Polo this is a 'hybrid mode between a conceptual framework and a phenomenological approach': see Alejandro Zaera Polo, 'A Conversation with Steven Holl', in *El Croquis*, no 78 (1996), p 11.
93 Holl thus demonstrates his preference by contrasting an intellectual figure, attentive to the analysis of sensation and phenomena such as Maurice Merleau-Ponty (1908–61), with the more intellectual Derrida, entirely projected towards the philosophy of language. However, as architectural Deconstruction has little to do with its philosophical counterpart, an architecture that is attentive to the phenomena of light and matter, such as that of Holl, has equally few points of contact with phenomenological philosophy.

Steven Holl, Stretto House,
Dallas, Texas, USA, 1990–2:
model.

The design of the Stretto House
is the result of the transposition
into architectural form of a musical theme by the composer Béla
Bartók. The theme is suggested
by the site, with its four dams,
which in turn recall the movements of the composition.

taken from a musical composition by the composer Béla
Bartók, whose four-four times were in turn inspired
by the observation of the site, which contained four
pre-existing dams.[94]

The most interesting works produced by Holl, other
than the Stretto House, are the residences in Fukuoka,
Japan (1998–91) and the DE Shaw & Co Office and Trading Area in New York (1992). In both cases Holl plays
with the dialectic between the simplicity of the structure and the variety of the components. In Fukuoka,
he does this by making each apartment different from
the next, and articulating each according to an elegant
system of coloured and pivoting screens, inspired by
the Japanese ideal of fluid, flexible space. In New York
this is achieved by designing a central atrium illuminated by multiple windows, each of which filters a different colour of light.

# 1.9 The Minimalist Approach: Herzog & de Meuron

The German-speaking part of Switzerland,
towards the end of the 1980s, was home
to the development of a line of research
that was antithetical to that of Deconstructivism. This was discovered in 1991
by *The Architectural Review* and presented
in an issue dedicated to the phenomenon,
introduced by an article written by Peter
Buchanan.

'There is,' states the critic, 'an up and coming generation of architects whose work is a welcome relief after
the fashionable formal excesses of the '80s. Some of
them, such as Jacques Herzog & Pierre de Meuron and
the very un-Swiss Santiago Calatrava are starting to
achieve near cult status internationally; others deserve

94 The idea of translating a musical
composition into space is not new in
architecture. We need only look to
the Renaissance, the Baroque or the
work of Le Corbusier, who collaborated
with the musician Iannis Xenakis
(1922–2001). Towards the end of the
1980s there were a number of architects interested in this issue: many
of these were tied to the Architectural Association (Holl, to be precise,
completed his studies at this school),
whilst some were American. However,
while architects such as Eisenman or
Tschumi were primarily interested in
understanding how to translate one
system of signs into another, broaden-
ing their research beyond music and
transposing, for example, poetic or
literary texts into architecture, Holl
proved to be little interested in the
exquisitely linguistic aspects of the
issue, focusing on the theme of space,
and its rhythmic and perceptive
aspects.

Herzog & de Meuron,
Ricola Warehouse,
Laufen, Switzerland, 1986–7.

In an era marked by the aesthetics of Deconstructivism, the
Ricola Warehouse stands out for
its absence of expressive rhetoric, its use of economic materials
and the simplicity of the design,
based on the proportions of the
golden section.

**95** Peter Buchanan, 'Swiss Essential-ists', in *The Architectural Review*, no 1127 (January 1991), p 19.

**96** Jacques Herzog (born 1950) and Pierre de Meuron (born 1950) studied at the Eidgenössische Technische Hochschule in Zurich (ETH) with Aldo Rossi, Luigi Snozzi (born 1932), Bruno Reichlin (born 1941) and Dolf Schnebli (born 1928). Their first projects, including the Frei photographic studio in Weil am Rhein, Germany (1981–2), the Stone House in Tavole, Italy (1982–8) and a house for an art collector in Therwil, Switzerland (1985–6), employ simple and traditional technologies and forms, including the sloped roof. The studio has two associates: Harry Gugger (born 1956) since 1991 and Christine Binswanger (born 1964) since 1994.

to be better known. Except for Calatrava, most of these architects share a continuing fascination with Modernism, with its early architecture and its contemporary art, both of which inspire a common concern to distil and express essentials.'[95]

Buchanan's insights revealed themselves to be accurate: in only a few years Herzog & de Meuron[96] acquired enormous renown, as did at least one of the other architects mentioned in the issue: Peter Zumthor.[97] A no less famous future awaited the Spanish-born Santiago Calatrava who, because he followed a different form of research than the rigorous Minimalism examined here, will be discussed in paragraph 1.11.

It was during the second half of the 1980s, with the Ricola Warehouse (1986–7) in Laufen, a city near Basel, that Herzog & de Meuron defined a strategy that went beyond the vernacular approach of their previous work, focusing, with more abstract and figuratively more efficient images, on the building envelope – what Robert Venturi had called the theme of the 'decorated shed'.[98] Here they proposed a simple rectangle whose facades are designed by the overlapping of concrete panels, installed in such a manner as to recall the stacking of products inside the building. The gap between the panels allows for internal ventilation. However, the vertical progression of the strips is organised according to the golden section, giving the building a quality reminiscent of a Minimalist sculpture. The exposed installation of the wooden slats, concrete panels and insulation recall the poetics of poor materials used in the architecture-sculptures of Gehry, though they

**97** Peter Zumthor (born 1943), after graduating and serving an apprenticeship with his father as a cabinet-maker, joined a company located in Chur responsible for historic buildings. The issue of *The Architectural Review* published his office in Haldenstein (1986) and the Saint Benedict Chapel (1987–9), two small projects characterised by simplicity and the sober use of traditional technologies.

**Herzog & de Meuron, Pfaffenholz Sports Centre, St Louis, France, 1989–93.**

The simplicity of the volumes of this sports complex serves to highlight the design of the glazing, with its etched pattern of chipboard, and the concrete panels, which feature an oversized and out-of-focus pattern of the material itself.

overturn the presuppositions, orienting their research no longer in the direction of Deconstructivism, but in a decidedly rigorist one.

'The Ricola warehouse,' Antonio Citterio once confessed to me, 'was a true revelation for the younger generation. It showed us that there was a way of working that was different from what had become the asphyxiated historicism of Post-Modernism and, at the same time, that was not lost in the excesses of form, as was the case with the Deconstructivists.'[99]

In the years around 1989, the change announced by the Ricola Warehouse was concretised in works in which the theme was progressively more that of the skin, the epidermis of the building. They include the signal building in Auf dem Wolf, Basel (1989–95), the SUVA Apartment Buildings in Basel (1988–93), the Pfaffenholz Sports Centre in St Louis, France (1989–93), the Goetz Gallery in Munich (1989–92) and the Schützenmattstrasse apartments in Basel (1984–93). These projects take the form of envelopes designed as if they were works of art, and thus use the same techniques employed by artists, such as decontextualisation, disorientation, perceptive deception and changes of scale.[100] The signal box in Auf dem Wolf, for example, is similar to a giant pop battery and, thanks to the delicate plays of chiaroscuro caused by the differing orientation of the copper bands that wrap it, appears like a vibrant Minimalist sculpture. The shutters on the Schützenmattstrasse building, based on the design of the sewer grates in Basel, create a per-

**98** For Robert Venturi (born 1925) there are two different approaches to architecture: the 'duck' and the 'decorated shed'. Those who make use of the 'duck' (the word comes from a duck-shaped kiosk built in Los Angeles to sell products made with duck meat) wish to represent the theme being dealt with through the form of the building: this is the case with the cross-shaped Catholic church. The 'decorated shed' is used by those who do not focus on form, but on the images used to decorate the container or overlapped upon it.

**99** Conversation with Antonio Citterio (born 1950), during preparation of a monographic publication: Luigi Prestinenza Puglisi, *Antonio Citterio* (two editions – one Italian and one English, Edilstampa (Rome), 2006. At the time Citterio was working in Weil am Rhein and thus often found himself in Basel.

**100** An in-depth analysis of the use of these techniques can be found in: Alessandro D'Onofrio, *Herzog & de Meuron: Anomalie della norma,* Kappa, (Rome), 2003.

103 Tony Fretton (born 1945) founded
his practice in 1982. He specialises
in the construction of spaces for art,
often developing his projects together
with artists.
104 David Chipperfield (born 1953)
studied at the Architectural Association, graduating in 1977. Although he
spent time working for Richard Rogers
and Norman Foster, his work quickly
moved towards a minimalist approach.

ceptive dislocation resulting from the fact that what we expect to find on the horizontal plane of the paving is found on the vertical facade. The etched panels of the Pfaffenholz Sports Centre – which reproduce, at a giant scale, the grain of concrete – play with the ambiguity that a visually poor material is decorated precisely with the same material, though shown under a virtual magnifying lens.

## 1.10 Minimalism in England, France and Japan

In the early 1980s, John Pawson[101] had already completed a number of clearly Minimalist works, including his 1982 renovation of the apartment of the author Bruce Chatwin, a 45-square-metre space, aesthetically furnished with a few carefully selected objects.[102] However, it is at the start of the 1990s that we can observe the beginnings of the definition, in Great Britain, of an alternative to Deconstruction and High Tech in the work of Pawson, Tony Fretton[103] and David Chipperfield.[104]

This was initially visible in the design of interior spaces, houses and shops, that employed a synthesis of clear and elementary forms, limiting the effects of decoration to plays of light and the contrast of materials, for example plastered surfaces (often white or grey) and the use of marble, wood or exposed concrete. This is the case with the Equipment stores designed by Chipperfield in London and Paris (1991) where the only bright colours are those of the shirts, displayed on a diaphanous, backlit shelf.

Perhaps the most well-known work from this period is the Lisson Galleries in London (1992) by Tony Fretton, with its sober exterior designed primarily with large

101 John Pawson (born 1949), after
studying at Eton College, left school
to travel in the Middle East, India,
Australia and Japan, where he was
introduced to the architecture of the
designer Shiro Kuramata (1934–91). In
1979 he registered at the Architectural
Association, which he left in 1981 to
set up his own practice.

102 The history of this project can
be found in 'Thinking up against a
wall', in *Domus*, no 901 (March 2007),
pp 68–71.

Tony Fretton, Lisson Galleries, London, England, 1992.

The facade of the Lisson Galleries is the result of the balance between the void of the large window on the ground floor and the solid form of the upper floors, animated by an asymmetrically placed opening.

Dominique Perrault, Bibliothèque Nationale de France, Paris, France, 1989–95.

The Bibliothèque Nationale de France is developed around a large sunken court, occupied by vegetation and defined at the corners by four L-shaped glass towers, reminiscent of an open book, that contain the stacks.

105 Yehuda Safran, 'Tony Fretton: Lisson Gallery a Londra', in *Domus*, no 738 (May 1992), p 44.

106 Dominique Perrault (born 1953) opened his own office in 1981. The ESIEE building was his first important work.

sheets of glazing that give the building an abstract appearance, almost out of time. Yehuda Safran, in an article for *Domus*, speaks of a rigorous, attentive and profound architecture and does not hesitate to recall the affirmation made by Mies van der Rohe: 'In my opinion only a relation that touches the essence of time can be real.'[105]

From the second half of the 1980s onwards, France was also home to the definition of a form of research that tended to favour essential forms. One of its forerunners, demonstrating his usual ability to anticipate the future, was Jean Nouvel. His work from this period manifests a growing interest in the theme of transparency. This would lead him to design the Tour Sans Fin for the La Défense neighbourhood in Paris (1989), a tower whose summit almost dissolves into the surrounding atmosphere; the building for the Les Thermes Hotel and Spa in Dax, France (1990–2); the Cartier factory in Villeret, Switzerland (1990–2); and, later, the Fondation Cartier in Paris (1991–4), a building that – as

we will see in the next chapter – uses a system of glass screens, both transparent and reflective, in an attempt to render tangible the theme of the disappearance of the architectural object.

Less loaded with atmospheric qualities is the Minimalist work of Dominique Perrault.[106] With his École Supérieure d'Ingénieurs en Électronique et Électrotechnique (ESIEE) in Marne-la-Vallée, France (1984–7) he had already proposed a building whose form was reduced to a large, sloping plane, to which were attached the linear volumes of the laboratories. However, it is with his Hôtel Industriel Jean-Baptiste Berlier in Paris (1986–90) that he proposes a glass box whose simplicity is the clear antithesis of the complex forms favoured by Deconstructivist architects. His objective, as noted by Frédéric Migayrou, was that of achieving a ground zero of form, a 'neutral state that precedes and conditions all expression'.[107] In practical terms this is rendered concrete in a building-display case that exposes the transparency of its internal spaces,

107 Frédéric Migayrou, 'Notes on the Architecture of Dominique Perrault', in *El Croquis*, no 104 (2001), p 259.

Dominique Perrault, Hôtel Industriel Jean-Baptiste Berlier, Paris, France, 1986–90.

The Hôtel Industriel is a wilfully inexpressive volume, a glass display case that is animated by what takes place inside.

**108** The definition of 'zero-degree envelopes' can be found in the book-interview *Tschumi on Architecture: Conversations with Enrique Walker,* The Monacelli Press (New York), 2006, p 92.
**109** The self-taught Tadao Ando (born 1941) quickly became famous for his buildings, including the Azuma Residence in Osaka (1975–6), which were inspired by the Minimalist reduction of Mies van der Rohe, Le Corbusier's poetics of *béton brut* (reinforced concrete) and the monumental geometry of Louis Kahn (1901–74).

occupied by about 40 different companies. The image of the building, consequently, while maintaining the constancy of its envelope, was destined to change over time in relation to the history of its inhabitants and the changes they made. Perrault won the competition for the Bibliothèque Nationale de France in 1989. The project, a large central void defined by four L-shaped corner towers, was completed in 1995.

This passion for simple forms also attracted Bernard Tschumi who, between 1990 and 1991, completed a pavilion in Groningen where, with the exception of the sloping floor resting on a few concrete piers, the walls, roof and load-bearing structure are all made of glass. It is the starting point for a form of research that favours the construction of neutral containers – 'zero-degree envelopes' – where architecture almost tends to disappear. [108]

In Japan this Minimalist approach was represented by two figures pursuing antagonistic lines of research: Toyo Ito and Tadao Ando.[109] For the former, as we have seen, transparency and lightness were the results of the IT revolution and its consequent dematerialisation of the real. For the latter, whose research began with his first works in the 1970s, formal reduction was, instead, an expedient for creating new aesthetic spaces, essential and qualitatively excellent – inspired by the imperative of an almost Miesian nothingness, and in opposition to a world that, precisely because of the domination

**Bernard Tschumi, Glass Pavilion, Groningen, The Netherlands, 1990–1.**

The Glass Pavilion is a small, glazed structure that contains information counters. It materialises the need for transparency and the lightness of a society in which flows of information have a growing relevance.

**Tadao Ando, Contemporary Art Museum, Naoshima, Japan, 1988–92: aerial view.**

The Contemporary Art Museum balances the geometric rigour typical of Tadao Ando's compositions with the softness of the curves of the landscape into which it is inserted.

110 This is one of the reasons why Tadao Ando was so appreciated by Kenneth Frampton (born 1930) who, in the 1980s, saw him as one of the representatives of critical regionalism, a phenomenon that focused on opposing the growing globalisation of architectural languages; and by traditionalists such as Vittorio Gregotti who saw him as the champion of a rigorist approach to architecture.

111 Kazuyo Sejima (born 1956) opened her own practice in 1987, having been apprenticed to Toyo Ito. Between 1987 and 1988 she completed the Platform 1 house in Katsuura, Chiba, Japan, that partially recalls Ito's ideas of contemporary dwelling expressed in his *Pao 1* and *Pao 2* projects.

112 Toyo Ito speaks of this in 'Diagram Architecture', in *El Croquis*, no 77-I (1996), pp 18–20.

of new technologies, was chaotic, unauthentic and consumerist.[110] The result is a certain quality that could be called rhetorical, class-conscious and monumental, compromising even the best examples of his work where, fortunately, architecture confronts its natural environment, almost absorbing and disappearing into it, thanks to studied cuts and the use of light.

A third approach to Japanese Minimalism was discovered at the beginning of the 1990s by an architect who had been apprenticed to Toyo Ito: Kazuyo Sejima.[111] Sejima is extraneous to the temptations of technology and, at the same time, far removed from the monumentalism of Ando. She experimented with this approach in the Saishunkan Seiyaku Women's Dormitory in Kumamoto, Japan (1990–1), a building composed of elementary forms that are joined to one another by an additive and almost diagrammatic logic[112] that recalls the abstract space of comics. The relations between the parts are essential, objects are reduced to primary and elementary characteristics – colours and geometric

forms – and the absence of points of reference or qualitatively relevant nodes leads to the creation of a homogenous and isotropic space that, as in a video game, allows for a freedom of movement, theoretically in all directions. Finally, there is also the cancellation of almost any expressive or stylistic desire. This research was re-proposed by Koolhaas in a competition that he organised in 1992 for the magazine *The Japan Architect*, which called for the design of a 'House With No Style', a project that aspired to anonymity.[113]

# 1.11 The Development of High Tech

Initially launched in the 1970s and consolidated in the early '80s, High Tech continued to spread in a variety of different directions: from the neo-organic work of Santiago Calatrava,[114] to the neo-humanist

**Kazuyo Sejima, Saishunkan Seiyaku Women's Dormitory, Kumamoto, Japan, 1990–1.**

The Minimalist buildings of Kazuyo Sejima are abstract and often diagrammatic, setting them apart from the more classical and monumental works of Tadao Ando and the vibrant and organic works of Toyo Ito.

113 The competition results were published in Volume 9 of *The Japan Architect* (1992): 'Japanese Architecture Scene in 1992. Results: Shinkenchiku Residential Design Competition. Judge: Rem Koolhaas'.

114 After studying in Valencia, Santiago Calatrava (born 1951) studied engineering in Zurich.

115 After completing the Centre Pompidou, Renzo Piano (born 1937) began to move towards a less aggressive architecture where technology was better reconciled with the human dimension. This was the direction taken by his mobile workshop for the urban expansion of Otranto (1979), with which he attempted experiences of involvement and participated in urban planning; the temporary IBM pavilion (1982–4), built using a wood structure; and the musical space (1983–4), similar to a ship, constructed for *Prometheus*, the opera by the composer Luigi Nono, presented in Milan and Venice.
116 In 1990 Will Alsop completed the Hamburg Ferry Terminal. From this year onwards he was involved with the Hôtel du Département des Bouches-du-Rhône, better known as 'Le Grand Bleu', completed in 1994, launching him on the international scene.

approach taken by Renzo Piano,[115] to the playful work of Will Alsop.[116]

The Spanish Santiago Calatrava earned international attention with his Hall for the Lucerne Station in Switzerland (1983–9) and the Stadelhofen Station in Zurich (1983–90). They recall the wrapping forms of 1950s and '60s architecture, experimented with by Eero Saarinen, Jørn Utzon and Felix Candela[117] and the neo-gothic and neo-organic forms of Antoni Gaudí.[118]

In particular, the Stadelhofen in Zurich is a railway station marked by a lightweight steel canopy that recalls the articulations of a living organism, fixed in a moment of equilibrium and, in its commercial spaces, the entrails of a prehistoric animal, whose rhythm is marked by a powerful structure of flat arches in reinforced concrete.

Fascinated by nature, Calatrava also experimented with complex moveable elements: for example the Kuwait Pavilion for Expo '92 in Seville, whose roof, made of shaped wooden beams, was able to assume infinite intermediate positions between closed and open. We can also mention the competition for the addition to and restoration of the Reichstag in Berlin (1992), where he designed the assembly halls with an operable glass roof that allowed the public to follow the parliamentary sessions. Calatrava reached his maximum poetic intensity in his bridge designs, for example the Alamillo Bridge in Seville (1987–92), or the Devesa in Ripoll, Spain (1989–91), where elegant, asymmetric structures balance a dynamic image.

Renzo Piano is an architect who is poorly represented by the moniker High Tech. In 1986 he completed the Menil Museum in Houston, Texas, where he attempted to demonstrate that a technologically innovative work could use traditional materials, such as wood, and achieve, not unlike the ancients, delicate effects of light. Between 1987 and 1990 Piano was presented with the opportunity to design the Institut de Recherche

117 Eero Saarinen (1910–61), Jørn Utzon (born 1918) and Felix Candela (1910–97) are, respectively, the designers of the John F Kennedy Trans World Airlines Terminal Building in New York (1956–62), the Sydney Opera House (1957–73) and the Lomas de Cuernavaca 'open' chapel in Palmira, Mexico (1958), all of which are characterised by their technological advances and their curving forms that recall those of the natural world.

118 Antoni Gaudí i Cornet (1852–1926) is the world-famous designer of the gigantic and complex church of the Sagrada Família in Barcelona, begun in 1883 and still under construction.

**Santiago Calatrava, Stadelhofen Station, Zurich, Switzerland, 1983–90: view of the canopies.**

Calatrava's structures recall the forms of nature by which they are inspired. In the case of the Stadelhofen Station, the lightness of the canopies in the upper levels is contrasted by the heavier and bone-like concrete structures of the shopping centre below.

**Renzo Piano, Columbus International Exposition, Genoa, Italy, 1988–92.**

For the Columbus International Exposition, Piano was responsible for the renovation of the port of Genoa. The project is crowned by a panoramic elevator that humanises the image of the winch used in the port to lift goods.

et Coordination Acoustique/Musique (IRCAM). The building, located beside the Centre Pompidou in Paris, refuses the aesthetic of exposed building services and large glazed surfaces: it is primarily below-ground, and the exposed portion, inserted with much discretion within the historical block, is clad in cleanly designed terracotta bricks. The only memory of the futuristic components of High Tech is the elevator, the glass cabins of which are exposed, and some exposed air-conditioning ducts, aligned, well ordered and protruding above the street level.

The separation from his earlier works is even clearer in his later work, including the design of the Columbus International Exhibition in Genoa, Italy (1988–92), the UNESCO Research Laboratories in Vesima, Italy (1989–91) and others, such as the passenger terminal at Kansai International Airport in Japan (1988–94), the church of Padre Pio in San Giovanni Rotondo, Italy (1991–2004), the Potsdamer Platz in Berlin (1992–2000) and the Jean-Marie Tjibaou Cultural Center in Noumea,

New Caledonia (1991–8). Despite the fact that they are highly different works, they are all united by the desire to humanise technology, to recover the materials and atmospheres of the past, and to mediate between the old and the new, without renouncing innovation or falling into the trap of nostalgia.

Even Norman Foster,[119] Richard Rogers,[120] Michael Hopkins[121] and Nicholas Grimshaw,[122] whom we can consider as the most canonical representatives of High Tech, were experimenting at this time with a softer approach, part of an attempt to create relationships with context and move in a more ecologically responsible direction.

Between 1989 and 1991 Norman Foster completed the Sackler Galleries at the Royal Academy of Arts in

**119** Norman Foster (born 1935) came to the fore with his offices for Willis Faber & Dumas in Ipswich, UK (1971–5) and the Sainsbury Centre for the Visual Arts in Norwich, UK (1974–8). Between 1979 and 1985 he completed the Hong Kong and Shanghai Banking Corporation Headquarters in Hong Kong, considered by many to be his masterpiece due to its complex structural system, clearly visible on the facade, with its enormous trusses used to hang the floors below.
**120** After completing the Centre Pom-pidou in Paris, Richard Rogers (born 1933) continued to design buildings with a highly technological impact and exposed services and structures. His most famous work is probably the Lloyd's Building in London (1978–86).
**121** Michael Hopkins (born 1935), once a partner with Foster Associates (1965–75), opened his own office in 1976. His primary works include the Schlumberger Research Centre in Cambridge (1982–5), which features plastic tent-structures suspended from a lightweight steel frame.

**122** Nicholas Grimshaw (born 1939), once a partner with Terry Farrell, founded his own company specialising in prefabricated elements. He built the English Pavilion for Expo '92 in Seville, with its attractive water wall that helped to balance the energetic qualities of the building.

**Norman Foster, London Stansted Airport, Essex, England, 1987–91: view of the entrance.**

The decision to separate the distribution of the weight of the roof onto four connected columns allows for a lightweight structure that is both modular and highly flexible.

**Norman Foster, Sackler Galleries, Royal Academy of Arts, London, England, 1989–91: interior view.**

In this impeccable project for the Royal Academy of Arts, where the cornice of the old building is used as a pedestal for statues, Foster demonstrates that High Tech can also be used to enhance historical structures.

**Norman Foster, Carré d'Art, Nîmes, France, 1987–93: view of the building in its archaeological context.**

The slender columns of the new glass and steel project are clearly inspired by those of the nearby Roman temple.

**Renzo Piano, Institut de Recherche et Coordination Acoustique/Musique (IRCAM), Paris, France, 1987–90: view from the plaza in front of the Centre Pompidou.**

Clad with terracotta panels, the IRCAM appears to have been designed by a different hand than that responsible for the neighbouring Centre Pompidou. It testifies to Renzo Piano's decisive moving away from the High Tech aesthetic of exposed services and building systems.

**Santiago Calatrava, Alamillo Bridge, Seville, Spain, 1987–92: view from the riverbank.**

The Alamillo Bridge, built for Expo '92 in Seville, owes its elegance to the asymmetrical structure and slope of the pylon that exposes the dynamics of the forces at play.

London, demonstrating that a contemporary structure, lightweight and transparent, can contribute to the functional reorganisation and enhancement of a historical one. This experiment was successfully repeated with the Carré d'Art in Nîmes, France (1987–93) where he inserted, in the midst of the historical centre and in front of a Roman temple, a five-storey cultural centre (with an equal number of storeys below ground). Thanks to the simple, almost classical design of the glazed facades and the insertion of a high portico, supported by slender columns, the building easily dialogues with its Roman counterpart, demonstrating the unfounded nature of the negative accusations made against High Tech which are based on the idea that the style is necessarily cold and a-contextual. Between 1989 and 1991 Foster completed the Century Tower in Tokyo which marks, with respect to the more machine-like Hong Kong and Shanghai Banking Corporation Headquarters in Hong Kong (1981–6), a moment of formal simplification – a simplification that is reinforced in the elegant structure of London's third airport at Stansted in Essex (1987–91), supported by slender structures that create a rectangular grid of square modules.

More characteristic in expressive terms are the buildings of Richard Rogers from this period. We can mention the Kabuki-cho Tower in Tokyo (1987–93), the Channel 4 Headquarters in London (1990–4) and the Human Rights Tribunal in Strasbourg, France (1989–94). His unbuilt works include the Tokyo Forum (1990), a complex architectural machine which was to have contained three large halls connected by escalators and panoramic elevators that, in turn, covered large spaces of daily life, including shops, cafés, cinemas, restaurants, exhibition spaces, musical workshops and theatres.

**Richard Rogers, Tokyo Forum, Tokyo, Japan, 1990: longitudinal section.**

This project develops the Archigram-inspired ideas based on freedom, flexibility, technology and lightness that informed the Centre Pompidou in Paris. Below, a large covered plaza open to the public; above, suspended spaces host events.

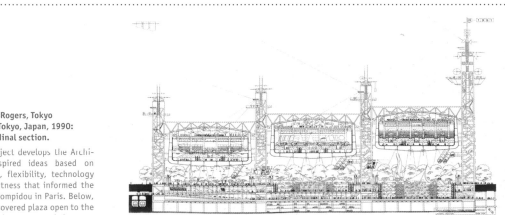

**Venturi, Scott Brown & Associates, Sainsbury Wing, National Gallery, London, England, 1986–91: view from Trafalgar Square.**

The new project blends into its urban context. The only hint that it is a new building can be found in the large openings that seem to cut the facade, reducing it, through a typically Post-Modern gesture, to a sort of theatre backdrop.

**Rafael Moneo, Atocha Train Station, Madrid, Spain, 1984–92: view of the plaza in front of the station.**

The Atocha Train Station in Madrid uses themes dear to the metaphysical tradition, such as porticoes, bell towers and monumentality. Even the choice of materials and colours is functional to the idea of an architecture that seeks to reconcile the ancient and the modern.

## 1.12 Post-Modernism and Modernism Continued

While it is true that the five years between 1988 and 1992 were witness to the emergence of new lines of research, it is also true that while some were consolidated, others were exhausted. Though Post-Modernism can be said to have exhausted itself, it continued to produce a variety of works, some even very interesting.[123]

Undoubtedly the most worthy of note is the Sainsbury Wing at the National Gallery in London (1986–91) by Venturi, Scott Brown & Associates. Robert Venturi and Denise Scott Brown were awarded the commission after Prince Charles called the proposal by Ahrends, Burton & Koralek[124] 'a monstrous carbuncle on the face of a much-loved and elegant friend'.[125] The two American architects chose to create a backdrop whose style was not dissimilar to that of the adjacent museum, eliminating a piece through a decisive cut near the entrance that announced its modern qualities. A monumental stair on the interior, not without its ironic references to the past, leads to the upper rooms.

Completed in 1990 (the project dates back to 1985), another building worthy of mention is the Haas Haus in Vienna by Hans Hollein,[126] an exuberantly contemporary building, though not without its references to traditional Viennese architecture and the logic of excess and overabundance typical of Post-Modern taste.

**123** It is interesting to note that during these years new and old trends tended to overlap, mix or join with one another. For example, the Nexus World Housing complex, built in Fukuoka, Japan, at the end of the 1980s/beginning of the 1990s, features the work of Post-Modern architects such as Arata Isozaki, Oscar Tusquets Blanca (born 1941) and Christian de Portzamparc together with the 'Deconstructivist' Koolhaas and the 'phenomenologist' Holl.

**124** Ahrends, Burton & Koralek (ABK) was founded in 1961 by Peter Ahrends (born 1933), Richard Burton (born 1933) and Paul Koralek (born 1933). Their designs employ a Modernist idiom.

**125** The phrase was pronounced on 30 May 1984 during the celebrations of the 150th anniversary of the Royal Institute of British Architects (RIBA). This declaration (henceforth known as the 'Monstrous Carbuncle Speech') was followed by other initiatives, including the publication of *A Vision of Britain: A Personal View on Architecture,* Doubleday (London and New York), 1989, a book in which the Prince defines 10 points that characterise good architecture: place, hierarchy, scale, harmony, enclosure, materials, decoration, art, signs and lights, community. In 1989 he also promoted the Summer School in Civic Architecture in Oxford and Rome that, in 1992, was transformed into The Prince of Wales's

Institute of Architecture. In 1994 he published *Perspectives on Architecture.* For a more in-depth investigation and critical evaluation of the origins of this story, see 'Prince Charles and the Architectural Debate' in *Architectural Design,* no 5–6 (1989).

**126** Hans Hollein (born 1934) graduated from the Academy of Fine Arts School of Architecture in Vienna in 1956, completing his education in the United States in Chicago and at Berkeley. Initially a protagonist of the radical European avant-garde, producing writings and visionary projects including the 1967 *Alles ist Architektur* (*Everything is Architecture*), he was later a key figure of the Post-Modern movement. He earned recognition

**Álvaro Siza, Meteorological Centre in the Olympic Village, Barcelona, Spain, 1989–92.**

The head of the Portuguese school, Álvaro Siza is able to bring together Modernist sympathies and the materials and forms of Mediterranean traditions. In many of his works, such as this Meteorological Centre, it is possible to observe references, in this case tempered, to the organic form and lessons of Alvar Aalto.

The same year was also witness to the inauguration of the Cité de la Musique in Paris (1984–90) by Christian de Portzamparc,[127] a project that well represents a desire not to design giant buildings, proposing balanced urban environments of smaller, more articulated buildings in order to avoid rigid hierarchies or monumental compositions.

The Disney Building by Arata Isozaki[128] in Orlando, Florida (1987–91) is a giant toy composed of vividly coloured stereometric volumes that culminate in an enormous chimney which functions as the entry hall.

During the same years Aldo Rossi,[129] at the time an internationally recognised star – he was awarded the Pritzker Prize in 1990 – completed his Il Palazzo Hotel in Fukuoka, Japan (1987–9), the Bonnefanten Museum in Maastricht, The Netherlands (1990–4), the addition to Linate Airport in Milan, Italy (1991–6), the Walt Disney Headquarters in Orlando, Florida (1991–6) and the Schültenstrasse block in Berlin (1992–8), all composed of fragments taken from an imagination inspired by forms, often archetypal, of the city of the past.

There was also another approach that, while reducing the concessions to Post-Modernism to a minimum, sought to unite the tradition of the Modern Movement with more conservative approaches focused on recovering a relationship with historical architecture and/or local traditions of building. Members of this group include the Spaniard Rafael Moneo,[130] the Portuguese Álvaro Siza,[131] the Ticino-Swiss architect Mario Botta[132] and the Italian Vittorio Gregotti.[133] Active for many years in the field of architecture (Botta, the youngest, fully experienced

with some refined interior projects, completing, in 1982, the Museum Abteiberg in Mönchengladbach, Germany, a project that contributed to his receiving the Pritzker Prize in 1985.
**127** Christian de Portzamparc (born 1944) earned international recognition with his residential complex in rue des Hautes-Formes in Paris (1975–9), which criticises Modernist principles of building the city, returning to more traditional ones and a closer relationship between buildings and the public spaces of streets and squares. He was awarded the Pritzker Prize in 1994 after completing the Cité de la Musique in Paris.
**128** Arata Isozaki (born 1931), after a Metabolist period with Kenzo

Tange (1913–2005), oriented his work towards elementary geometric forms, such as those of the Los Angeles Contemporary Art Museum in Los Angeles, California (1981–6).
**129** Aldo Rossi (1931–97) is one of the most important Post-Modern architects. His work, marked by a nostalgia for the architecture and urban spaces of the paleo-industrial world, contains elements from his personal imagination (figures of environments or simple domestic objects with clear and well-defined forms) and the metaphysical tradition, in particular the paintings of Giorgio de Chirico (1888–1978). His most emblematic works are the San Cataldo Cemetery in Modena, Italy (1971–84), organised like a metaphysi-

cal city, and the Teatro del Mondo, a floating wooden theatre built for the 1980 Venice Biennale which was entitled 'La Presenza del Passato' ('The Presence of the Past').
**130** (José) Rafael Moneo (born 1937) graduated in Madrid and later worked in Denmark with Jørn Utzon, designer of the Sydney Opera House in Australia. In 1985 Moneo was made Chairman of the Architecture Department at Harvard University Graduate School of Design, a position he held until 1990. His most well-known projects include the National Museum of Roman Art in Mérida, Spain (1980–6) where he built a large space marked by brick arches that allude to the spaces of Roman architecture.

**IM Pei, Bank of China, Hong Kong, 1982–9: view of the building and its urban context.**

The Bank of China, like Pei's other buildings, is characterised by its volumetric solidity and precise construction, down to the most minute detail.

**Christian de Portzamparc, Cité de la Musique, Paris, France, 1984–90.**

Adjacent to the Parc de la Villette by Tschumi, the Cité de la Musique uses a language that is less radically modern, employing new elements together with traditional ones – in this case the composition of volumes as urban blocks.

element of protest. While Botta and Gregotti continued to act from a progressively more conservative, and at times reactionary, position, Siza and, above all, Moneo – who demonstrated a more open, pragmatic and, on occasion, experimental attitude – became, respectively in Portugal and Spain, the points of reference for a younger generation who, while critical of the formal excesses of post-Deconstructivist trends, sought to update their personal architectural language.[134]

The same years, finally, were also witness to the activities of professionals who completed quality projects, working laterally with respect to the trends of the time, though no less important as a result. At the head of this group we find Richard Meier[135] and IM Pei.[136] The former, in projects such as The Hague City

the Post-Modern season), they placed themselves in opposition to Deconstructivism and what they felt to be the ephemeral trends of the time. Beyond the specific interest of their architecture, they coagulated an

**131** Álvaro Joaquim de Meio Siza Vieira (born 1933) is the head of the so-called Porto School. His work involves the recovery of Portuguese traditions filtered through a modern language of simple and essential forms, where light, screened by thick walls and focused through carefully designed openings, plays a primary role. He received the Pritzker Prize in 1992.

**132** Mario Botta (born 1943) graduated under the tutelage of Carlo Scarpa (1906–78) in Venice and went on to collaborate with Le Corbusier and Louis Kahn, from whom he declares to take inspiration. He earned recognition with a collection of single-family dwellings built in the 1970s and '80s in Ticino, followed by monumental

public buildings, including the San Francisco Museum of Modern Art in San Francisco, California (1989–95). He is considered, together with Aurelio Galfetti (born 1936), Livio Vacchini (1933–2007) and Luigi Snozzi, to be one of the exponents of the Ticino School.

**133** Vittorio Gregotti (born 1927), after working with Ludovico Meneghetti (born 1926) and Giotto Stoppino (born 1926), founded Gregotti Associati in 1974, completing numerous works characterised by a dry and severe rigorism. Involved since the 1950s with the world of publishing, between 1979 and 1998 he was the director of *Rassegna* and, between 1982 and 1996, of *Casabella*.

**134** The Spanish miracle, the result of a happy coincidence of political, cultural and economic aspects that developed after the introduction of democracy following the death of the dictator Francisco Franco on 20 November 1975, was documented in the exhibition 'On-Site: New Architecture in Spain' curated by Terence Riley and presented at the MoMA in New York (12 February to 1 May 2006)

**135** Richard Meier (born 1934) graduated from Cornell University and worked with Skidmore, Owings & Merrill (SOM, founded in 1936 by Louis Skidmore and Nathaniel Owings) and for Marcel Breuer (1902–81), before opening his own office in 1963. He was launched onto the international

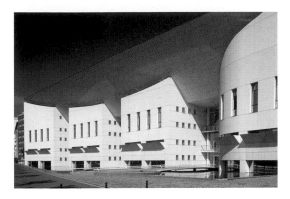

Hall and Central Library (1986–95), the Royal Dutch Paper Mills Headquarters, Hilversum, The Netherlands (1987–92) and the Canal+ Headquarters in Paris (1988–92), continued to experiment with his personal language of forms taken from the purist vocabulary of Le Corbusier. The latter, after completing the pyramid at The Louvre in Paris (1982–9) and the elegant Bank of China in Hong Kong (1982–9), was actively involved in numerous projects, including the Miho Museum in Kyoto, Japan (1991–8), where the primary theme was that of the insertion of the architectural object within a natural context.

## 1.13 The Inheritance of Deconstructivism

There is no doubt that between 1988 and 1992 Deconstructivism was the most relevant and controversial phenomenon. It would be fair to state that precisely this

phenomenon, paradoxically not embraced by any architect in particular,[137] brought an extraordinary impulse to contemporary architecture. In fact Deconstructivism was responsible for the renewed interest of an entire generation of young designers in spatial research, the setting aside of the iconic excesses of the Post-Modern period, and re-elaboration of projects that were capable of giving form to the yearnings for freedom and experimentation expressed by contemporary society.

Deconstructivism can claim the merit of having produced a season of unprecedented theoretical reflection and stimulating and heated discussions that led in turn to the elaboration of contrasting and alternative lines of research. This makes it difficult to share the opinion

scene in 1972 by the exhibition held at the MoMA, curated by Arthur Drexler, of the New York Five Architects (the others were Peter Eisenman, Michael Graves, Charles Gwathmey (born 1938) and John Hejduk). His work is based on the repetitive use of candid geometric forms, organised in complex and spatially captivating articulations, for example the High Museum of Art in Atlanta, Georgia (1980–3), which earned him the Pritzker Prize in 1984.
**136** Ieoh Ming Pei (born 1917) studied at the Massachusetts Institute of

Technology and later at Harvard with Walter Gropius. He is the designer of numerous public buildings – the most well-known being the East Building of the National Gallery of Art in Washington, DC (1974–8) – that are appreciated for, amongst other elements, the accurate geometric organisation of the plan and perfect detailing.
**137** As mentioned, not even the seven architects invited to participate in the 'Deconstructivist Architecture' exhibition referred to themselves as Deconstructivists.

**Richard Meier, Canal+ Headquarters, Paris, France, 1988–92: exterior view.**

The designer of refined and spatially involving buildings, Richard Meier elaborates his own Modernist language in the Canal+ Headquarters. As in his other works, there are numerous references to the Purist period of Le Corbusier.

**138** For Vittorio Magnano Lampugnani, for example, 'the central cultural contribution of deconstructivism entered into an irremediable contradiction with the fundamental obligations of architecture'. See under 'Deconstructivism' in Vittorio Magnano Lampugnani, *Lexicon der Architektur des 20.Jahrhunderts,* Verlag Gerd Hatje (Ostfildern-Ruit), 1998, translated, expanded, reviewed and updated for the Italian edition: *Dizionario Skira dell'Architettura del Novecento,* Skira (Milan), 2000.
**139** The rediscovery of the Constructivist avant-garde from the beginning of the 20th century is related to the experimental tradition of the 1960s and '70s: from Frederick Kiesler (1890–1965) to John M Johansen (born 1916); from Archigram to Buckminster Fuller; from Vittorio Giorgini (born 1926) to Superstudio; from the Japanese Metabolists to the American group SITE.

of those who see it as merely another formalism, the degeneration of Post-Modernism and a style of excesses, if not the very negation of architecture.[138] Whatever opinion we have of this phenomenon, it is undeniable that one of the merits of the architects of Deconstructivism was that of having rediscovered, and recovered, the avant-garde[139] tradition, or of having introduced, and reinvented from scratch, new techniques of designing space, turning it into a shared heritage of architectural research, even non-Deconstructivist. These include experimentation with the in-between; with folds and changes of points of view; with the dynamics of the contemporary metropolis; with deformations, vibrations and oscillations; with new relationships between the natural and the man-made; with the exasperation of opposites in order to stimulate the perception of the observer; with a more involving relationship between the body and architecture.

A further merit of Deconstructivism was that of having demonstrated – after the Post-Modern conformism that favoured plaster, stone and brick – that almost any material, from sheet metal to chipboard to plastic fencing used to protect construction sites, can be successfully used. It is difficult to consider the post-Minimalist research into the skin of buildings without this anti-classical and liberating premise.

Beginning in 1993, as we will see in the next chapter, Deconstructivism would be declared superseded, even by those who were so strongly influenced by it. Nonetheless, because its design techniques continued to be employed (and many young architects will clearly recognise this debt), or because many buildings designed during its heyday were now being completed, the phenomenon did not cease to have an important influence – at the very least until October 1997 when, with an unprecedented media whirlwind, the world was witness to the inauguration of Gehry's Guggenheim Museum in Bilbao; or January 1999, this time on the occasion of the opening of Libeskind's Jewish Museum in Berlin.

**1** *Architectural Design*, 'Folding in Architecture' (1993), guest-edited by Greg Lynn. In 2004, some 10 years later, a revised edition was published with an introduction by Lynn and an essay by Mario Carpo.
**2** Greg Lynn (born 1964) worked in Eisenman's office – where he was lead architect for the Cincinnati School of Design, Architecture, Art and Planning and the Carnegie Mellon Institute – and for Antoine Predock (born 1936), before founding his firm, Greg Lynn FORM, in 1992.
**3** Kenneth Powell, 'Unfolding Folding', in *Architectural Design*, 'Folding in Architecture', revised edition, 2004, p 23.
**4** The issue featured writing by, amongst others, Peter Eisenman, Greg Lynn, Jeffrey Kipnis, Stephen Perrella, Kenneth Powell, John Rajchman and Frederik Stjernfelt.
**5** 1993 was the year of the English translation of the book by the French philosopher Gilles Deleuze (1925–95): Gilles Deleuze, *Le pli: Leibniz et le baroque*, Éditons de Minuit (Paris), 1988. English translation: *The Fold: Leibniz and the Baroque*, foreword and translation by Tom Conley, University of Minnesota Press (Minneapolis), 1993.
**6** René Thom (1923–2002) was a scientist and inventor of the theory of catastrophes, which seeks to study mathematical models capable of describing natural phenomena and, in particular, discontinuous ones such as catastrophes marked by sudden changes. This theory was applied to physical sciences such as meteorology, physics, engineering and biology

# NEW DIRECTIONS: 1993–7

## 2.1 The Turning Point

The beginning of the end the Deconstructivist movement was sanctioned by the publication, in 1993, of a monographic edition of *Architectural Design*[1] magazine, 'Folding in Architecture', guest-edited by Greg Lynn.[2] 'Deconstruction has done its job,' Kenneth Powell declared in the introduction.[3] The other critics invited to write for the issue were all in agreement.[4]

The turning point was also a reflection of changes in philosophical interests. Derrida was no longer in vogue and other philosophical theories were now being explored: Deleuze's[5] folds, the morphogenesis of René Thom,[6] and the sciences of complexity proposed by theoreticians at the Santa Fe Institute.[7]

What is more, there was also a change in taste that led to the obsolescence of fragmentation, acute angles and broken lines in favour of an aesthetic focused on the theme of continuity. This was expressed in a return to soft curves – a reflection of the teachings of Deleuze – and the Baroque. The circle, so admired for its perfect simplicity and Renaissance traits, was no longer the ideal figure; instead, it was superseded by the soft and wrapping folds of the drapery of statues and the whirling spaces of the 17th century. These are the more appropriate references for a culture that loves to play with the themes of complexity, of the ineffable dialectic between chaos and order. Greg Lynn states: 'For the first time perhaps, complexity might be aligned with neither unity nor contradiction but with smooth, pliant mixture;' and later: 'Where Deconstructivist Architecture was seen to exploit external forces in the familiar name of contradiction and conflict, recent pliant projects by many of those architects exhibit a more fluid logic of connectivity'.[8]

and to human and social sciences, including linguistics, semiotics and economics. Precursors of the application of the theory of catastrophes in architecture include Carmine Benincasa's *Architettura come dis-identità: Teoria delle catastrofi e architettura*, Dedalo libri (Bari), 1978.

7 The Santa Fe Institute (SFI) was founded in 1984, with the mission of developing and disseminating a general theory of complexity. It is interesting to note that between 1992 and 1993 various works dedicated to the theory of complexity were published, including: M Mitchell Waldrop, *Complexity: The Emerging Science at the Edge of Order and Chaos*, Simon and Schuster (New York), 1992; Stuart A Kauffmann, *The Origins of Order: Self-Organization and Selection in Evolution*, Oxford University Press

(New York), 1993. With his usual timeliness, Charles Jencks edited the book *The Post-Modern Reader*, Academy Editions/St Martin's Press (London and New York), 1992.
8 Greg Lynn, 'Architectural Curvilinearity: The Folded, the Pliant and the Supple', in *Architectural Design*, 'Folding in Architecture', revised edition, 2004, pp 24 and 26.

**Rem Koolhaas (OMA), Jussieu Library, Paris, France, competition, 1992.**

The interior of the building is defined by sloping planes that create a continuous space. Koolhaas' objective is that of transforming the different activities that take place inside the library into events along a continuous promenade architecturale that begins on the ground floor and ends on the roof.

Two architects were recognised as the precursors of this new trend: Frank O Gehry and Peter Eisenman – the former for his museum in Weil am Rhein, completed in 1989, and the latter for Rebstock Park (1990–1).[9] Both projects make ample use of curves: the museum in order to achieve a sculptural conception, where the object, even while referring to the forms of the landscape, is clearly separated from it; and the park in order to immerse itself in nature, creating a more empathic and less aggressive relationship. Both approaches were tested in later experiments: the first led to highly plastic buildings, the second to landscape architecture.

In any case, in order to proceed, there was an abandonment of the old ways of designing, which were based on hand drawing, and they were replaced by a new faith in the computer. The use of new technologies was made necessary by the complexity of the spatial configurations obtained by the process of folding, as well as the necessity of abandoning the empiricism that, in other historical periods, in particular the 1970s, characterised research into the use of soft and wrapping forms.[10] This was further made possible by a market that, year after year, proposed more advanced computers at progressively lower costs, and the parallel diffusion of ever more sophisticated software capable of managing three-dimensional surfaces and complex volumes.[11]

The final element that favoured the birth of a new generation of 'Natural Born CAADesigners'[12] was an initiative that was quickly emulated by other universities: in 1994 Bernard Tschumi, Dean of Columbia University's Graduate School of Architecture, Planning and Preservation in New York since 1988, introduced the first 'paperless design studios', entrusting them to such professors as Greg Lynn, Hani Rashid and Scott Marble.[13]

9 These are the same years when Eisenman adopted, for the first time, what would become the keyword of this research: fold. In fact, the term appeared in *Unfolding Frankfurt*, Ernst & Sohn (Frankfurt), 1991, a publication on the Rebstock Park Project with essays by Eisenman and John Rajchman.

10 From this point onwards there is a rediscovery of the architecture of the 1960s, and in particular the work of Buckminster Fuller, Frederick J Kiesler, John M Johansen, Claude Parent (born 1923), John Lautner, Archigram and radical groups. Books that have dealt with this theme include Luigi Prestinenza Puglisi's *This is Tomorrow: Avanguardie e architettura contemporanea*, Testo&Immagine (Turin), 1999.

11 A history of the development of software can be found in the chapter 'New Tools of the Trade' in the book by John K Waters, *Blobitecture: Waveform Architecture and Digital Design*, Rockport Publishers (Gloucester), 2003, pp 50–63.

12 Christian Pongratz and Maria Rita Perbellini, *Nati con il computer: Giovani architetti americani*, Testo&Immagine (Turin), 2000. Published in English as: *Natural Born CAADesigners: Young American Architects*, Birkhäuser (Basel, Boston and Berlin), 2000.

13 The history of the 'paperless studios' is told in the article 'The Computer School' by Ned Cramer and Anne Guiney, in *Architecture* (September 2000), pp 93–8. Later professors include: Lise Anne Couture (Asymptote); Karen Bausman (born 1958); Mark Rakatansky; William Sharples (born 1963), Coren Sharples (born 1965) and Gregg Pasquarelli (born 1965) (SHoP); Sulan Kolatan and William Mac Donald (Kolatan/Mac Donald); Winka Dubbeldam (born 1968) (Archi-Tectonics); Mark Wigley; and Stan Allen.

**Frank O Gehry, 'Fred & Ginger', Prague, Czech Republic, 1992–7: exterior view.**

The two volumes are reminiscent of the dancing figures of Fred Astaire and Ginger Rogers. Torsional forces result in the elimination of the corner, allowing for a better view of the river, and creating a level of harmony between the new building and the Baroque city of Prague.

14 Jeffrey Kipnis, 'Towards a New Architecture', in *Architectural Design*, 'Folding in Architecture', pp 57–65.

They would contribute to the diffusion, primarily among young architects, of what Jeffrey Kipnis, in one of his essays for *Architectural Design* in 1993,[14] baptised with the term the architecture of DeFormation. They were accompanied by other, previous experiments that were also stimulated by a reflection on new technologies.[15] There were those that hypothesised a lightweight and transparent architecture that designs its own disappearance;[16] those that sought to transform the facades of buildings into screens for the projection of information and events;[17] or those that designed works of architecture which mutated according to the variation of flows of communication.[18]

To these approaches to research we must add another, developed during the second half of the 1990s, and generated by progressively more complex virtual computer-generated models. It consists of the ideation and creation of digital simulations of spaces that are particular and multidimensional. This is the case with Marcos Novak's[19] notions of 'transArchitecture', which coincided with the enthusiasm for cyberspace architecture and forecast the unravelling of new territories in our brains. Or the works of Diller +

15 Kipnis classifies them as the architecture of InFormation. Citing two cases that he considers representative, he states: 'The strategy of InFormation of which Koolhaas' Karlsruhe and Tschumi's Le Fresnoy are exemplary cases, is to form a collecting graft, usually by encasing disparate formal and programmatic elements within a modernist monolith'. In 'Towards a New Architecture', p 59.
16 This is what was proposed by Nouvel, Fuksas and even Koolhaas in buildings that play with the properties of glass. Coop Himmelb(l)au, in order to go one step beyond this metaphor of our times, imagined a building with

the form of a cloud, 'Cloud no 9', for the United Nations Plaza in Geneva (1995).
17 Venturi, in the book *Iconography and Electronics upon a Generic Architecture*, The MIT Press (Cambridge, MA and London), 1996 compares the electronic image to Byzantine mosaics. This is the solution that, as we have seen, was tested by Rem Koolhaas for the main facade of the Karlsruhe Arts and Communications Centre (1989); by Toyo Ito in the *Egg of Winds* in Okawabata (1988–91); and later, using photographic and not cinematic images, when Herzog & de Meuron wrapped their precious buildings with silk-screened facades.

18 For example the Institut du Monde Arabe by Jean Nouvel, which manifests the passage of solar energy through the movement of oculi controlled by photoelectric cells; or again in the Tower of Winds (1986) by Toyo Ito, whose luminosity mutates in relation to its exterior context.
19 Marcos Novak (born 1957): architect, artist and musician. From 1989 to 1996 he taught at the University of Texas in Austin and from 1996 to 1999 he was a professor at UCLA in Los Angeles. He is the inventor of the term 'transArchitecture', a discipline that, in reality, is rather obscure and which tends to use the computer to test multidimensional spatial realties.

**Peter Eisenman, Aronoff Center for Design and Art, Cincinnati, Ohio, USA, 1991–6: exterior view.**

The design of the Aronoff Center is generated by the vibration of elementary volumes. Changes of colour and brusque shifts in alignment create a sensation of imbalance and structural precariousness.

**Frank O Gehry, Walt Disney Concert Hall, Los Angeles, California, USA, 1988–2003: exterior view.**

Designed before the Guggenheim (it was completed after due to problems with funding), the Walt Disney Concert Hall in Los Angeles anticipates the design strategy defined in Bilbao. The steel volumes are a translation into form of the music produced inside the building.

Scofidio[20] and Asymptote,[21] who place fragments of the virtual within everyday reality: for example, by inserting video cameras connected to monitors that look beyond the physical space that architecture allows us, or projecting graphics on the floor, offering an immediate, three-dimensional perception of data and information about a site.

## 2.2 Explosive Buildings

Completed in 1994, the Vitra Fire Station in Weil am Rhein, Germany, by Zaha Hadid met with an almost unanimous chorus of acclaim. Writing for *Architecture* magazine, Joseph Giovannini stated: 'This building tricks the eye and body into feeling sensations of Einsteinian speed.'[22] Ziva Freiman wrote in *Progressive Architecture*: 'the ostensibly dynamic building, executed as it is with great precision, inspires rather restful contemplation.'[23] For *Domus*, Michael Mönninger spoke of the building as a milestone in the history of architecture.[24]

The commission was the result of a series of coincidences. Rolf Fehlbaum, the director of Vitra, having seen an article in *Vogue* magazine, contacted Hadid to design some furniture. His visit to the architect's office in London was followed by a reciprocal visit to Switzerland by Hadid. A few months later she received a proposal to design a small, 800-square-metre, two-storey building, for five vehicles and 24 firemen who were to protect Vitra's highly flammable productive equipment and furniture warehouses. Designed for a utilitarian purpose, the building was also to be used for occasional exhibitions, promotional activities and meetings.

The objective was that of creating a building of significant architectural value that would complement the factory designed by Nicholas Grimshaw and the museum

20 Diller + Scofidio was founded in the 1980s by Elizabeth Diller (born 1954) and Ricardo Scofidio (born 1935). They earned their fame through interdisciplinary works presented as art, video and electronic installations. Their work investigates changes in our point of view generated by the use of new media, such as video cameras, scanners and x-rays.
21 Asymptote was founded in 1988 by Hani Rashid (born 1958) and Lise Anne Couture (born 1959). In 1989 they designed the Steel Cloud,

a visionary project for the post-information age, 'without perspective, without depth, structure or enclosure'. Their later work involved the interaction between reality and the virtual, culminating in 1999 with the materialisation of the data of the New York Stock Exchange into a spatial entity.
22 Joseph Giovannini, 'Zaha Hadid', in *Architecture* (September 1993), p 69.

23 Ziva Freiman, 'The Concrete Evidence', in *Progressive Architecture* (August 1993), p 54.
24 'Small-scale buildings often become milestones in the history of architecture.' Michael Mönninger, 'Zaha M Hadid: Fire Station, Weil am Rhein', in *Domus*, no 752 (September 1993), p 60.

25 A brief history of the Vitra campus, up to 1993, can be found in John Morris Dixon's essay 'The Vitra Campus', in *Progressive Architecture* (August 1993), pp 60–3.
26 Michael Mönninger, 'Zaha M Hadid: Fire Station, Weil am Rhein', p 60.
27 In Zaha Hadid, *Zaha Hadid: The Complete Buildings and Projects*, Thames and Hudson (London), 1998, p 64.

by Frank O Gehry, under construction at the time (the buildings by Álvaro Siza and Tadao Ando came later).[25]

Built in reinforced concrete at a cost of 2.6 million German Marks, while – in Mönninger's words – 'the building does not "speak" and does not represent anything either ... [i]t could be seen as a starfighter or a speedboat, as a collapsing bridge structure or an exploding spaceship.'[26] However, the most convincing image comes from Hadid herself: it is a structure that vibrates like a fire alarm bell when it first sounds. 'The whole building is frozen motion, suspending the tension of alertness, ready to explode at any moment.'[27]

Completely different than the Monsoon Restaurant, so much so that it appears to have been designed by another hand, the Vitra Fire Station in reality presents

the same scenographic sensitivity, this time projected towards the organisation of the exterior spaces. In fact, the building functions as a wall to the exterior and a backdrop to internal circulation, reorganised in offsets and shifts in perspective.

There is also a similar logic, founded on the highlighting of the encounter-confrontation of opposing principles, primarily between the unit of composition and the multiplicity of compositional elements, each of which is highlighted and treated with specific care. In particular we can observe three longitudinal elements that seem to have been caused by the vibration – from the right to the left and upwards – of a single linear mass, while the roof reinforces the horizontal qualities of the composition, blocking the upward movement, and opening up the entire construction in other directions.

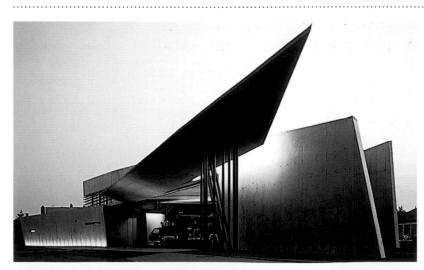

**Zaha Hadid, Vitra Fire Station, Weil am Rhein, Germany, 1989–94: view of the entrance.**

The canopy over the entry, skewed with respect to the axis of the street, draws attention to the building, while the simple grey surfaces of the exposed concrete are a wilful contrast to the variety of plastic effects obtained by the articulation of planes and volumes.

**Zaha Hadid, Vitra Fire Station, Weil am Rhein, Germany, 1989–94: interior view.**

Chromatic changes and unusual perspectives give the interior space an intensely dynamic quality, despite its modest dimensions.

The second opposition is between volume and plane. The building is more than a composition of lines; it is a play of volumes that intersect with one another. However, if we look closely we see that the volumes are obtained by planes that, as much as they are connected, folded and tormented, never lose their planar characteristics or, in the end, their dynamism.

The third opposition is between the weight of reinforced concrete – serious, material and sculptural – and the lightness of an immaterial energy, rendered possible precisely by the fundamental quality of concrete: that of eliminating the duplications between structure and cladding and thus creating a poetic of subtraction, where signs are reduced to their pure essentiality, stripping volumes down to their essence and transforming them into pure lines of force.

In 1995, thanks in part to the success of the Fire Station, Hadid was already a star. Of her more interesting projects from this period we can mention the recasting of an area in New York, near Times Square, between 8th Avenue and 42nd Street. The project called for two blocks with the same number of commercial plates, atop which were to be built, respectively, a 22- and a 45-storey tower. The lower tower comprises a simple, almost elementary envelope, inserted as an ordering element within the urban fabric. The taller tower, instead, has a fragmented form, created by the alternation of glass and opaque walls, which can also contain the brightly lit screens and publicity banners of Times Square. The glass walls define the residential functions and the opaque service spaces that can be lit with fluorescent lighting, such as conference rooms, banquet halls, a gymnasium and a pool.

The fragmentation of the building into blocks, other than permitting the alternation of glazing and advertising banners, is also reflected in the vertiginous, full-height atrium. This space is overlooked, in a controlled disorder, by private and public spaces, re-creating, on the inside of the building, the vitality of flows of people

**Zaha Hadid, Vitra Fire Station, Weil am Rhein, Germany, 1989–94: painting.**

The station relates to its environment by attacking it from different directions.

**Zaha Hadid, Habitable Bridge, London, England, 1996: project model.**

Inspired by famous inhabited bridges, such as the Ponte Vecchio in Florence, Hadid has designed an infrastructure that, in addition to resolving traffic issues, also manages to be a catalyst for urban activities.

and activities that are, on the exterior, integral to the urban environment that is New York.

The same strategy used for the 42nd Street Hotel – the decomposition of form into elementary units that are later recomposed into a new, typologically innovative organism – was also applied by Hadid to the project for the Boilerhouse Extension to the Victoria and Albert Museum (1996) and, later, the Contemporary Arts Center in Cincinnati, built and inaugurated in 2003. The difference, however, is that in these later works the elementary units are assimilated to pixels – minute fragments of light which, as they are composed and recomposed, allow the screens of televisions to produce a flow of images that complete architectural space. This space is characterised by the flexible and ample covered plaza that welcomes visitors ('the urban carpet'); by the variety of display spaces suspended in the air, in order to offer, through their strange intersections, unusual views ('the jigsaw puzzle'); and by a double facade system that creates a cushioning layer between the interior and the exterior. This facade system can simultaneously be a membrane, an interface or a fully autonomous form ('the skin/sculpture').

The Habitable Bridge on the River Thames in London (1996) transforms the bridge typology into a double system of lines of force, rendered concrete by the cluster of long-limbed elements placed along the two banks of the river. These latter, used for commercial and cultural activities, generate an intense attraction that creates a physical and ideal connection between the two sides of the city, otherwise separate. At the same time, the paths, placed at various levels and oriented along shifting directions, offer new openings towards this natural space of the river and the artificial skyline.

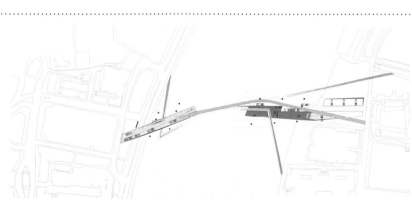

**Zaha Hadid, Habitable Bridge, London, England, 1996: site plan.**

The bridge is a node that serves as the focal point for various events that converge here from different directions.

Eric Owen Moss, Samitaur Complex 1, Culver City, California, USA, 1989–96: exterior view.

The Samitaur Complex, like Moss's other buildings, is a unified composition of geometric principles that were once held to be incompatible. This mixture produces dissonant and spatially captivating structures.

## 2.3 Los Angeles, Graz and Barcelona

Morphosis, the Los Angeles-based office[28] run by the partners Thom Mayne and Michael Rotondi,[29] earned its initial fame with a few small projects, mostly interiors, completed during the 1980s. These were composed of sharp and decisive forms executed in industrial materials (cor-ten steel, steel mesh, exposed bolted steel beams), the junctions between different geometries constituting exploding or syncopated and fragmented spaces. Coherent with a form of research that, during this period, was also being pursued by protagonists like Zaha Hadid and Coop Himmelb(l)au, Morphosis demonstrated a preference for the intense over the beautiful and energy over harmony, pursuing an aesthetic of the sublime that led them to introduce forces and tensions. This approach has been referred to as Dead Tech,[30] a poetic form of High Tech in the wake of an atomic disaster. It must be said, however, that while the term suggests a state of devastation, the objective here, on the contrary, is that of alluding to the tension and vital force of matter during deflagration.

Completed between 1994 and 1997, the Sun Tower in Seoul, South Korea is the result of the confrontation within the same form of two 10-storey towers for two different clients, with a shared foyer. The complex and, in parts, chaotic volumes of the whole are exalted by the use of perforated sheet steel that wraps the build-

28 At least since 1972, when Ray Kappe founded the Southern California Institute of Architecture (SCI-Arc), Los Angeles has been home to a common approach. Other offices that have passed through Los Angeles include Coop Himmelb(l)au and Archigram. In the 1990s, besides Frank O Gehry, the city was also home to a group of young experimental architects: Thom Mayne, Michael Rotondi, Eric Owen Moss, Frank Israel (1945–96) and Michele Saee (born 1956). See Aaron Betsky, John Chase and Leon

Whiteson, *Experimental Architecture in Los Angeles*, Rizzoli (New York), 1992; Introduction by Frank O Gehry.
29 Morphosis was founded in 1972 by Thom Mayne (born 1944) and Michael Rotondi (born 1949). In 1991 Michael Rotondi left the practice to found his own office, RoTo.

30 The term can be found in Matteo Zambelli, *Morphosis: Operazioni sul suolo*, Marsilio (Venice), 2005, p 32. The definition can be attributed to the science-fiction writer William Gibson (born 1948).

**Odile Decq, Benoît Cornette, Highway Bridge and Control Centre, Nanterre, France, 1993–7: exterior view.**

The project consists of a building, located under a highway overpass, set within a park. The overall compatibility with the environment is guaranteed by the horizontal nature of the project, glazed surfaces and light and aerodynamic forms.

ing like a skin, creating effects of transparency that help to lighten the overall image. At night, thanks to artificial lighting from the interior, the tower becomes a gigantic billboard, an urban landmark.

Between 1992 and 1996 Morphosis were busy completing the Blades Residence in Santa Barbara, California, a single-family dwelling skilfully fragmented into multiple nuclei. It is an example of 'landform architecture', an approach that Mayne had been pursuing for years. It consists of works that became landscape, abolishing the opposition between figure and ground, building and context, artifice and nature.

Eric Owen Moss[31] can be considered, together with Morphosis, as one of the most important points of reference for new Los Angeles architecture. He owes much of his fame to numerous projects in Culver City, an abandoned industrial area in Los Angeles, many of which were commissioned by Frederick and Laurie Samitaur Smith, two enlightened clients who saw the regenerative potential of a new and unusual architecture in attracting businesses and innovative activities, generating public interest and offering a new and more desirable way of inhabiting space. His more important works include Box (1990–4), an off-kilter steel box with a large window that erodes the corner, containing a conference room, built on the roof of a restored industrial building; the Beehive/Annex (1996–2001), a conference centre whose spiral form is interrupted by a stair that functions as a roof; the Samitaur Complex 1 (1989–96); the Samitaur Complex 2 (begun in 1997); the Pittard Sullivan Building (1994–7); and the Wedgewood Holly Complex (1989–2001), also known as 'Stealth' for its resemblance to the aeroplane of the same name, designed to elude radar interception. All of these projects are marked by a form of spatial research, in some cases exasperated, that questions traditional forms, materials and relationships in order to arrive at what Moss calls Gnostic architecture: 'Gnostic architecture is not about a faith in a movement, a methodology, a process, a

31 Eric Owen Moss (born 1943) studied at Berkeley and Harvard, where he earned his second Master in Architecture in 1972. In 1973 he opened his own practice in Los Angeles.

**Günter Domenig, GIG Headquarters, Völkermarkt, Carinthia, Austria, 1994–5: exterior view.**

In Domenig's work the tension of Expressionism is made manifest in gestures that open the building towards the landscape.

**Thom Mayne (Morphosis), Sun Tower, Seoul, Korea, 1994–7: view from the street.**

The use of perforated steel cladding renders the building's impact on the city both light and airy and, at the same time, favours the integration of the towers within the disarticulated landscape of this Korean city.

**Günter Behnisch, Geschwister-Scholl-Schule, Römerstadt, Germany, 1992–4: exterior view.**

As in Behnisch's other works, this project is a union of his taste for colour and material, refined technological detailing and an attention to environmental sustainability.

technique, or a technology. It is a strategy for keeping architecture in a perpetual state of motion.'[32] An extraordinarily talented designer, Moss in many ways recalls Antoni Gaudí. He takes a metaphysical approach to architecture, seen as a discipline that is capable of rendering spatially concrete that which, going beyond the banal, is truly important.[33]

Oriented towards an expressive, and in some cases mystic, vision of architecture we find the architects of Graz, in Austria, dominated by the figure of Günter Domenig.[34] *The Architectural Review* first brought them to the world's attention in 1995 in a monographic issue entitled 'New Graz Architecture'. They were: Konrad Frey; Bernhard Hafner; Heidulf Gerngross; Helmut Richter; Manfred Kovatsch; Szyszkowitz-Kowalski; Klaus Kada;

and Volker Giencke.[35] For the critic and historian Peter Blundell Jones, the author of the introduction to the issue, their work led to the emergence of eight themes of significant importance for contemporary research: an ability to engage historical relations by contrast; an attention to functional aspects; an interest in mega-structures; the use of curves, skews, asymmetries and irregularities; composition using bridges and voids; an interest in new technology, exposed structures and details; the rediscovery of the roof as more than a simple flat plane; and an attention to the participation and involvement of the building's users.

32 Eric Owen Moss, *Gnostic Architecture*, The Monacelli Press (New York), 1999, p 18.
33 During conferences to present his work, Moss showed images of Phobos, one of the two moons of Mars. The objective was that of demonstrating that this hidden moon, with its non-spherical form and inverse rotation, placed scientific preconceptions in question, stimulating the birth of new theories. For more information on Phobos and the philosophy of Moss, see Paola Giaconia, *Eric Owen Moss: The Uncertainty of Doing*, Skira (Geneva and Milan), 2006.
34 Günter Domenig (born 1934) graduated from the Technische Universität of Graz in 1959. His first projects were marked by a zoomorphic

form of expressionism. In the 1970s he completed two precursory works: the multifunctional hall in Graz-Eggenberg, Austria (1972–7) together with Eilfried Huth and the Zentralsparkasse in Favoritenstrasse in Vienna (1974–9). The first, with its organic form, recalls an archaic monster; the second features a facade that has been deformed and torn away by an external force. On the interior, as noted by Paolo Vincenzo Genovese: 'Entrails of steel piping wrap the walls that, suddenly, slant down below a cascade of glass that opens towards the sky.' In Paolo Vincenzo Genovese, *Günter Domenig: Lanci di masse diroccate*, Testo&Immagine (Turin), 1998, p 51.
35 Konrad Frey (born 1934), Bernhard

Hafner (born 1940), Heidulf Gerngross (born 1939), Helmut Richter (born 1941), Manfred Kovatsch (born 1940), Michael Szyszkowitz (born 1944), Karla Kowalski (born 1941), Klaus Kada (born 1940) and Volker Giencke (born 1947). As with the Deconstructivists and architects of Los Angeles, it is risky to speak of a school. As Peter Blundell Jones notes in his introduction: 'The vigorous rejection by Graz architects of the term Grazer Schule had a basis that has become ever more evident: there is not one school but rather a range of tendencies spanning all the way from Domenig at his most expressionistic to the cool minimalism of Rieger Riewe.' Peter Blundell Jones, 'Comment', in *The Architectural Review*, no 1184 (October 1995), pp 6–7.

Another centre of new architectural expression was the city of Barcelona, home to Enric Miralles, initially partnered with Carme Pinós and, from 1990 onwards, with Benedetta Tagliabue.[36] In 1991 *El Croquis* magazine published a monographic issue[37] of the work of Miralles and Pinós, giving ample importance to what many consider to be the couple's masterpiece: the Igualada Cemetery in Spain, that was about to be completed. The project has a formidable expressive power: inserted within the topography of an arid Spanish landscape, it becomes part of it and, at the same time, emerges as a privileged microcosm with a powerful symbolical impact. Plantings, reinforced concrete and gabion baskets (steel cages filled with small and large stones) define a long facade that is simultaneously artificial and natural, based on principles that are not unlike those of landform architecture tested by Morphosis and Domenig. Between 1993 and 1994 Miralles completed the Centro de Gimnasia Rítmica y Deportiva in Alicante (1989–93) and the Sports Facility in Huesca (1988–94), both in Spain. These projects offered him an opportunity to display his talent, typically Catalan, of playing with spaces, light and materials, even those that belong to the world of technology.[38] International success arrived in 1997 when the French architectural magazine *L'architecture d'aujourd'hui* dedicated a monographic issue to his work. This was also the year that Miralles won the competition for the new Scottish Parliament in Edinburgh.

36 Enric Miralles (1955–2000) and Carme Pinós (born 1954) graduated from the Escuela Técnica Superior de Arquitectura de Barcelona (ETSAB) respectively in 1978 and 1979. Their professional partnership lasted from 1983 to 1990, when Miralles teamed up with Benedetta Tagliabue (born 1963) who, after his death in 2000, continues to run the office, completing many unfinished projects. Tagliabue graduated in Venice in 1989.

37 *El Croquis*, no 49/50 (1991). This was the second issue dedicated to the couple, after *El Croquis*, no 30 (1987).

38 Catherine Slessor, for example, places the Centro de Gimnasia Rítmica y Deportiva in Alicante amongst the examples of Eco-Tech in her book *Eco-Tech: Sustainable Architecture and High Technology*, Thames and Hudson (London), 1997.

**Enric Miralles, Carme Pinos, Centro de Gimnasia Rítmica y Deportiva, Alicante, Valencia, Spain, 1989–93: exterior view.**

The large, exposed steel trusses are used to lighten the building, connecting it to the sky. The effect transforms a High Tech structure into a sign at the scale of the landscape.

**Gaetano Pesce, Jay Chiat Offices, New York, USA, 1994: detail.**

The large mouth that defines the display window reminds us of the inflatable dolls found in a sex shop. It is one of Pesce's numerous contributions to the world of Pop Art, from which this project takes its inspiration.

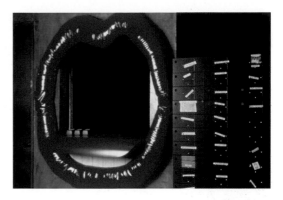

## 2.4 The Radicals and Coop Himmelb(l)au

Rediscovered and appreciated after a lengthy period of silence, radical architects, particularly active in the 1960s and '70s, once again captured media attention. Given that most of them were still practising and teaching in major institutions, their new work demonstrated an affinity with the advanced research of their young contemporaries.

In 1994, for example, Jay Chiat, the owner of the same advertising agency that hired Gehry to design the binocular-building in Venice, California, decided to renovate his offices in New York, entrusting the work to Gaetano Pesce.[39] Perhaps the most notable feature of Pesce's project for Chiat is the highly iconic and striking

paving: red, blue and yellow resins define the fields in a design with the form of a face, seen from the front and in profile, and an enormous arrow that indicates the direction of entry. The choice of materials is equally strong: some are recycled, such as overlapping video cassettes that create the wall of the media library; others have a strong tactile impact, such as the felts that cover the fronts of the computer tables; others still are shaped in ways that suggest anthropomorphic images, some of which are unsettling: of these latter there is a perforation, in a plastic material, that recalls the lips of the inflatable dolls sold in pornographic shops around the world.

We are undoubtedly dealing with a work that is outside the functionalist canon, fresh with an air of innocence, and that does not hesitate to recover the useless, the arbitrary and the unnecessary, even if it is based on a paradoxical reasoning: in a complex and advanced society, the useful is that which goes beyond function, while it is not necessarily – almost never to be precise –

**39** Towards the end of the 1960s Gaetano Pesce (born 1939) designed a series of pop furnishings, such as the Moloch Lamp, a floor lamp created by significantly oversizing a common desktop lamp; Il Pugno, an inviting sofa with the form of an open hand; and the feminine Up series of armchairs, which use an oversized chain to support an oversized spherical footrest. He later worked with felt, fabrics and resins, a precursor to new types of furnishings. He also designed buildings made from plastic or recycled materials.

40 For an insight into the client's opinion of the work, see 'Federica Zanco Interviewing Jay Chiat' in *Domus*, no 769 (March 1995), pp 54–5.

41 Alessandro Mendini (born 1931) is one of the protagonists of the Radical design movement. Architect, designer and painter, he was the director of *Casabella* (1970–6), *Modo* (1977–9) and *Domus* (1979–85). In 1979 he founded his own office, Studio Alchimia, producing Post-Modern objects. Since 1989 he has run Atelier Mendini.

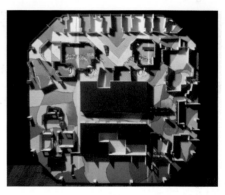

**Gaetano Pesce, Jay Chiat Offices, New York, USA, 1994: aerial view of the model.**

The paving of the office is a representation of a face seen simultaneously from the front and the side. The face is visible in its entirety only from an ideal point of view, while in reality it is fragmented by the layout of the interior, such that it appears to be an abstract design.

that which we obtain in a strict and rigorous manner.[40] A substantially similar position was taken by Alessandro Mendini,[41] the promoter of Radical design in Italy, who had been highly critical since the outset of products sold simply to respond to practical uses, though lacking in evocative and emotional terms. In 1994 Mendini completed the Groninger Museum in The Netherlands. His collaborators included Philippe Starck,[42] Michele De Lucchi[43] and Coop Himmelb(l)au, in an attempt to underline that the completion of such a complex undertaking, such as a home for art, can no longer be achieved through individual syntheses. The entire work is surprisingly varied. On the exterior, the stereometric forms of the portion designed by Mendini recall the work of the Italian metaphysical artists[44] – though they are destabilised by an excess of decoration, some of which is clearly Mediterranean in flavour, if not Islamic. The structure designed by Coop Himmelb(l)au contrasts the former with its sharp walls that almost seem to slip from the building, and the highly decorative flavour of the unusual chromatic patterns. On the interior

Starck works to create an evanescent language in the pavilion of decorative arts, using transparent drapery; De Lucchi, for the pavilion of archaeology and history, employs elements from the rationalist tradition; Mendini, called on to design the temporary exhibition halls, uses images with a metaphoric meaning; and Coop Himmelb(l)au's ancient arts pavilion is a strident and mechanical space.

In the Groninger Museum, the contributions of four teams of designers overlap, without any real sense of continuity, proposing a chaotic microcosm of meanings and spaces that refer to cultures and trends which are both extraneous and incommunicable: closed volumes and fragmented walls, transparency and opaque masses, flashy polychrome effects and pallid monochromes, traditional and industrial materials, warm and inviting spaces, and cold, uncomfortable ones.[45] The result, as Mendini states, is focused on disorienting the visitor 'to render the variety of architectural types ambiguous. In that museum every now and again you feel you are

42 Philippe Starck (born 1949). This self-taught figure designed some of the rooms in the residence of the President of the French Republic – François Mitterrand – in 1982. In 1988 he won the Grand Prix de la Création Industrielle. In 1989 he founded Starck Products. He is the designer of highly successful and widely sold pieces, such as the Juicy Salif, designed for Alessi in 1990. Between 1989 and 1990 he completed the Flame Building for Asahi in Tokyo, a hyper-iconic building

with a giant golden blob-like object on the roof.

43 Michele De Lucchi (born 1951) opened his own practice in 1984. He is the designer of many objects for Studio Alchimia and Memphis. In 1989 he designed the Tolomeo lamp, one of the most popular objects of contemporary design.

44 The Metaphysical movement was an artistic movement from the early 19th century. One of its major protagonists was Giorgio de Chirico. Metaphysical painting, composed largely of objects

made up of elementary volumes, sought to represent a work of archetypal figures that went beyond the physical appearance of reality. After the Second World War the architects of neo-Traditionalism and, later, Post-Modernism, were inspired by the movement, above all in Italy, including Aldo Rossi.

45 We must remember that in 1985 Fuksas, Steidle, Alsop and Nouvel had worked on the Europe Tower using a similar method. This form of working with multiple hands has a lengthy

in a house, every now and again in a church, and then every now and again you seem to be in a theatre or in an office. We tried in fact to surprise the visitor by continuing to transform the system of spatial sensations vis-à-vis the works exhibited.'[46]

## 2.5 Nouvel: Beyond Transparency

In July 1994 Jean Nouvel created a new company, Architectures Jean Nouvel,[47] abandoning his previous partnership with Emmanuel Cattani that, though positive in terms of the quantity and quality of work, was a disaster in financial terms. Having handed over the economic management of the company to experts, Nouvel now fulfilled the exclusive role of artistic director. This allowed him to capitalise, in terms of image, on the success of five important works completed between 1993 and 1994: the residential complex in Bezons, France (1990–3); the Lyons Opera House (1986–93); the Congress Centre in

history in the art world: for example, Surrealism. It is also very interesting to note that while Mendini was completing the Groninger Museum, Rem Koolhaas, Bernard Tschumi and Peter Eisenman were working on projects that placed the concept of organic totality in discussion. The Villa Dall'Ava (1985–91) and Euralille (1989–96) are two examples of design, one at the small scale, the other at the scale of urban planning, where the logic of unity is replaced by that of combination.

46 'Juli Capella interviews Alessandro Mendini', in *Domus*, no 813 (March 1999), p 62.
47 Jean Nouvel's professional history is traced in Françoise Fromont's 'Ateliers Nouvel. Boîtes à concepts', in *L'architecture d'aujourd'hui*, no 296 (December 1994), pp 28–35.

**Mendini, De Lucchi, Starck, Coop Himmelb(l)au, Groninger Museum, Groningen, The Netherlands, 1986–94: view of the complex.**

The museum is a collection of four different projects by four different groups of architects. The resulting complex has three souls: the Radical, the Post-Modern and the Deconstructivist.

Tours (1989–93); the Fondation Cartier in Paris (1991–4); and the Shopping Centre in Lille (1991–4).

The consecration of his professional status was assisted by monographic issues of *L'architecture d'aujourd'hui* and *El Croquis*, both published in 1994.[48] They high-lighted the creative talents of an architect who is difficult to label as belonging to a particular style or trend. In the Tours Congress Centre Nouvel works with fluid and precise forms, similar to those of a car body. In Lyons, he covers a historical stone building with a steel barrel vault, while the Fondation Cartier plays with the theme of transparency and lightness. The nine-storey

..........................................................................................

**Mendini, De Lucchi, Starck, Coop Himmelb(l)au, Groninger Museum, Groningen, The Netherlands, 1986–94: view of the project by Coop Himmelb(l)au.**

Coop Himmelb(l)au destructure and fragment planes. The lively colours of the decorative patterns contribute to the extraneous nature of the building with respect to its surroundings.

48 *L'architecture d'aujourd'hui*, no 296 (December 1994) and *El Croquis*, no 65–6 (1994).

**Jean Nouvel, Fondation Cartier, Paris, France, 1991–4: view from the street.**

The extension of the glass facade beyond the edges of the building makes the structure seem to dissolve into the surrounding atmosphere.

building, located along the Boulevard Raspail, is little more than a simple glass box with a Miesian flavour. The project is a composition of transparent and reflective screens that dematerialise the construction. Some of the glazed facades are extended by approximately 10 metres beyond the volume of the building, becoming transparent backdrops through which one has a glimpse of the park that surrounds the building. Further confusing the perception of the building, the project features an 18-metre-high glass perimeter wall. The final result

49 Dan Graham (born 1942) is a conceptual artist and pioneer of video art. His work confronts the relationship between art and the public using video cameras connected to monitors that allow visitors to observe themselves as they observe the work of art. Beginning in the 1980s Graham built steel and glass pavilions that allowed for the multiplication of infinite reflections.

50 Pierre Chareau (1983–50), together with Bernard Bijvoet (1889–1979), is the designer of the Maison de Verre in Paris (1927–31), a work notable for its glass block facade and the invention of rotating, tilting, folding and extending furnishings whose movements allowed for different configurations of the interior spaces.

recalls the installations of the American artist Dan Graham:[49] an infinite space that appears to be devoid of any solidity or materiality.

Nouvel thus moves away from the functionalist aesthetic – that would find such a waste of material inconceivable – and towards a poetic of appearance, where the identity of the building is the result of its context, of a continually variable interaction with the sky, the weather and passing traffic.

Further underlining Nouvel's interest during this period in Minimalist trends is the collection of furniture designed specifically for the Fondation Cartier, produced by Unifor under the name Less. However, that the homage to Mies van der Rohe and Minimalism is more form than substance can be observed in the fact that reduction does not in any way lead, as with the German master, to a clarification of the structure of the object, but rather to a poetic of evanescence. This can be seen, for example, in the fact that the table

– surely the strongest piece of the collection – is so thin that it seems to disappear. At the same time, for example with the rotating containers, Nouvel looks at other inspirations, in this case the 'mobile' furnishings designed by Pierre Chareau.[50] The same can be said of his architectural research. In 1993 he started building two projects that test new poetic approaches: the City of Justice in Nantes and the Lucerne Cultural Centre (KKL). The latter will be discussed in the next chapter.

## 2.6 Herzog & de Meuron and the Skin of the Building

In 1993 Herzog & de Meuron completed four buildings whose success would contribute to orienting a progressively more consistent segment of architectural research from the theme of space, something dear to the Deconstructivists,

The architects chose to focus on
a simple volume that exalts the
materials used: etched designs
on the long sides and exposed
concrete on the short sides, where
water runs down the facade,
changing their appearance and
colour over time.

to that of the building envelope, or in more popular terms, mutated from the world of biology, its skin.[51] The projects were: the Schützenmattstrasse apartments and the SUVA offices and apartments, both in Basel, Switzerland; the Pfaffenholz Sports Centre in St Louis, France; and the Ricola Europe Factory in Mulhouse-Brunstatt, France.

The Schützenmattstrasse building (1984–93) features cast-iron shutters that mimic, at an enlarged scale, the decorative motif of the sewer covers in Basel. Their inspiration is likely to be found in the work of Frank Gehry.[52] However, while the works of the latter are visually exciting, the Schützenmattstrasse is discretely inserted within its context.[53] The unusual and

continuous facade of shutters replicates, as mentioned, the decorative motif of the sewer grates so familiar to the residents of Basel. What is more, because they fold back, and in some cases hide away, they give the building a lightweight and changing appearance.

The SUVA office and apartment building project (1988–93) consists of the modernisation of a building from the 1960s and the addition of a new volume. The formal coherence of the whole is obtained by using a continuous curtain wall to cover the existing building and the new construction. In this way the building, while presenting a contemporary appearance, through the stratification of successive interventions, demonstrates its history, becoming a sort of palimpsest.[54] What makes this transparent skin interesting, aside from panels with the etched logos of its tenants and strips of windows with different functions, is that some are moved by the

**51** The metaphor of the skin is, in reality, taken from an intuition of the media researcher Marshall McLuhan for whom within our society, dominated by electronic communication, objects acquire sensibilities and are clad with a sensitive epidermis that, exactly like human skin, allows for communication between the interior of the body and the exterior of the world. One of the first books to deal systematically with the theme of the skin of the building as one of the emerging motifs of

design research in the 1990s is Daniela Colafranceschi's *Architettura in superficie: Materiali, figure e tecnologie delle nuove facciate urbane*, Gangemi Editore (Rome), 1995. This book was followed, the next year, by a collection of interviews with the protagonists of this form of research: Daniela Colafranceschi, *Sull'involucro in architettura. Herzog, Nouvel, Perrault, Piano, Prix, Suzuki, Venturi, Wines*, Edizioni Librerie Dedalo (Rome), 1996. **52** Gehry, inspired by the aura of pop culture permeating the American West

Coast, in 1986 completed the Chiat/ Day offices, whose entrance is marked by a pair of oversized binoculars, designed in collaboration with the artist Claes Oldenburg. **53** It must be remembered that Herzog & de Meuron were students of Aldo Rossi at the ETH in Zurich – from whom they perhaps discovered the passion for the *objet trouvé* before Gehry. What is more, the duo were in constant contact with artists who defined the second half of the 20th century – in 1978 they had collaborated with Joseph Beuys (1921–86) and, as part of an exhibition held at the Canadian Centre for Architecture (CCA) in 2002, they proposed a series of ideal interlocutors, ranging from Beuys to Alberto Giacometti (1901–66), Donald Judd (1928–94), Andy Warhol (1928–87) and Dan Graham.

54 A palimpsest is a hand-written manuscript page subject to cancellations and successive rewritings. In the 1990s the term was widely used by architects to indicate those interventions that leave a trace of a pre-existing condition. In this way the new architectural text becomes the completion of and/or comment on the preceding elements.

inhabitants themselves in relationship to their specific requirements while others, functioning as brises-soleil, are oriented by a centralised and electronically controlled system to match the angle of the sun's rays.

The play of perception is also central to the design of the Pfaffenholz Sports Centre (1989–93). The main building – an extremely simple volume – sports dark green glazing covered with an etched pattern of the chipboard cladding behind it, and the latter can be seen through the glass, creating a pleasurable and disorienting effect of optical redundancy. The smaller volume of the changing rooms – equally elementary – is constructed using concrete decorated with an oversized and out-of-focus image of the material itself.

Another building that is notable for the extreme rigour of its architectural lines and, simultaneously, the richness of its envelope, is the Ricola Europe Factory (1992–3). Similar to a large packing crate, the two long sides are open and raised above ground level. What makes this building captivating are the etched poly-carbonate panels featuring the motif of a hand and 11 leaves, a reference to nature. Meanwhile the short sides, in exposed concrete and without any guttering, are stained by rainwater run-off, giving the building a material quality whose colouration and visual effects vary over time.

In 1995, Herzog & de Meuron had just completed the signal tower in Auf dem Wolf, Basel and were working on the design of a second one, completed in 1997. They are two prisms clad in thin bands of copper, which fold up in correspondence with the windows behind to allow for the passage of light. The copper bands create a Faraday cage that protects the delicate equipment inside the building. They are similar to a giant transformer, wrapped with thin metal windings: a sculpture at the urban scale that could easily be a work of Minimalism or Pop Art, depending upon whether we look at it as a pure volume or an *objet trouvé*.

**Herzog & de Meuron, Ricola Europe Factory, Mulhouse-Brunstatt, France, 1992–3: interior detail of the facade.**

The natural motifs of the polycarbonate facade panels, in addition to highlighting the Ricola logo, also create a sophisticated dialogue with the building's natural surroundings.

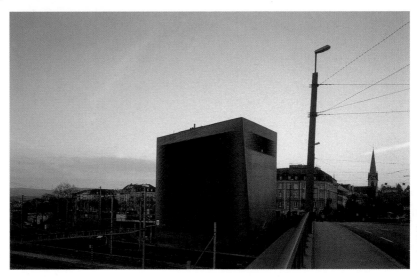

Herzog & de Meuron, Signal
Box 4, Auf dem Wolf, Basel,
Switzerland, 1992–5: exterior
view.

The building owes a great deal to
Minimalist and Pop sculpture. Its
essential form recalls the first,
while its resemblance to a large
battery ties it to the second.

The result is that complexity is once again avoided: the banality of the composition, as in the field of conceptual art or Minimalist sculpture, serves to exalt the materials, textures and relationships that would otherwise risk fading into the background. Between 1993 and 1994, Herzog & de Meuron began exploring a more involving spatial research. We can mention, for example, the Koechlin house in Riehen, Switzerland (1993–4) that relates to the undulating terrain and, at the same time, is organised around a central patio, deftly playing with double-height spaces. There is also the caricature museum in St Alban Vorstadt, Basel, Switzerland (1994–6) where the small available space is multiplied by using an enlivened path, rendered interesting by the transparent and reflective qualities of glass.

## 2.7 Minimalisms

From 1993 to 1997 and beyond, the word Minimalism appears more and more frequently in architectural publications and exhibitions. In 1993 *El Croquis* published a monographic issue entitled 'Minimalismos', edited by Josep María Montaner,[55] with *Lotus International*[56] and *Architectural Design*[57] following suit in 1994. The year 1995 was witness to the publication of essays by Ignasi de Solà-Morales, with a reprinted essay on Mies van der Rohe and

Annette Gigon, Mike Guyer,
extension to the Art Museum
in Winterthur, Switzerland,
1993–5: exterior detail of
the facade.

This addition is characterised
by the simplicity of the volumes
and the widespread used of
transparent walls. Slightly
oversized sheet metal-clad
skylights vaguely recall an
industrial building, making the
project hover between reality and
abstraction.

55 Edited by Josep María Montaner, *El Croquis*, no 62–3 (1993), special issue on 'Minimalismos'.
56 *Lotus International*, no 81 (1994).
57 'Aspects of Minimal Architecture', *Architectural Design*, vol 64, no 7–8 (1994).

SANAA (Kazuyo Sejima +
Ryue Nishizawa), N-Museum,
Wakayama, Japan, 1995–7:
interior view.

The building, like many other
projects by Sejima and Nishizawa,
is characterised by the extreme
rigour of the composition and
the dematerialisation of the volumes, obtained by using transparent walls.

Minimalism.[58] In 1995 the MoMA in New York inaugurated the exhibition 'Light Construction'.[59] On 26 June 1996 the exhibition 'Less Is More: Minimalismo en arquitectura i d'altres arts'[60] opened in Barcelona. On 30 September 1996 the show entitled 'Monolithic Architecture' opened in Pittsburgh, Pennsylvania, curated by Rodolfo Machado and Rodolphe el-Khoury.[61] All the same, as is often the case, the more one investigates a theme, the greater the difficulty in clearly identifying the precise objective of the research: in this case, Minimalism in architecture.

This can be seen, for example, in the introduction to the catalogue of the 'Less Is More' exhibition, where the two curators, Vittorio E Savi and Josep María Montaner, list eight characteristics that can be found – individually, or as a collection – in the buildings that belong to this trend. They are: a taste for pared-down, simple and traditional forms; geometric rigour; the ethics of repetition; technical precision combined with a love of matter; the search for unity and simplicity; a leap in scale; the formal predominance of structure; and a pure expression that renounces historical or expressive allusions. Thus, in line with these premises, the catalogue illustrations included famous buildings, such as the Farnsworth House by Mies van der Rohe, or more recent examples, such as Nouvel's Fondation Cartier and the signal tower in Basel by Herzog & de Meuron, in addition to many others from varying periods

58 'Mies van der Rohe y el Minimalismo', in Ignasi de Solà-Morales, Dif-
erencias: Topografía de la arquitectura
contemporánea, Editorial Gustavo Gili
(Barcelona), 1995.
59 The exhibition entitled 'Light
Construction', curated by Terence
Riley, ran from 21 September 1995 to
2 January 1996. Catalogue: Terence
Riley, Light Construction, The Museum
of Modern Art (New York), 1995.

60 The show closed on 28 July 1996
and was held in the Sala d'Exposicions
del Col·legi d'Arquitectes de Catalunya. Catalogue: Vittorio E Savi and
Josep María Montaner, Less Is More:
Minimalisme en arquitectura i d'altres
arts / Minimalism in Architecture and
the Other Arts, Col·legi d'Arquitectes
de Catalunya and Actar (Barcelona),
1996.

61 The show closed on 11 February
1996. Catalogue: Rodolfo Machado
and Rodolphe el-Khoury, Monolithic
Architecture, Prestel (Munich and New
York), 1995.

David Chipperfield, River and Rowing Museum, Henley on Thames, Oxfordshire, England, 1989–97: exterior view.

The building represents the confluence of different figurative aspects: the Minimalist simplification of volumes, a rigorous classicism with hints of Japan and experimentation with materials.

62 They include the Steiner Villa in Vienna (1910) by Adolf Loos (1870–1933); the Leça de Palmeira Pool in Spain (1955) by Álvaro Siza; the Monument to the Unknown Political Prisoner (1952) by Max Bill (1908–94); the Salk Institute in La Jolla, California (1959–65) by Louis Kahn; and the Student Residence in Chieti, Italy (1976–9) by Giorgio Grassi.

in the history of 20th-century architecture.[62] However, if this was a true representation of the situation, it was clear that the term Minimalism ran the risk of becoming generic and losing its meaning in order to express, in the best manner possible, only the need – particularly felt in these years by a growing number of architects – to purify the language of architecture of formal excesses by focusing attention more on the envelope than on the design of complex formal and spatial dynamics.[63]

John Pawson, Pawson House, London, England, 1999: interior view.

Considered one of the principal exponents of the Minimalist movement, Pawson focuses on the simplicity of lines and the extreme poverty of decoration: in this case a large shelf, whose colour and graining differ only slightly from the other materials used in the same space.

## 2.8 Questions of Perception

In 1994 the Japanese magazine *A+U* published a special edition entitled 'Questions of Perception'.[64] The issue was guest-edited by Steven Holl, Alberto Pérez-Gómez and Juhani Pallasmaa. Pallasmaa, with an emblematic essay entitled 'An Architecture of the Seven Senses', denounced the particular danger of an architecture that privileged visual aspects over the other senses. This leads to a loss of sensuality, a 'drift towards a distancing, a kind of chilling, de-seasonalisation and de-eroticisation of the human relation to reality'.[65]

How can we avoid this danger? By recovering, as the central part of the issue claims, 11 distinct 'phenom-

63 This programme, in reality accepted by many young architects in the 1990s, is synthesised with clarity in the text that Iñaki Ábalos (born 1956) and Juan Herreros (born 1958) presented at the Col·legi d'Arquitectes de Catalunya during the conference entitled 'A Fragile Skin'. The text is published in Ábalos & Herreros, *Áreas de impunidad / Areas of Impunity*, Actar (Barcelona), 1997, pp 9–47.

64 The issue was recently republished: Steven Holl, Juhani Pallasmaa, Alberto Pérez-Gómez, *Questions of Perception: Phenomenology of Architecture*, William Stout Publishers (San Francisco), 2006.
65 Juhani Pallasmaa, 'An Architecture of the Seven Senses' in Steven Holl, Juhani Pallasmaa, Alberto Pérez-Gómez, *Questions of Perception*, p 27.

**Álvaro Siza, University Library, Aveiro, Portugal, 1988–94: exterior view.**

Siza's debt to the work of Alvar Aalto can be sensed in the slight curvature of the wall. The remainder of the composition features a more severe approach to form, whose origins can be sought in Italian neo-Rationalist architecture.

**Steven Holl, Chapel of St Ignatius, Seattle, Washington, USA, 1995–7: exterior view.**

The result of the ingenious use of prefabricated concrete panels, this church is punctuated by numerous openings that allow sunlight to filter into the building.

enal zones': where the figure and the ground coexist; where perspectival perception is the source of continual surprises; where colour is employed; where effects of light and shadow are considered; where the building is conceived in terms of its nocturnal appearance; where perception implies a concept of duration, where water plays a role; where sound contributes to giving quality to space; where plays of tactility of surfaces are employed; where concepts of scale and proportion are used; and where an idea connects architecture to its context.

The result is a captivating architecture, though in some cases excessively loaded with impressionistic effects. This is undoubtedly different from the work of Herzog & de Meuron, whose use of materials is more detached, though intellectually more involving.

Completed in 1997, the Chapel of St Ignatius in Seattle, Washington (1995–7) is perhaps one of Steven Holl's most successful projects due to the tactile qualities of the materials employed: concrete, zinc, plaster and coloured glass. There is also the ingenious method of using large, prefabricated panels, not to mention the complex volumetric moves based on the multiple lighting effects, though fundamentally the result of a very simple, rectangular plan.

However, the most 'phenomenological' and critically successful work is by Peter Zumthor, making it, by default, the building that most exalts the values of perception and tactility: the Thermal Bath Complex in Vals, Switzerland (1994–6). Built of overlapping layers

**Steven Holl, Chapel of St Ignatius, Seattle, Washington, USA, 1995–7: interior view.**

Passing through coloured glass, natural light produces suggestive effects reminiscent of Le Corbusier's Notre Dame du Haut, Ronchamp, from which this project freely takes its inspiration.

**Peter Zumthor, Thermal Bath Complex, Vals, Switzerland, 1994–6: interior view.**

The alternation of large spaces and small rooms, of humid and dry spaces, of darkness and light is enhanced by the choice to finish the walls and floors in stone, based on the principles of historical local techniques.

36° Winter   30° Sommer

Massimiliano Fuksas, Maison
des Arts, Bordeaux, France,
1992–5: exterior view.

Two volumes, each of which is
clad with a different material,
create a level of dynamic tension.
A deep cut, made by a continuous
line of windows, divides the two
copper-clad volumes, lightening
the composition.

such weight can translate into lightness and the spatial envelope produce such a clear sensation of freedom as in this work by Zumthor.'[66]

A similar line of research was being pursed in the United States by Tod Williams and Billie Tsien.[67] In 1995 they completed the Neurosciences Institute in La Jolla, California. Three buildings define a public square that gives unity to the entire complex. Light and materials are the focus of the architects' attention, clearly visible in the auditorium with its delicate origami folds.

of stone and reinforced concrete, using a technique inspired by local traditions, the baths owe much of their fascination to the sober and rigorous pool that is obsessively and minutely detailed. The project is articulated in ample spaces that alternate with cubicles that are as suggestive as they are small, each of which has its own effects of light, colour, acoustic and, as a result of the use of various perfumes, distinct smell. What most impresses, however, is the ability with which the architect managed to unite the values of an architecture of the past with contemporary geometries, a love for extreme precision and the essential nature of the whole. In the words of Friedrich Achleitner: 'While it is possible to capture the various landscapes that define the project and the enormous effort behind each detail, at first sight it remains a mystery as to how

Tadao Ando, Museum of Wood,
Mikata-gun, Hyogo, Japan,
1991–4: view of one of the
internal courtyards.

Ando's work is characterised by
a cold and austere appearance,
reinforced by the use of exposed
concrete, even in interior spaces.
In this wood-clad courtyard these
qualities are mitigated, in favour
of an appearance that is more
tactile and involving, though no
less monumental.

..........................................................

**66** Friedrich Achleitner, 'Elementare profondità', in *Casabella*, no 648 (September 1997), p 59.
**67** Tod Williams (born 1943) studied at Princeton and Cambridge. Billie Tsien (born 1949) has worked with Tod Williams since 1977 and has been a partner in the office since 1986. They share the Louis Kahn Chair at Yale.

Álvaro Siza, Oporto School
of Architecture, Portugal,
1987–94: exterior view.

In Siza's architecture an important role is played by volumes
and their composition. Openings,
kept to a minimum, recall the
strip windows favoured by the
Modern Movement.

## 2.9 Koolhaas: Euralille

It is difficult to think of an architect who is less Minimalist and more inclusive than Rem Koolhaas. 'Architecture,' he states, 'is by definition a chaotic adventure,' adding that '[c]oherence imposed on an architect's work is either cosmetic or the result of self-censorship.'[68]

During the 1990s Koolhaas was already widely known, though his definitive international consecration took place in 1996, following the publication of his 1,345-page tome entitled *S,M,L,XL* (Small, Medium, Large and Extra Large), a book-manifesto that met with extraordinary success, also thanks to the innovative graphic design by Bruce Mau. *S,M,L,XL* abandons typological and morphological distinctions. 'Small' deals with the display pavilion and 'Medium' the building, while the neighbourhood is 'Large' and urban planning 'Extra Large'. In addition to Koolhaas' projects the book contains numerous essays that, in the words of the author, are autonomous episodes and not to be seen as elements of interconnection.

The objective is that of giving life to what Koolhaas calls 'a new realism'. It consists of a disenchanted vision that adheres to things as they are forecast by the society in which we live: a metropolitan reality that is no longer founded on the ordered development of the city, but on the chaotic localisation of urban agglomerates and networks of connection. What is the destiny of architecture – Koolhaas asks – within this context? We cannot avoid seeing it as an obstacle to change, as the chain around the ankle of a prisoner, robbed of the ability to move as he wishes. The best building is thus that which does not exist: it is the space in which no wall hinders or directs the body. What inspires Koolhaas is surely the almost nothing of Mies, a master to whom the Dutch architect has always made reference, though it is not difficult to see in these reflections a personal

Juan Navarro Baldeweg, Mahon
Courthouse, Mahon, Spain,
1993–5: exterior view.

Baldeweg attempts to unite the
principles of the Modern Movement with the forms of local
traditions, cladding the building
with materials other than simple
stucco.

68 'Introduction' in Rem Koolhaas and
Bruce Mau, *S,M,L,XL*, The Monacelli
Press (New York) and 010 Publishers
(Rotterdam), 1995, p XIX.

**Rem Koolhaas/OMA, Euralille, Lille, France, 1989–96: overall aerial view.**

Koolhaas' project avoids the re-proposal of a traditional urban context, composed of streets and public spaces. The majority of Euralille's public spaces are covered, including the dominant shopping centre designed by Jean Nouvel, completed in 1995.

re-elaboration of the problems of Minimalism that, during this period, were capturing the attention of architectural research.

The year 1996 was also the year that Euralille – the first large masterplan entrusted to Koolhaas, and conceived between 1989 and 1994 – took form. This design opportunity was made possible when the city of Lille, which found itself at the centre of new important axes of European mobility thanks to the construction of new high-speed rail lines, decided to convert itself into a centre of metropolitan attraction. The project, which covers some 120 hectares, is centred on the new TGV station located approximately 200 metres from the old station, to which it is connected by a road artery emblematically named Rue Le Corbusier. The project called for the construction of numerous commercial and business premises, awarded to different architects: Koolhaas was responsible for the Congrexpo; the TGV station was designed by Jean-Marie Duthilleul;[69] the shopping centre by Jean Nouvel; the Crédit Lyonnais tower by Christian de Portzamparc; and the World Trade Centre by Claude Vasconi.[70]

Euralille contains all of the design techniques honed by Koolhaas in his previous projects: assembly by strips and layers; design by nodes and networks; the dramatisation of movement; and the dialectic between the needle and the globe.

Assembly by strips and layers is the result of the meeting of two different systems: the infrastructural and the architectural. This occurs in the station, which is overlapped, a posteriori, by the office tower and the commercial building. There is a dominance of the poetic

**Rem Koolhaas/OMA, Euralille, Lille, France, 1989–96: view of the towers by Claude Vasconi and Christian de Portzamparc.**

Fascinated by the aesthetic of congestion, Koolhaas called for the towers to be built above the railway station, entrusting their design to different architects.

69 Jean-Marie Duthilleul (born 1952), architect and engineer, graduated from the Ecole National de Ponts et Chaussées (1979). He is the director of projects of 'développement urbain et architecturaux' for the Société Nationale des Chemins de Fer (SNCF), the French rail company.

70 Claude Vasconi (born 1940) is
known for the organisation of Les
Halles in Paris (1994–2000), which he
won together with Georges Pencreac'h
(born 1941) in a 1973 competition. He
is the designer of numerous Modernist
buildings and was responsible for the
redesign of the Borsig factory in Berlin
(1994–2000).

**Rem Koolhaas/OMA, Euralille, Lille, France, 1989–96: detail view of the Congrexpo.**

Entire portions of the Congrexpo were designed to be seen from automobiles travelling along the adjacent highway. The objective was to create forms suitable for the dynamic uses of space imposed by the metropolis.

of the list, of overlapping, of encounter-confrontation: for example, the Congrexpo, where three different buildings, each with their own architecture and logic, come together to form a single building with an elliptical plan.

Conceived of as a collection of nodes linked to various systems of networks (automotive, railway, pedestrian),

Euralille is animated by a succession of dynamic spaces: the only open-air plaza is triangular in form and, in any case, represents a moment of transition from the shopping centre to the TGV station. The remaining public spaces are all located inside the buildings, in large cavities from which depart paths of all types. Movement becomes a generating principle of form. The traffic that runs along the Rue Le Corbusier cuts the TGV station in two; the elevation of the Congrexpo changes if looked at from a distance and at different speeds; signage and indications acquire predominance over the facades; the buildings are articulated in order that they open towards the spaces of movement of automobiles, trains and other vehicles in movement. Finally, Koolhaas invents a large, void space at the point of connection between the TGV, the parking structure and the highway. It is a new *espace piranesien* that testifies to the fact that movement – the form of events – is the sublime of our era, that which spellbinds us and terrorises us: the driving force of a new aesthetic.

**Rem Koolhaas/OMA, Euralille, Lille, France, 1989–96: view of the *espace piranesien*.**

Koolhaas uses the term *espace piranesian* to describe urban nodes located on multiple levels that allow for exchanges between different infrastructural systems. It is within these spaces, crowded with people in movement, that we find the unsettling fascination of Modernism.

72 Sir D'Arcy Wentworth Thompson
(1860–1948) was a biologist, math-
ematician and scholar of classical
culture and author, in 1917, of the
book *On Growth and Form* in which he
examines the nexus between the form
of organisms and their development.

## 2.10 The Poetics of the Electronic: Between the Blob and the Metaphor

Blob[71] architecture (or Blobitecture) was launched in 1995 by Greg Lynn. It consists of amoeba-like buildings generated and controlled by special software that, on par with complex natural forms, are the result of the transformation of simpler objects, caused by the concomitant action of external and internal forces. Using extremely sophisticated technologies Lynn pursues a recurring objective in the history of architecture: copying nature in order to cancel any box-like appearance of the built works, rendering them integral with the environment that surrounds them, using common forms, histories and processes. This led to references to the work of the early 20th-century biologist D'Arcy Thompson,[72] to whom we owe studies on the morphological evolution of organisms.

In 1995 Charles Jencks published *The Architecture of the Jumping Universe*. The book expresses the urgency of returning to the study of the complex forms of nature, ensuring the coexistence of ecological and cybernetic forms.[73] Jencks cites Ilya Prigogine[74] and, as Lynn had done in the issue of *Architectural Design* dedicated to folding, the School of Santa Fe and Thom's theory of catastrophes. The universe, according to the model posited by these scholars, is a complex system that evolves by leaps and bounds (hence the title), the latest of which has led to the current situation, characterised by enormous ecological and demographic problems, in addition to important opportunities. The

71 The essay 'Blobs' was originally published in the *Journal of Philosophy and the Visual Arts*, no 6 (1995), pp 39–44, as part of a special issue enti-tled 'Complexity: Architecture/Art/Philosophy'. Reprinted in Greg Lynn, *Folds, Bodies & Blobs: Collected Essays*, La Lettre Volée (Brussels), 1998.

73 Charles Jencks, *The Architecture of the Jumping Universe – A Polemic: How Complexity Science is Changing Architec-ture and Culture*, Academy Editions (London), 1995. Jencks underlines how many new ideas were already present in Deconstructivism, citing Eisenman with his constructions based on morphogenetic principles; Gehry for his level of vital energy and ability to organise the complex; Zaha Hadid for the planetary force of form; Libeskind for his cataclysmic tension and the violence of mass; and Koolhaas for his ability to overlap and collide simple elements in articulated structures. He also manages to give a role to the exponents of High Tech, such as Renzo Piano, Santiago Calat-rava or Nicholas Grimshaw, who render organic structures complex through engineering. Finally he recovers – list-ing them as precursors – the principal exponents of the modern organic movement, from Erich Mendelsohn (1887–1953) to Bruno Taut (1880–1938), and from Frank Lloyd Wright (1867–1959) to Bruce Goff (1904–82).

**76** Jencks does not hesitate to praise Eisenman – praise that Eisenman would return in the cover notes of the same book: 'Jencks has the uncanny capacity to announce a new movement in architecture before it has begun. With Post-Modernism he was looking to the past. Now, for the first time, with his new book on morphogenesis he is taking a look at the future.'

objects of our era, in fact, are humanised and, at the same time, man is transformed into an object in what is, undoubtedly, a positive process. The refinement of these machines corresponds with the roughness of an architecture based on the formative concepts of a pseudo-rationalist era that makes no consideration of the fact that new technologies are able to be developed because science, having reached a post modern state, has conquered the four legendary terms of determinism, mechanism, reductionism and materialism; it has thus begun to look at the world as a system with life and an ability for self-regulation, similar to an organism that seeks a progressively better equilibrium through continual changes of state.[75]

How can architecture render this process visible? By acquiring a spiritual dimension and mutating the nature of the forms of its development. This leads Jencks to become interested in organic configurations, fractals and structures that curve and move like the waves of an atom and in anything that represents the spiritual side of mankind, whose role is that of leading the universe towards self-recognition as part of an uncovering of the idea, similar to Hegel's dialectical process. This also generates an interest in blob architecture, Greg Lynn and, above all, Eisenman, who begins to move towards the neo-organic and the neo-Baroque.[76]

Launched by such culturally authoritative sponsors, blob research, especially in schools of architecture, was extraordinarily popular, though actual built examples are rare. Notwithstanding the efforts of Lynn and many others, focused on the digitalisation of the process through to construction, it is particularly difficult to obtain a convincing result. The construction of complex forms using traditional materials requires a vast and unacceptable amount of labour and the use of numerically controlled machinery to produce complex components. The process is economically unviable for an industry such as that of construction, which is technologically less advanced than other industrial sectors.

---

**74** Ilya Prigogine (1917–2003) was a Nobel Laureate and researcher in thermodynamics and complex systems. His theory raises questions about the principle according to which entropy, or disorder, is the ultimate state of the universe. In the 1990s his books were widely read even by those in other fields.

**75** This generates the image of the butterfly as opposed to that of the trap. The latter symbolises the mechanical conception of the universe, the architecture of *existenz*

*minimum,* the machine for dwelling. It is activated only when provoked by cause. It swallows its prey and restores less than what existed prior to its action. The butterfly, which renders the image of the universe much more organic, is the product of a series of creative steps: from a simple organism it becomes a larva, and from larva a chrysalis, and finally a winged insect.

Jakob + MacFarlane, Restaurant Georges, Centre Pompidou, Paris, France, 1997–2000: interior view.

The project consists of the restoration of the restaurant in the Centre Pompidou by inserting four blobby, aluminium-clad volumes, each with a different colour and function.

In 1997 Kolatan/MacDonald[77] designed a blob for the addition to the Raybould House in Fairfield Corner, Connecticut. They called for a skeleton in wood that recalls a traditional boat hull, the difference being that the wooden 'ribs' were cut by numerically controlled machinery. The same year Jakob + MacFarlane[78] won an invited competition for the design of a new rooftop bar at the Centre Pompidou in Paris with a project based on four computer-generated, aluminium-clad blobs, each of a different colour. The project was completed in 2000. In 1997 the Dutch group NOX[79] completed the Water Pavilion for Delta Expo 'Waterland' in Neeltje Jans, The Netherlands. The interior, the result of the succession of 14 ellipses, recalls the stomach of a whale. It is rendered particularly interesting by the use of interactive lighting, sounds and projections. The neo-organic is transformed into the neo-Baroque. The seal on this new aesthetic came with the Staten Island Institute of Arts (1997) by Peter Eisenman. Its wrapping, curved forms are the result of the digital manipulation of pedestrian and automotive paths.

While this passion for complex forms raged, Toyo Ito was pursuing an aesthetic that sought to unite Minimalism with electronics. In 1997 the architectural magazine *2G* published his projects together with an essay entitled

77 Kolatan/MacDonald was founded in 1988 by William MacDonald (born 1958) and Sulan Kolatan (born 1956). They are interested in experimenting with new forms related to digital space and, in particular, add-on structures that shape new spatial patterns and protocols.

78 The two partners of Jakob + Mac-Farlane are Dominique Jakob (born 1966) and Brendan MacFarlane (born 1961). Jakob graduated in Paris in 1991; MacFarlane, a graduate of SCI-Arch in Los Angeles, completed his Masters studies at Harvard.

79 NOX takes it name from a humanoid extraterrestrial population of the same name, the most advanced race in the universe in the science fantasy television programme 'Stargate'. The group was founded in 1990 by Lars Spuybroek (born 1959) and Maurice Nio (born 1959), who left in 1996 to work in the office of BDG (Bureau de Gruyter).

80 Toyo Ito, 'Tarzans in the Media Forest', in *2G*, no 2 (1997), pp 122–44.

'Tarzans in the Media Forest'[80]. In the essay Ito refers to Marshall McLuhan's theory whereby the visual society that preceded us has been overtaken by a tactile one. The first manages quantity, forces and weights, while the second works with flows, interrelations and immaterial values.

Let us look – Ito says – at a young boy from our present day and age. It would appear that he cannot live without a cellular phone and other electronic gadgets. These instruments, which wrap him like clothing, are indispensable to him for remaining in contact with the world around him: they keep him within a loop. However, the same need to be a part of and interact with context can also be found in buildings and cities. For example, we can compare a traditional building with a contemporary one. The first is defined by its mass, the organisation of solids and voids, colours, patterns, the system of construction and functional organisation. The second surprises us, instead, because of how it interacts with the surrounding environment: the way

in which it captures light and relates to external and internal climatic conditions, placing us in relationship with sounds, smells and colours and ensuring our comfort. If we wish to compare it to a body, we could speak of perceptive and self-regulating systems.

However – Ito continues – if architecture is like an antenna that places us in relation with the external world, 'it must function as a highly effective sensor to detect the flow of electrons'.[81]

Man, having reacquired this renewed natural dimension, like a new Tarzan can move through a world that has finally been reunified: a world of integral communication and a forest of media.

The metaphor of new architecture is the fluid and, in particular, water – the water in which Mies's Barcelona Pavilion appears to hover, in which ancient Japanese philosophers saw the principle of life and in which the electronic images on computer screens seem to

81 Toyo Ito, 'Tarzans in the Media Forest', p 140.

**Richard Rogers, Channel 4
Headquarters, London, England,
1990–4: exterior view.**

Of the protagonists of the High
Tech movement, Rogers remains
closest to its industrial origins.
This can be seen in his interest in
the sincerity of construction, the
poetics of the structures and the
exposed building systems.

float. Water is the material that this Japanese architect chooses as the inspiration for his masterpiece: the
Sendai Mediatheque, about which more will be said in
the next chapter.

## 2.11 Eco-Tech

According to the critic Catherine Slessor,
there are six aspects that define Eco-
Tech.[82] Firstly there is the design of
expressive structures, resulting from the
influx of genial consultants, such as Peter
Rice of Ove Arup or engineer-architects like
Santiago Calatrava, who do not hesitate
to abandon the coldness of High Tech in
order to pursue more complex, and even
organic, principles. This is followed by the
desire to model space with light and play
with transparency, something permitted
by innovations in glazing technology
(larger sheet sizes, structural glass, etc).
The third aspect relates to the increased
awareness of energy savings, using new
materials and products and renewable
and natural sources of energy. The fourth
characteristic is an attention to context,
in order to obtain buildings that are both
inviting spaces of urban aggregation and
avoiding an appearance that is extraneous
to their environment. There is also an
attention to interconnections, with traffic
networks and systems that manage flows
dedicated to the exchange of information.
Finally there is an attempt to transform
buildings into symbols of society, non-

82 Catherine Slessor, *Eco-Tech: Sustainable Architecture and High Technology*,
Thames and Hudson (London), 1997.

**Thomas Herzog, Exhibition Hall,
Hanover, Germany, 1995–6:
exterior view.**

This building is a mixture of
organic and High Tech sugges-
tions. The objective is that of
humanising technology by creating a machine that is visually
attractive and environmentally
sustainable.

**Nicholas Grimshaw, Waterloo International Terminal, London, England, 1988–93: interior view.**

The beauty of this international rail terminal is the result of the elegant structural system of steel trusses and the choice to divide the roof into two halves: one of which is primarily opaque and the other predominantly transparent.

rhetorical monuments, conceived of at the urban scale as public landmarks.

In 1993 the British Government under John Major authorised the extension of the Jubilee Line, the underground railway infrastructure that connects the centre of London with the Docklands. The stations were awarded to: Michael Hopkins (Westminster); Ian Ritchie Architects[83] (Jamaica Road); Norman Foster (Canary Wharf); Will Alsop (North Greenwich); and MacCormac Jamieson Prichard[84] (Southwark).

1993 was also the year of the completion of another important infrastructure: the Waterloo International Terminal, designed by Nicholas Grimshaw. It is the English terminal of the high-speed rail line that crosses the Eurotunnel, connecting Paris and London. Grimshaw later inaugurated the Regional Control Centre in Bristol, a building with a studied elegance, in 1994.

During this period Foster completed the Carré d'Art in Nîmes (1984–93), the University of Cambridge Faculty of Law (1990–5) and the Microelectronics Park in Duisburg (1988–96), all of which demonstrate a desire to find a classical scale, while later this architect – perhaps influenced by the digital neo-Baroque aesthetic – would be tempted by curvilinear forms.

83 Ian Ritchie Architects was founded in 1981 by Ian Ritchie (born 1947), the co-founder, in 1986, of the engineering firm of Rice Francis Ritchie (RFR). His interventions throughout the 1980s explored fabric and textile structures, light-transmitting fabrics, high-performance glass systems, robotics and light-memory coatings.
84 MacCormac Jamieson Prichard was founded in 1972 and is run by Sir Richard MacCormac (born 1938).

**Norman Foster, University of Cambridge Faculty of Law, England, 1990–5: exterior view.**

The design of the Law Faculty building displays a classic approach obtained by the simplicity of the plan and the accuracy of the construction detailing.

**Rafael Viñoly, Tokyo International Forum, Tokyo, Japan, 1989–96: interior view.**

The International Forum, which contains a conference centre and display spaces, has become one of the most interesting urban spaces in Tokyo. The interior street, crossed by paths and covered by a roof of curved trusses, is undoubtedly spectacular.

Richard Rogers completed the Channel 4 Headquarters in London (1990–4) and the European Court of Human Rights (1989–95), using forms that are more faithful to the original language of High Tech, composed of exposed building systems and glass and steel.

In 1994 Will Alsop completed the Hôtel du Départment des Bouches-du-Rhône in Marseilles, known as the 'Le Grand Bleu', a work that, in the light of the lesson of Ce-

dric Price, declines technology in a fantastic and often playful manner, an approach akin to Pop Art.

A progressively greater tribute to structure can be found in the neo-organic work of Santiago Calatrava. His more important works from this period include the BCE Place Gallery in Toronto (1987–93); the project for the dome of the Reichstag, which opened in four pieces, in Berlin (1995); and the Lyon TGV station (1989–94), with its unsettling organic appearance. His bridges remain his more elegant and essential works, such as the Trinity in Salford (1993–5), supported by a single, inclined pylon and slender steel cables.

Another important work from this decade, though only partially related to the world of High Tech, is the Tokyo

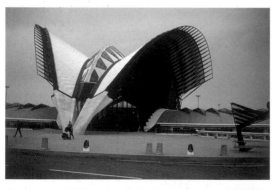

**Santiago Calatrava, TGV station, Lyon, France, 1989–94: exterior view.**

Inspired by the observation of living organisms and filtered through a typically Spanish predilection for Baroque forms, Calatrava's structures conjure up the forms of fantastic animals.

**Santiago Calatrava, TGV station, Lyon, France, 1989–94: interior view.**

Even the interior spaces of Calatrava's station are dominated by the structures and their rhythmic placement.

85 Rafael Viñoly (born 1944) studied
in Buenos Aires, graduating in 1968.
In 1979 he moved to New York where
he founded Rafael Viñoly Architects
in 1983.

International Forum (1989–96) by Rafael Viñoly:[85] an imposing conference and exhibition centre – so much so that it quickly became an urban landmark – containing a gigantic and scenographic plaza with a glass canopy supported by fusiform beams.

## 2.12 Renzo Piano's Soft-Tech

In 1997 the Centre Pompidou, only 20 years after its inauguration, was closed for renovations, the result of its immense success: a daily flow of 25,000 visitors, instead of the forecast 5,000. The project called for a renovation of decaying elements and an addition to the existing 70,000 square metres of another 8,000, to be used for cultural activities and services. The project prepared by Piano, for whom High Tech was now a distant memory, did not hesitate to question some of the ideological presuppositions of the original building: he transformed the hall on the ground floor, originally conceived of as a large,

**Renzo Piano, Kansai International Airport Terminal, Osaka, Japan, 1988–94: general view.**

The airport building has a distinctive undulating roof, supported by giant and lightweight steel trusses. It is the proof that even complex projects of this type can manage technological requirements, an attention to the landscape and respect the human scale.

Will Alsop, Hôtel du
Département des Bouches-
du-Rhône, Marseilles, France,
1990–4: exterior view.

Nicknamed 'Le Grand Bleu' as a
result of its distinctive colour,
the complex is composed of a low
building, whose fusiform shape is
reminiscent of a subway station
or naval construction. The taller
building is crowned with motifs
that pick up on the geometric
decoration of the low building.

covered plaza, into an elegant commercial space; he closed the exterior escalator connection to the first two floors; he limited access to the terraces, now open only to paying customers; and he compromised the flexibility of the interior spaces by introducing new elevators. In short, he thwarted two of the guiding concepts that informed the philosophy behind the building, designed in 1971 together with Richard Rogers and Gianfranco Franchini: total public permeability and unlimited transformation.[86]

What is more, the work produced by the office of this Genoese architect was progressively more extraneous to the formal harshness typical of avant-garde research. With the completion of the Kansai International Airport Terminal in Japan (1988–94), perhaps his masterpiece, Piano definitively earned a place in the firmament of the Star System. He was also on the cusp of obtaining new commissions from important clients, attracted by his innovative, though non-radical, research, that was attentive to the psychological comfort of its users, nature and traditional technologies. The Kansai project features an elegant, double-curving roof, whose interior spaces make use of traditional Japanese colours.

In the project for the Fondation Beyeler in Basel, Switzerland (1991–7), the contrast between two

86 So much so that Richard Rogers cannot help but note that, after the renovation, the museum abdicated its role and was institutionalised, losing its characteristic of being a 'building designed for people'.

87 Giorgio Grassi (born 1935) graduated from the Politecnico di Milano in 1960. In 1967 he published *La costruzione logica dell'architettura*, Marsilio (Padua), 1967, a book in which he sought to give scientific foundations to the themes of disciplinary autonomy sustained during the same period by Aldo Rossi and the Tendenza movement. His works of architecture, inspired by metaphysical painting, share a geometric simplicity, structural rigidity and monumental appearance.

88 Helmut Jahn (born 1940) studied at the Technische Hochschule of Munich and in 1966 at the Illinois Institute of Chicago (IIT). In 1967 he joined CF Murphy Associates. The firm was renamed Murphy/Jahn in 1981. Charles Francis Murphy (born 1890) died in 1985, leaving Jahn in control. The works of Murphy/Jahn include the State of Illinois Center in Chicago (1979–85).

different technologies – a heavy and material system of stone walls and an airy and light glazed roof – is attenuated by the brilliant idea of inserting a dematerialising reflecting pool, inhabited by nymphs, and the decomposition of the volume into planes. Furthermore, the dynamism suggested by the cantilevered roof is contrasted on the interior by square rooms that allow for the ordered distribution of the works of art.

His subsequent works follow the same approach. For example, the Jean-Marie Tjibaou Cultural Center in Noumea, New Caledonia (1991–8) and the project for the Potsdamer Platz in Berlin (1992–2000). The centre, dedicated to the Kanak culture, is notable for the happy invention of wooden apses that recall historical local structures and which vibrate in the wind, integrating the building within its natural surroundings. Unfortunately, with respect to the original design that called for an internal space surrounded by a cluster of these structures, the final project is a linear slab that is much more banal, though still faultless. In the Potsdamer Platz, Piano manages to reconstruct a fragment of the European city, with its typical urban spaces, avoiding both the excessive rigour of the nearby project by the Italian Giorgio Grassi[87] and the chaos, similar to a shopping mall, of the project by Helmut Jahn[88] for the adjacent Sony Centre. Piano's project also has the merit of

**Renzo Piano, Fondation Beyeler, Basel, Switzerland, 1991–7: interior view.**

In this museum Piano unites stone-clad walls with a lightweight roof in steel and glass. The most successful space in the building is the room that contains the paintings by Monet, whose large glazed surfaces allow for a view of the reflecting pool that contains the nymphaeum.

89 Hans Kollhoff (born 1946) graduated in 1975 in Germany, after which he moved to the United States to study at Cornell University. In 1978 he opened his own practice in Berlin. Since 1990 he has been a professor at the ETH, Zurich. His work is characterised by a rigour and historicism influenced by Aldo Rossi and Oswald Mathias Ungers (1926–2007).

90 Bart Lootsma, 'Une tradition de l'innovation', in *L'architecture d'aujourd'hui*, no 306 (September 2006), p 51.

maintaining the unity of a complex that, other than the blocks designed by his office, also features buildings by architects as diverse as Richard Rogers, Rafael Moneo, Hans Kollhoff[89] and Arata Isozaki.

in London and American architecture faculties, like those of Cooper Union, Columbia, Princeton and Harvard.'[90]

## 2.13 PAYS-BAS_perspectives

The September 1996 issue of *L'architecture d'aujourd'hui* was entitled 'PAYS-BAS_perspectives', dedicated to Dutch architects, and presented by Bart Lootsma, who stated: 'they take advantage of the current climate of international exchange generated in the eighties, but their ideas, their plans and their buildings can all be described without any qualifications as being original. They relate more to the theoretical developments that have taken place in the Architectural Association

The issue featured a list of emerging talents who would later become the protagonists of one of the most important architectural phenomena of the late 1990s. They were the architects educated in the wake of Rem Koolhaas, a figure whose intellectual provocations made him an intellectual reference, while his international success made him a professional one. The issue featured Wiel Arets, van Berkel & Bos (UNStudio), Adriaan Geuze & West 8, MVRDV, NOX, Koen van Velsen and Ton Venhoeven CS.

Wiel Arets[91] came to the public's attention for his pared-down and schematic works, precise like mathematical calculations, and a prelude to a research oriented towards Minimalism.

**Rem Koolhaas/OMA, Educatorium, Utrecht, The Netherlands, 1993–7: exterior view.**

The complexity of the spatial configuration corresponds with the brutal treatment of the materials and the play of transparencies, made possible by the use of different types of glass.

91 Wiel Arets (born 1955) has taught at the Architectural Association, Columbia University and Cooper Union. In 1995 he was nominated Dean of the Berlage Institute in Amsterdam, home to the most important postgraduate programme in The Netherlands.

**UNStudio, Rijksmuseum Twenthe extension, Enschede, The Netherlands, 1992–6: exterior view.**

This contemporary project is clearly different from its pre-existing surroundings. The sloping form is the result of the possibility of using the new building to connect various existing floor levels.

Van Berkel & Bos (UNStudio) [92] had just completed the Erasmus Bridge in Rotterdam, The Netherlands (1990–6), an urban landmark that, while perhaps too reminiscent of Calatrava's work, had an important impact on the skyline of the city. They are also the architects of the Villa Wilbrink in Amersfoort (1993–4), a single-family residence in which they successfully applied a design method based on diagrams: the transposition of a functional programme into a geometric scheme that, in turn, was translated into architectural form. This method was later applied in the Möbius House in Het Gooi, The Netherlands (1993–8). This single-family dwelling is organised like a Möbius strip in order to optimise relations between the spaces of work and dwelling.

Adriaan Geuze, with West 8,[93] pursues a form of experimentation with the themes of the natural and artificial landscape, seen no longer as alternatives but as strictly interrelated systems, open to the changing needs of those who inhabit them. One example of this approach is the Schouwburgplein in Rotterdam, The Netherlands (1990–6), a flexible public square capable of hosting numerous events, also made possible by a system of lighting mounted on moveable steel structures that can be adjusted at will, in theory even by local citizens.

MVRDV[94] are moved by the constant search for a rational base upon which to found their projects. However, it is a rationality that, as per the teachings of Koolhaas, always leads to complex buildings that are spatially interesting and substantially anti-classical. This is the case of the De Hoge Veluwe Park in The Netherlands (1994–5), where the apparently traditional entry pavilions are obtained by deforming and readjusting, in a Modernist key, the archetypal model of the house-parallelepiped with its double-pitched roof.

Of the work of NOX, *L'architecture d'aujourd'hui* chose to present the Water Pavilion for Delta Expo 'Waterland' in Neeltje Jans, The Netherlands, which has already been mentioned.[95] Koen van Velsen's[96] firm were represented

92 Ben van Berkel (born 1957) was a student and subsequently a teacher at the Architectural Association. He founded the Amsterdam-based practice of van Berkel & Bos, also known as UNStudio, in 1988, with the art historian Caroline Bos (born 1959).
93 West 8 was founded in 1987 by Adriaan Geuze (born 1960) and Paul van Beek (born 1961).
94 MVRDV was founded in 1991 by Winy Maas (born 1959), Jacob van Rijs (born 1964) and Nathalie de Vries (born 1965).

95 See paragraph 2.10: The Poetics of the Electronic: Between the Blob and the Metaphor.
96 Koen van Velsen (born 1952).

**West 8, Schouwburgplein, Rotterdam, The Netherlands, 1990–6: exterior view.**

The extreme flexibility of this public square is guaranteed by the system of adjustable lighting that, in theory, can be manipulated by its users.

**MVRDV, Villa VPRO, Hilversum, The Netherlands, 1993–7: exterior view.**

The complex organisation of the interior spaces and the design of the exterior facades of the Villa VPRO recall the work of OMA. It is a testament to the significant qualities of works produced under the influence, primarily theoretical, of Koolhaas.

**Mecanoo, Faculty of Economics and Management, Utrecht, The Netherlands, 1991–5: exterior view.**

The building is designed like a glass box that contains other, coloured boxes. It is also a source of spatial surprises that culminate in three courtyards, each different from the other.

97 Ton Venhoeven (born 1954).

by their Megabioscoop in Rotterdam, The Netherlands (1992–6), the cinema built beside the Schouwburgplein, designed based on the principles of diagrammatic architecture. Finally, Ton Venhoeven[97] was presented in two photomontages that demonstrated the numerous spatial themes found in even the most banal buildings.

Though very different from one another, these Dutch architects share common forms of research: an interest in a rational method that justifies the project, an attention to the relationship between architecture and its context and the landscape, an articulated spatiality capable of containing complex events, the use of poor and industrially produced materials, and a purposefully Calvinist and brutalist approach, with a resulting lack of attention to the precious nature of finishes and

**Neutelings Riedijk, Minnaert Building, Utrecht, The Netherlands, 1994–7: exterior view.**

The Minnaert is characterised by its closed appearance, rendered unsettling by the air-conditioning ducts and piping that, similar to excrescences, can be seen on the facades. On the interior, as part of a planned contrast, the spaces are welcoming, pleasant and well lit.

detailing. These are the preferences that would allow them to escape on the one hand from the excessive complexity of the hyper-organic nature of digital architecture and, on the other, from the pure surfaces of post-Minimalism. The result is a formidable contribution to the phenomenon of landscape architecture, which we will discuss in the next chapter.[98]

........................................................................

**98** Of the publications that have dealt with the Dutch phenomenon, see: Bart Lootsma, *Superdutch: New Architecture in the Netherlands*, Thames & Hudson (London), 2000; Hans Ibelings, ed., *The Artificial Landscape: Contemporary Architecture, Urbanism, and Landscape Architecture in the Netherlands*, NAi Publishers (Rotterdam), 2000.

**Mecanoo, Faculty of Economics and Management, Utrecht, The Netherlands, 1991–5: view of one of the courtyards.**

Inspired by Zen gardens, this courtyard re-proposes their typical elements: the use of wood, paving in river gravel, larger stones and, finally, a tree.

NOX, Water Pavilion and Interactive Installation, Delta Expo 'Waterland' Neeltje Jans, Zeeland, The Netherlands, 1997: exterior and interior views.

The exterior of the pavilion resembles a steel sculpture, while the interior is a welcoming and interactive space, enlivened by suggestive lighting and audio effects.

**MVRDV, WOZOCO Housing for the Elderly, Amsterdam, The Netherlands, 1994–7: exterior view.**

The numerous balconies, each of a different colour, enliven the building and allow its inhabitants to live outdoors during the warmer seasons, conversing with one another and observing the activities that take place in the surrounding park.

**MVRDV, WOZOCO Housing for the Elderly, Amsterdam, The Netherlands, 1994–7: exterior view.**

The large cantilevers that project from the main volume of the building are justified by the need to provide more space in the living units with respect to local planning.

## 2.14 Pro and Versus a New Architecture

Shaken by new fermentations − blobby forms, the use of new materials, facades covered with large projection screens, dematerialisation, superficial effects − the academic world reacted: often randomly, accusing the new of being nothing other than the product of a civilisation continually more interested in ephemeral trends, in other cases with more even-tempered and reasonable considerations. This is the case with Harvard Design Magazine that, in 1997, dedicated a monographic issue to the theme of 'Durability and Ephemerality'.99 Kenneth Frampton, Luis Fernández-Galiano, Henry Petroski and Gavin Stamp sounded the alarm: the danger for new architecture was the loss of consistency, of solidity. The lack of interest in tectonic100 values, the use of facades separated from buildings, the transformation of facades into projection screens and the wilful application of short-lived materials appeared to confirm this.

Traditional materials, such as brick, stone and wood, Frampton states,[101] were used to create structures that were built to last. For example, the Villa Mairea by Aalto[102] that, after almost 70 years, was still an exemplary construction in which nature and culture, present and past, interact to the point where they almost overlap.

The problem of the duration of materials is, Frampton concluded, a problem of architecture, with its roots in the 1930s, when Le Corbusier dedicated himself to vernacular forms and traditional materials. There are also later examples, such as the research of the Greek architect Dimitris Pikionis[103], the Italian neo-rationalists[104] and, finally, the Spaniards, led by Rafael Moneo.

An equally traditionalist position was held by Luis Fernández-Galiano[105] who cited Loos, for whom if art is revolutionary, architecture is conservative. Too many designers, Fernández-Galiano claimed, were theorising an ephemeral architecture, preferring the concept of

99 *Harvard Design Magazine* (Fall 1997), monographic issue on 'Durability and Ephemerality'.
100 The theme of tectonics (the way in which buildings demonstrate, through their form, how they are actually constructed) was being examined at the time by Kenneth Frampton in his book *Studies in Tectonic Culture: The Poetics of Construction in Nineteenth and Twentieth Century Architecture*, The MIT Press (Cambridge, MA), 1996.

101 Kenneth Frampton: 'Intimations of Durability', in *Harvard Design Magazine* (Fall 1997), pp 22−8.
102 The Villa Mairea by Alvar Aalto (1898−1976) is located in Noormarkku, Finland. It was built between 1938 and 1939.

103 Dimitris Pikionis (1887−1968) is the Greek architect responsible for the landscaping of the ruins of the Acropolis in Athens.
104 The term neo-rationalist refers to those architects who also operate under the umbrella term La Tendenza. Their point of reference was Aldo Rossi.
105 Luis Fernández-Galiano, 'It's the Economy, Stupid', in *Harvard Design Magazine* (Fall 1997), pp 44−6.

**106** The Roman architect and theorist Vitruvius – in his ten-volume treatise *De architectura*, written in the 1st century BC and highly influential during the Renaissance – defined the qualities of architecture as *'firmitas, utilitas, venustas'* – durability, functionality and beauty.
**107** Gavin Stamp, 'The Durability of Reputation', in *Harvard Design Magazine* (Fall 1997), pp 54–7.

**108** James Stirling (1926–92) was one of the most influential architects during the second half of the 20th century. After an initial phase in which he revisited the forms of the Modern Movement, he was one of the leading exponents of Post-Modernism. His most important work is considered to be the Neue Staatsgalerie in Stuttgart, Germany (1977–84), which features an enchanting *promenade architecturale*.

**109** Ellen Dunham-Jones, 'Temporary Contracts', in *Harvard Design Magazine* (Fall 1997), pp 4–11.
**110** Botond Bognar, 'What Goes Up, Must Come Down', in *Harvard Design Magazine* (Fall 1997), pp 33–43.

*venustas* to that of *firmitas*.[106] They transform buildings into icons, admired and revered, in the hope that society will care for them in the long term, independently of any maintenance and management costs, using the example of the Aronoff Center by Eisenman.

For Gavin Stamp,[107] many buildings by Stirling,[108] Foster and Rogers revealed themselves to be failures. However, thanks to the architects' superstar status, the press kept silent about the defects, preferring instead to cover them with exaggerated praise.

A different opinion was held by Ellen Dunham-Jones[109] and Botond Bognar[110]. For the former the problem of durability, beyond any architectural consideration, was now directly connected with production and thus it made little sense to design imperishable buildings. The latter was in full agreement, making reference to the Japanese situation: the Nomad Restaurant designed by Toyo Ito in 1986 was demolished in 1989; the U House, also by Ito, was demolished in 1986; a house in Yokohama designed by Kazuo Shinohara in 1984 was substituted in 1994; the Tokyo City Hall by Kenzo Tange, completed in 1952, was demolished in 1992. Not to mention the Imperial Hotel by Wright that was demolished in 1960 to make way for a local branch of an international chain of hotels. Rather than mourning the loss of monumentality and durability, it would be well to assume, as part of one's poetic, the sign of precariousness, above all if this allows the building to fluctuate through the use of new, sensitive and transparent materials, within an ever more immaterial and dynamic metropolitan reality. Kazuyo Sejima, Kazuo Shinohara, Itsuko Hasegawa, Hiroshi Hara,

**Sauerbruch Hutton, GSW Headquarters, Berlin, Germany, 1995–9: exterior view.**

This project, now a landmark in the city of Berlin, features an ingenious use of different colours and an uninhibited play of different architectural forms.

111 Kazuyo Sejima (born 1956), Kazuo Shinohara (born 1925), Itsuko Hasegawa (born 1941), Hiroshi Hara (born 1936), Riken Yamamoto (born 1945) and Toyo Ito (born 1941).
112 *Domus*, no 795 (July/August 1997), pp 2–3.
113 François Burkardt, 'Editoriale', in *Domus*, no 795 (July/August 1997).
114 Pierre Restany, 'An Illusion: The Humanist Myth of Duration', *Domus*, no 795 (July/August 1997), pp 104–8.

117 Marina Abramovic (born 1946) is a Body Art artist who investigates, through performance, the relationship between the body, space and symbolic systems.
118 Yves Klein (1928–62): known for his monochrome paintings, he

also worked with performances in which bodies were used as paint brushes to create abstract canvases. In a 1960 performance an elegantly dressed public watched as he created a painting using nude, paint-covered models while an orchestra played his *Monotone Symphony*, composed in 1949, using a single, continuous note. His interests also included the theme of the void and lightness, rendered concrete in a famous image in which he seems to take flight as he jumps off a wall.

Riken Yamamoto and, above all, Toyo Ito, demonstrate that it is possible to build masterpieces without being reactionary or conservative, even in the best possible Loosian understanding of the term.[111]

The same theme was also confronted by *Domus*[112] in a monographic issue entitled 'Durability', published the same year. There are articles in favour, for example that of Gregotti. However, the conclusions, in the end, agree with the thesis put forth by Botond Bognar: 'history,' affirms the director of the magazine, François Burkardt,[113] 'is an unstoppable process and there is no way to turn it back around'; durability is not, in and of itself, a value. For Pierre Restany[114] it was the society founded on the eternal that was obsessed with the values of permanence and materiality; today, instead, we share the understanding, matured from the 1960s onwards, that what is real is not eternal. We can look, for example, at Allan Kaprow,[115] who reduced artistic practice to the spontaneous and volatile action of happenings and performances. Or Christo and Jeanne-Claude,[116] whose works were destined to last for a mere 15 days. We could also mention artists from the world of Body Art and, in particular, the extraordinary investigator of relationships between the body and space Marina Abramovic;[117] or Yves Klein[118] and his living brushes, the blue revolution and the imaginary flights that intensely rendered man's need for lightness and immateriality; or Arte Povera, with its use of simple, perishable and consumable materials. Finally we can look at the landscapes that were made to resonate by the genius of Robert Smithson, or anthropicised and conceptualised by Richard Long[119] and the artists of Land Art. The danger for contemporary culture is not the freshness of the image, its here and now, but rather its freezing, mummifying it in a form that remains immutable over time. The obstinate hope for perennial monuments in the end testifies to a headstrong obtuseness that we have dragged behind us since the time of the Egyptians, and which consists of wanting, at all costs, to exorcise death and refuse the deeper meaning of life, which is precisely that of mutability.

115 Allan Kaprow (1927–2006) was an American artist who was one of the first to introduce the technique of happenings and public performances within the art world.

116 Christo (born 1935) and Jeanne-Claude (born 1935) are two artists known for their performance pieces, some of which consisted of wrapping famous monuments, such as the Pont Neuf bridge in Paris (1985) or the Reichstag in Berlin (1995).

119 Richard Long (born 1945) is one of the exponents of Land Art, an artistic movement that sought to abolish the distance between the artwork and the landscape, transforming large portions of the latter into works of art.

## 2.15 The MoMA Extension

In 1997, some of the world's leading architects confronted one another in a highly symbolic competition: the addition to the Museum of Modern Art MoMa[120] in New York, resulting from the acquisition of new spaces required to give breathing room to another structure that was at the point of collapse due to its popularity. Ten internationally famous architects between the ages of 40 and 50 were invited: four Europeans – Rem Koolhaas, Wiel Arets, Dominique Perrault and Herzog & de Meuron; four Americans – Bernard Tschumi, Steven Holl, Tod Williams and Billie Tsien and Rafael Viñoly; and two Japanese – Yoshio Taniguchi and Toyo Ito.

In June of the same year three finalists were selected, one from each continent: Tschumi (American by adoption), Herzog & de Meuron (Switzerland) and Yoshio Taniguchi[121] (Japan).

The winning project was announced in December. Unexpectedly it was Taniguchi's. While a very elegant project, it was conceptually inferior to expectations, and admittedly a balance between nostalgia for the traditions of Modernism and cautious explorations of the new.

The other projects were much more interesting. Koolhaas' entry was presented, as per the Dutch habit, in theoretical terms. What is the form of a museum for mass society? In what way should we move through its interior spaces? What role is played by storage spaces and vaults with respect to the display spaces? What is the proper lighting for a museum? The answers provided by Koolhaas are offered in two keys: individuality and

120 The competition entries can be found in: Barbara Ross, ed., *Imagining the Future of The Museum of Modern Art*, Museum of Modern Art (New York), 1998.

121 Yoshio Taniguchi (born 1937), after studying in Tokyo, graduated from the Harvard University Graduate School of Design in 1964. From 1964 to 1972 he worked for Kenzo Tange. Much of his fame is owed to the completion of museums in Japan, such as the Toyota Municipal Museum of Art in Toyota City (1991–5).

Koolhaas' project takes advantage of the building volume to create an interior enriched by a dynamic succession of spaces, where elevators move both horizontally and along inclined paths.

kinetic effects. *Individuality* in the sense that the museum – unlike other spaces so intensely used by the public, such as shopping malls or amusement parks – is a space that must create a private relationship with the works of art in individual spaces, almost micro-cells, one for each visitor. *Kinetic effects* in the sense that the landscape of the museum, totally artificial, must make use of mechanical devices, lights and other equipment to guarantee the high-speed mobility of users and the works on display. The result was a new Otis elevator that allowed flows of visitors to move, not only vertically, but also horizontally, along sloping surfaces. The project also explored the virtual, in all its simulatory possibilities, in order to expand the experience of the visitor and transform the museum into a film set, with continually changing stage sets for the paying public.

A similar approach was taken by Bernard Tschumi. The keyword of his research is the term 'interconnection' that – as he suggests in the project description – is to be understood in both spatial and conceptual terms: for example, through a sequence of closed and open spaces along paths that alternate environments for art and encounter; through a spectacular hanging garden, above, visible from the street, that represents an element of attraction; and finally, by creating interconnections between the permanent and the temporary, the collections of painting and sculpture, between the latter and other departments, between the public space and the spaces of education, between the galleries and the theatre.

For Toyo Ito the museum is also a metaphor of the city, in particular, a metropolis like New York, supported by a hierarchical logic: the succession of skyscrapers, the floors of buildings piled atop one another to infinity, rooms that repeat along the same plane. The new museum could be a *lying-down skyscraper*, a skyscraper with no centre, that develops horizontally, composed of spaces that follow one another in order to ensure the maximum freedom of use, exactly like a bar code, composed of lines of different thicknesses that follow

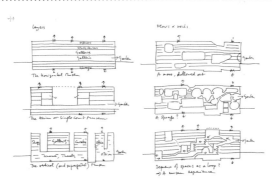

Bernard Tschumi, MoMA
Extension, New York, USA,
1997: competition drawings.

Tschumi focused on the interconnection based on the discovery of a method that allowed him to build a museum filled with both traditional and new and unexpected relations.

Toyo Ito, MoMA Extension, New
York, USA, 1997: competition
photomontage.

Toyo Ito proposed a lying-down
skyscraper based on the logic of
a barcode: the random succession
of spaces of varying dimensions.

no predetermined geometrical design.

Finally, for Herzog & de Meuron, a museum is not
Disneyland, or a shopping mall, or a media centre. It is a
sequence of open and closed spaces, offering different
levels of transparency. There are few special effects, no
futurist space, but simply a collection of rooms based on
a consideration of the artists to be displayed and their
sensibilities, not to be mortified by the preponderant
ego of the architect. The position of the two Swiss
architects is clear. They take note of the discontent for
the egocentric approach of the architect, always ready
to sacrifice the needs of the user in order to conserve
disciplinary values that are often incomprehensible.
However, paradoxically, this justifies the choice made
by the MoMA curators who, having to choose between
Tschumi, Herzog & de Meuron and Taniguchi, in the end
opted for the latter, who guaranteed a professionally
unquestionable project, inaugurated on schedule,
in 2004, in a city that was blanketed with posters
declaring: New York is Modern Again.

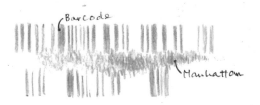

## 2.16 The Beginnings of a New Season

The controversy between blobs and
the almost nothing, in short between
the Baroque and the Minimalist that
characterised the period between 1993 and
1997, allowed for a completion of the work
begun by Deconstructivism. This process

**Yoshio Taniguchi, MoMA
Extension, New York, USA,
1997: exterior view.**

The winning project, designed by
Taniguchi, returns to the Modernist tradition, which coexists here
with the elegance of Minimalism
and hints of the Orient. It also
expresses a wilful indifference to
the important conceptual questions that the construction of a
museum such as the MoMA should
have investigated.

consisted of erasing those architectural trends, for example neo-historicism and Post-Modernism, that focused on what was referred to as autonomy: the design of buildings based on the correct rules of composition, passed down and evolved throughout the lengthy history of the discipline.

In fact, notwithstanding their significant differences, both Blobitecture and Minimalism tended to negate the architectural object – the former in order to transform it into a fragment of nature, the latter to dissolve it entirely.

The freedom from any regulation – which led to forms that ranged from neo-Baroque curves to the transparency of glass boxes – allowed for experiments, in perfect and never-before-seen liberty, with unusual materials, envelope/skins of all types, and unexpected relationships. It also allowed for the introduction within architectural debate of a different notion of the landscape, where architecture and nature play equal roles, to the point where they become confused with one another.

What is more, thanks to new technologies, even the most complex spatial organisations could now be realised. This made it possible to complete projects that would have previously been considered avant-garde utopias, destined to remain on paper. Freed of the esoteric and abstract rules of composition, and closer to the sensibilities of a vaster public, these buildings met with significant success. This success in turn led to the emergence of a new generation of architects, and the beginnings of a new season for contemporary architecture.

# 3 A SEASON OF MASTERPIECES: 1998–2001

## 3.1 The Guggenheim in Bilbao by Frank O Gehry

The inauguration of the Guggenheim Museum in Bilbao, Spain, on 18 October 1997 was the first in a series of events that signalled the beginning of a period which, from 1998 onwards, would be witness to the completion of numerous works of extraordinary architectural interest. Designed by Frank O Gehry, the building forced a reconsideration of the very idea of the museum; something that neither the bland renovation of the Centre Pompidou nor the sanitised addition to the MoMA had been able to do. The success of Gehry's building exceeded all expectations: in terms of the flow of visitors, during the first year ticket sales tripled the forecast figure of 500,000; and in terms of publicity, for the media the building in Bilbao was the building of the century, a cathedral to art capable of competing with the Guggenheim in New York designed by Frank Lloyd Wright.

The success of the Bilbao Guggenheim was further assisted by the voices of dissent, transforming the work into a building-symbol, emblematic of the mutations taking place in the way of designing, financing, building and advertising architecture. One of its most authoritative critics was Peter Eisenman. While he did not attack the building directly, he saw it as an example of the excessive spectacularisation of the practice of architecture.[1] For Rafael Moneo, Gehry's work was the ultimate example of an aesthetic of individualism and fragmentation,[2] while the Basque anthropologist Joseba Zulaika, in his *Crónica*

1 Peter Eisenman in 'Lo spettro dello spettacolo', *Casabella*, no 673/674 (December 1999/January 2000) began his article (p 85) by commenting on a statement made by the sculptor Richard Serra, for whom 'Gehry's Bilbao is more spectacle than structure'.

2 This emerges, for example, in the conversation between Rafael Moneo and William JR Curtis published in *El Croquis*, no 98 (2000), in particular pp 21–2.

**Frank O Gehry, Guggenheim Museum, Bilbao, Spain, 1991–7: aerial view.**

The project used three different types of cladding: marble, titanium and blue plaster. The marble is used for the more traditional exhibition spaces; the titanium is used to cover those with less than conventional forms, while the plaster is used for the offices. The entrance is located between the wings, which open towards the city in an embrace.

*de una seducción,*[3] spoke of the building as the epitome of cultural imperialism, the indication of a society of images and spectacle, of deception hiding in the shadows of consumerism.

In fact, the entire operation behind the creation of the new museum was an extraordinary one. Primarily for the choice made by the director of the Solomon R Guggenheim Foundation, Thomas Krens, to propose a *franchise* of the museum, the same technique used by McDonald's or Pizza Hut to grant licences for fast-food chains around the globe. Secondly for the fact that the City Government was able to sidestep – in a location such as Bilbao, afflicted by serious financial and productive-economic issues – traditional policies related to the creation of employment in industry, and to choose to build, instead, a museum that would act as a catalyst for immaterial goods – in this case publicity and culture.

There is also the miracle of having given form to a one-of-a-kind sculpture, composed of thousands of components, each different from the next. Rumour has it that the building was designed by Gehry's office using computerised scanners to transfer information from study models directly into working drawings, and from the latter to machinery that automatically produced the pieces of the building (in reality the process made use of much more traditional techniques).[4] 'To build the unbuildable' was the term used by Catherine Slessor in *The Architectural Review,*[5] while Joseph Giovannini wrote in *Architecture* that 'the computer that has made clouds, waves, and mountains scientifically intelligible, and chaos science possible, is the same instrument that made Gehry's tumult practicable. The building exemplifies the shift from mechanics to the electronics of our post-industrial age.'[6]

....................................................................................................

3 Joseba Zulaika, *Crónica de una seducción: Museo Guggenheim Bilbao,* Editorial Nerea (Madrid), 1997.

4 Gehry's office uses an adapted version of CATIA (Computer-Aided Three-dimensional Interactive Application), a program used in the aeronautical design industry. The program, in addition to handling geometrically complex forms, also allows for the direct transfer of information to manufacturing equipment. This makes it possible – something viewed with great enthusiasm by many young architectural offices – to create one-of-a-kind products using an

industrialised process. This is similar to the passage from the rigidity of the typewriter (standard industrial procedures) to the inkjet printer (new digital technologies).

5 Catherine Slessor, 'Atlantic Star', *The Architectural Review,* no 1210 (December 1977), pp 30–42.

6 Joseph Giovannini, 'Gehry's Reign in Spain', *Architecture* (December 1997), p 66.

The Guggenheim has both all the fascination and all the volatility of a high-powered image. When asked to describe it, we cannot help but make recourse to a metaphor – perhaps an arbitrary or imperfect one, but in any case one that transcends the materiality of the architectural object: it is a fish, a flower, a phantom ship, a cauliflower, a cloud, a body in movement. It could not be otherwise in a world of architecture that seemed to have suspended the rules of composition, where the exterior no longer reflected the interior – where there is no longer an immediately recognisable correspondence between form and function, or any reference to tectonics, to structural coherence, to the very logic of building.

However, the ease with which the building accepts these images is what guaranteed its success. In reality it is the building, and not the works on display, that attracts the public, making it possible for the Guggenheim Foundation to renounce, without deluding the paying public, the presentation of Pablo Picasso's *Guernica*, as originally promised.

Bilbao thus became a symbol of an architectural renaissance. The sign that an architectural language – fragmented, complex, non-linear, and with a strong sensual impact – could finally renew a relationship between the public and the work of art. For others, as mentioned, it was proof of a definitive defeat: the collapse of formal values into the meat grinder of the Star System. However, as the building was turned into an emblematic work, used to prove the aforementioned theories, the real Guggenheim slowly disappeared from all discussion, only to be replaced by clichés.

**Frank O Gehry, Guggenheim Museum, Bilbao, Spain, 1991–7: aerial view.**

The exhibition spaces, each different from the next, wrap around the spiral created by the central atrium.

Let us take a look at a few:

One: the Guggenheim is a monument to excess. In fact, the 120-million-dollar cost of the museum remained in line with the original budget, franchising licence included. The cost per square metre was less than that of other museums, and many times lower than that of the Getty Museum built by Richard Meier in Los Angeles.

Two: Bilbao is the first building of the 21st century, a masterpiece of the electronic age. This is false: the potentials of the computer are to be found elsewhere and buildings with complex forms were already being completed before the arrival of the computer age. If we wish to speak of the electronic paradigm, it is only to speak of a new, anti-serial attitude managed by the use of the computer.

**Frank O Gehry, Guggenheim
Museum, Bilbao, Spain, 1991–7:
view from the river.**

The building passes beneath the
existing Puente de La Salve, integrating it within the design. The
tower at the end of the building marks the presence of the
museum.

Three: for Gehry the sign is more important than reason and the arbitrary takes precedence over the logical. These are inconsistent theses. Bilbao is the result of a specific rationale – which can seldom be reduced to a simplified formula – where each decision was evaluated in relation to external context, to the formal structure of the building, to the choice of materials, to the control of dimensions.

At least four elements of the project are influenced by its context.

The first is the Puente de La Salve, an intrusive and graceless highway infrastructure that crosses the site. Gehry embraced it, building around it and transforming it into a structuring axis of the composition: the bridge acquires the fascination of a colourful and dynamic pop insertion, while the museum, otherwise located along only one bank of the river, appears to occupy both sides, taking on a territorial scale. The second element is the Nervión River. Gehry extends the building, such that it

appears to by lying down along the watercourse. The river facade contains most of the free forms covered with titanium scales: while allusions to the metaphor of the fish or the boat are possible, the primary reason for this decision was to take advantage of the reflections of the metal surfaces on the water. The work appears to grow out of the geography of the site, exalting its luminous qualities. The third landscape invention made by Gehry is the tower, a 60-metre-high object with no real function that wraps the Puente de La Salve, creating a landmark that can be seen from the public square in front of the City Hall: it is both a focal point and an urban landmark.

The fourth contextual move has to do with the integration of the consolidated city, made possible by the two wings that open to embrace the city, defining an urban space.

If we look at the building's interior spaces we note that circulation passes through 19 display halls, which

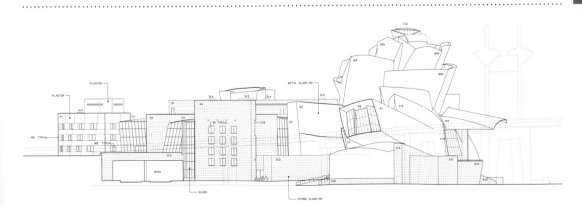

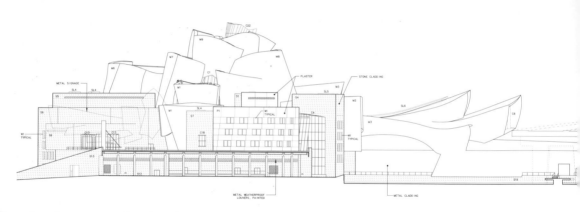

radiate from a central atrium that, at 50 metres in height (the atrium at the Guggenheim in New York is 35 metres high) becomes the fulcrum of the composition. To further exalt this space Gehry places the entrance to the museum one storey below, with the anti-rhetorical effect that, in order to access the museum, visitors must move down and not up, creating a spiral whose ascending motif is enriched by the intersection, cutting and overlapping of volumes: this is what generates the recurring metaphor of the flower, or the artichoke. For Gehry the error to be avoided was that made in Pei's expansion of the Louvre, where the entry hall is more akin to the lobby of a luxury hotel. More suitable references for Gehry's work would be the spatiality of Fritz Lang's *Metropolis*,[7] the *Merzbau* of Kurt Schwitters[8] or Wright's spiral-shaped Guggenheim in New York, all of which allude to a level of urban complexity – the same objective, though with very different results, that inspired Bernard Tschumi, Rem Koolhaas and Toyo Ito in the competition for the addition to the MoMA. Here it is also used to justify the pluralism of spatial solu-

tions and the diversity of functional choices, such as, for example, the three different typologies of display spaces of the 19 galleries radiating from the atrium: classical spaces with a traditional form for the permanent collection; non-conventional spaces for ad hoc artistic commissions; and a gigantic loft for temporary exhibitions.

Another important aspect of the project can be found in the materials of which it is made. Practical choices justified the use of the small titanium scales for the cladding of the complex forms. Stone is generally used for regular surfaces, with glazing mediating the joints between the two, otherwise impossible to resolve. The result is that each construction detail, even in such a complex structure, is easy to realise. This ensures a perfect level of finishing that enhances the formal decisions made. We can mention here, as an example, the disappointing finishing of the Groninger Museum in the portion designed by Coop Himmelb(l)au, which runs the risk of losing the dialectic of spaces imagined

........................................

7 Fritz Lang (1890–1976) was a film director and set designer. His masterpiece, *Metropolis* (1927), with its sets inspired by the Expressionist school, had a notable effect on the way of looking at and imagining Modern architecture.

8 Kurt Schwitters (1887–1948) was a German artist and painter and one of the masters of the Dadaist movement. His best-known work is the *Merzbau*, a sculpture-environment that grew over time through the insertion of new pieces, many of which were remnants of everyday life.

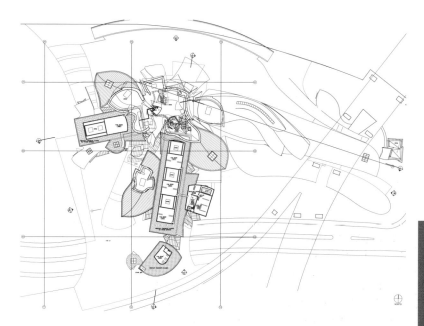

by the Austrian group in a confused, misshapen collection of forms.

In Bilbao, the titanium finish shines, above all along the river, while the stone, used in those areas that face the city, guarantees continuity with the urban structure. The blue-coloured volume differentiates the administrative functions and is entrusted with the role of enriching and enlivening the public space in front of the museum. The building contains a new synthesis in the work of Gehry, whose previous projects oscillated between simple, static forms, distinct from one another in terms of materials, colours and patterns, and complex and dynamic forms clad with a single material.

Lastly, there is the element of scale. Gehry, following the lessons of Frank Lloyd Wright, compresses and then explodes the spaces of the building; and, to create a perception of the large scale, he articulates them. This is why so many of the spaces that surround the atrium, including the entrance area, are small. This also explains the placement of the large sculpture by Richard Serra, which interrupts the otherwise excessively longitudinal development of the space dedicated to temporary exhibitions.

**Frank O Gehry, Guggenheim Museum, Bilbao, Spain, 1991–7: fourth-floor plan.**

Despite the complexity of its forms, the composition of the building is based on a very simple principle: a central volume, the 50-storey atrium, wrapped by 19 different spaces for the display of art.

## 3.2 The House in Floriac by Rem Koolhaas

A second work of extraordinary interest from the late 1990s is the house in Floriac, near Bordeaux, France (1994–8) designed by Rem Koolhaas. The house belongs to the set of projects in which the Dutch architect confronts the work of Mies van der Rohe.[9] The debt to Mies is clearly revealed in the external appearance of the building – the long perimeter wall that supports the house and the loggia overlooking the landscape are crowned and surmounted by a cumbersome masonry mass, reminiscent of the Riehl House designed in 1907 by the young Mies near Potsdam, Germany. However, the debt is both more stringent and less restrictive than the eclectic Dutch architect wishes to let on.

The Floriac house was designed for an enlightened couple of art collectors who also required spaces suitable for the reduced mobility of one of the two, confined to a wheelchair.

Faithful to his modus operandi, which includes a theoretical approach to any design issue, Koolhaas created a project-manifesto – perhaps his best synthesis of the theme of the dwelling.

The Floriac house oscillates between the polarity of the *private* and the *un-private*,[10] respectively representing the enclosed and restricted space of the interior, and the transparent and free space of the exterior. If we look at the courtyard, or the upper floor that contains the bedrooms, bordered by a massive masonry wall perforated by small 'portholes', the house appears to close in on itself. If, on the other hand, we shift our attention

---

9 Koolhaas has designed numerous homages to Mies during his career, including the reconstruction, for the 1985 Milan Triennale, of the Barcelona Pavilion (1929), in this case ironically curved to respond to the geometry of the space assigned to him, and in order to accentuate its spatial fluidity.

10 In fact, the house was presented at the MoMA exhibition 'The Un-Private House' in July 1999. See paragraph 3.5.

to the living room, a glass box that looks out over the landscape, we can observe two distinct references. The first is the model of the glasshouse and, in particular, the Farnsworth House, once again by Mies. The second is the work of the radical architects of Superstudio and Archizoom Associati who, during the late 1960s and early '70s, pursued the creation of isotropic and open spaces in which the body, free of any constrictions – unrestricted by walls, divisions or impediments of any sort – could move freely through space.

Mies, Archizoom and Superstudio: the only way to coherently combine such different influences and poetics is to generate forms in which the dialectic of opposites is dominant, for instance between the open and the closed, the compressed and the exploded, the transparent and the opaque. This approach is easy to find in all of Koolhaas' previous projects: in the Villa Dall'Ava in Paris (1985–91), where the glazed walls of the living room contrast with the compressed volumes of the bedrooms above; in the apartments in Fukuoka, Japan (1988–91), where a dark, rusticated wall protects the privacy of the patio houses that, thanks to the projecting and undulating roofs, appear to float freely as transparent volumes; in the housing projects in Rotterdam, The Netherlands (1984–8) and

**Rem Koolhaas/OMA, House in Floriac, France, 1994–8: exterior view.**

The house is composed of three overlapping pieces: a patio house, a glasshouse and a substantially closed and introverted box. The first contains the kitchen and service areas, the second the living spaces and the third the bedrooms.

**Rem Koolhaas/OMA, House in Floriac, France, 1994–8: interior view.**

A moving platform allows the owner, confined to a wheelchair, to access the various floors of the house. The size of the platform makes it more than an elevator: it is a moving room that becomes part of the various levels in the house.

nearby Amsterdam (1992–3), where the private spaces are gathered around introverted patios, one of which is even protected by a sort of drawbridge, while the public spaces open entirely towards the exterior.

In Floriac, the three levels of the house differ greatly from one another. In fact they are almost irreconcilable: the lower floor, with its underground spaces carved into the hill, is reminiscent of the spaces of a cave; the middle level, half covered and half open, affirms, as we have seen, the principle of the priority of the void and transparency over the solid and the opaque; finally, the upper level is a world of fragmented spaces, separated from one another by dividing walls that are, in turn, based on two opposing strategies – implosion in the central nucleus of the parent's apartment and a spiralling explosion in the children's apartment.

The play of opposites – in this case between stability and precariousness – can also be found in the structure. The house is striking for its technical virtuosity: the significant cantilever and the imposing volume of the third floor suggest the use of a large, reinforced concrete beam. These strong signs are juxtaposed against some unsettling details: the floors are slightly offset with respect to one another, resulting in the sensation of a disarticulated whole that appears almost to be disconnected; the use of different types of columns (double T, round, rectangular), one of which lands in the middle of the garden; a tension rod that pulls the building towards the earth, as if it wishes to take flight.

In order to further the use of differences and opposites, Koolhaas uses aluminium, resins and exposed concrete

11 Elevators have always fascinated
Koolhaas: he speaks about them in
*Delirious New York,* when he compares
the typology of the skyscraper with
the possibilities offered by mechanical lifting devices. The importance of
these devices is also underlined in the
more recent *S,M,L,XL.*

for ceilings and floors, while the walls are clad using materials with different colours and patterns.

There is also the difference between the stair that leads to the children's apartment and the elevating platform that connects the lower two floors with the parents' apartment. The circular stair is obviously impossible for someone in a wheelchair to use, almost an attempt to underline the autonomy of the couple's children. The square elevating platform, on the other hand, ensures access to all parts of the house: clearly oversized and little more than a simple element of vertical connection, it is also a room that allows the owner of the house to occupy a moving office that can be stopped, as necessary, near the kitchen, the living room or the sleeping area.[11] However, in this case, the elevator is more than a piece of technology. It is a machine that guarantees the co-penetration of continually changing points of view. It is an element of spatial liberty and, simultaneously, a multiplier of perception whose movement constantly changes the architecture of the house.

Koolhaas' choice to place a mechanism of movement at the centre of an otherwise static space has numerous precedents, including the structures designed by Archigram, whom he met at the Architectural Association in London. It is also no secret that Koolhaas was widely influenced by the first project for the Centre Pompidou designed by Gianfranco Franchini, Renzo Piano and Richard Rogers, which called for an entirely flexible structure and moving floors.

The debt to Archigram does not end with the invention of the room-elevator. We can also find it in the design of specific technical apparatus, which enriches the liveability of the house.

Nothing, suggests Koolhaas, can be taken for granted. Every desire can become the pretext for a formal invention. This is the case with the electrical rails used to hang paintings that can be slid out onto the terrace and contemplated *en plein air,* or the motorised glass door on the north facade that is over 8 metres long

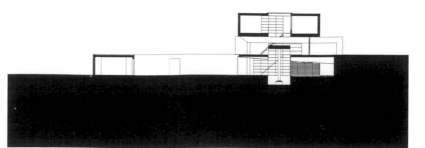

**Rem Koolhaas/OMA, House in Floriac, France, 1994–8: section.**

The section shows the location of the moving platform and its connections with the different levels in the house.

12 The Tugendhat House was built in Brno, in what is now the Czech Republic, between 1929 and 1930 by Mies van der Rohe.

13 Constant Nieuwenhuis (1920–2005) was a painter and one of the main exponents of the Situationist movement (1958) and unitary urban planning. He criticised functional urban planning and proposed a city, in this case New Babylon, focused on creativity and the ludic dimension.

14 The church of Notre Dame du Haut in Ronchamp, France (1950–5) is one of Le Corbusier's masterpieces from his Brutalist phase.

and which travels more than 11 metres.

In the Floriac house, as in all of Koolhaas' work, there is also an understanding that one form, as consolidated as it may be, can be replaced by another, and even more unusual one, if it represents the correct solution to a problem. The use of portholes instead of traditional windows does not affect the compactness of the wall and, at the same time, due to their being placed in strategic positions, they guarantee perspectival and visual perforations. Instead of the typical structural system of beams and columns, there is a preference for a more complex system of counterweights that, by channelling forces to the central part of the structure and the exterior of the built volume, drastically reduce the number of columns required inside the living room.

It is not difficult, in this play of formal inventions, to trace a repertory of references. The round, rectangular and T sections refer to the columns used by the protagonists of the Modern Movement; the electric track is an evident homage to the Maison de Verre by Pierre Chareau; the motorised glass wall is reminiscent of the Tugendhat House[12] by Mies van der Rohe; the 'Swiss cheese' wall, with its sequence of portholes, in some cases angled, can be traced back to New Babylon by Constant Nieuwenhuis,[13] alluding to the Modernist myth of transatlantic ships and, simultaneously, to the Post-Rationalist and Brutalist openings in Ronchamp,[14] in this case organised according to the logic of the strip window.

Intensely programmatic, the Floriac house makes no concessions to the sentiments and myths of domesticity. Aesthetics, Koolhaas suggests, have little to do with psychology in its intimate definition. It is the relationships between space and the body and the interrelations between interior and exterior that ensure the functioning of the object. 'This house,' the client stated, 'has been my liberation.'[15]

15 Beatriz Colomina with Blanca Lleó, 'A Machine Was Its Heart', Domus, no 811 (January 1999), p 60.

**Daniel Libeskind, Jewish Museum in Berlin, Germany, 1988–99: detail of the voids.**

The museum is filled with a series of void spaces, designed to remain empty. Their symbolic value is evident.

## 3.3 The Jewish Museum in Berlin by Daniel Libeskind

On 24 January 1999, little more than a year after the opening of the Guggenheim, the Jewish Museum by Daniel Libeskind was inaugurated in Berlin. The impressions generated by the work were in no way inferior to those of Gehry's museum. Crowds of visitors flocked to the building, once again more important than the exhibits on display (what is more, there was not enough time to properly set them up before the inauguration). A palpable sense of euphoria permeated the global architectural community. After the terrible 1970s and 1980s, they were now witnessing a particularly golden period for architecture, marked by the projects of what would become a new cultural and sociological phenomenon: the Star System, composed of such figures as Foster, Koolhaas, Hadid, Rogers, Piano, Nouvel, Fuksas, Calatrava and Herzog & de Meuron.

The history of the Jewish Museum project dates back to 1988. The 10 years that passed between the preparation of the project and its completion only slightly tempered the novelty of the proposal, certainly antagonistic with respect to contemporary cultural choices being made in Berlin.[16] Designed in the same year that Libeskind was invited to participate in the 'Deconstructivist Architecture' show, the museum is a product of this climate: disarticulated geometries, fragmented spaces, strident detailing and industrially produced materials. It is a Deconstructivist approach that alludes to the title 'Between the Lines', a reference to the motif of

16 We must remember that between 1988 and 1989 the IBA – Internationale Bauausstellung (International Building Exhibition) of Berlin – was still operative, pursuing a philosophy of conserving the historical urban fabric and traditional typologies. The IBA's huge programme of urban renewal of the city of Berlin began in 1979 and aimed to regain 'the inner city as a place to live in'. It involved some of the most internationally renowned architects of the time. It ended in 1987, but work continued on those buildings that had not yet been finished. The most representative works of this period were entrusted to Ungers, Rossi, Gregotti, Léon Krier (born 1946), Grassi and Stirling.

17 Arnold Schönberg (1874–1951) was
born in Vienna of Jewish descent.
He was a composer, theoretician and
the inventor of dodecaphonic music.
The work *Moses und Aron* was never
completed.

18 The Jewish writer Walter Benjamin
(1892–1940) is considered to be one
of the most acute scholars of his era.
*Einbahnstrasse* was published in 1928.

a snaking line intersected by a straight one. The first corresponds to the zigzag form of the display spaces, while the second is a longitudinal cut that carves into the others, creating inaccessible interior courtyards that symbolically represent the voids left by the Holocaust. The building is flanked by a concrete structure, the Holocaust Tower, another void, and an artificial garden – the Garden of Exile – composed of 49 sloping concrete prisms containing an equal number of trees.

Highly rhetorical, the work is built on a series of axes that translate the themes, symbols, geographies and vicissitudes of the Jewish faith into a spatial language and, in particular, the history of the Berlin community, prior to its extermination at the hands of the Nazis.

First and foremost there is a correspondence between the forms of the project and the home of Jewish intellectuals in Berlin. There is a reference to *Moses und Aron* by Arnold Schönberg[17] and the theme of the impossibility of the spoken word. There are also intersections between the project and the list of deportees recorded in the Gedenkbuch, the book containing the alphabetical lists of names, dates of birth, dates of deportation and places of extermination. Finally, there are correspondences with the Berlin evoked by Walter Benjamin[18] in his book *Einbahnstrasse* [One-Way Street].

All of these intersections, hermetically described in the writings and drawings that accompanied the presenta-

**Daniel Libeskind, Jewish Museum in Berlin, Germany, 1988–99: detail of the facade.**

The metal cladding is lacerated by the cuts created for the windows. For Libeskind their form is related to the addresses of the Jews living in Berlin before the Holocaust.

tion of the project, are at best obscure. However, this is precisely the fascination and secret of the game. We know that Libeskind, like a shaman, has revealed – or perhaps it would be better to say constructed – correspondences. We know that these correspondences between addresses, Schönberg, Benjamin and the Star of David are arbitrary to common sense but, at the same time, necessary for the poetic imagination. It is precisely for this reason that we are fascinated, accepting the de-structuring of the categories of the intellect in order to prefigure a more complex physical and metaphysical universe that we feel, or hope to intuit, as our own.

We are reminded of the reflections of Carl Gustav Jung[19] on synchronicity – man's ability to connect, in a single discourse, diverse phenomena, not tied to one another by any nexus of apparent causality, but in reality simultaneously present in the profound structure of history and our Id. There are also the poetic lessons of the masters chosen by Libeskind: from John Hejduk,

his professor at Cooper Union, and Aldo Rossi, with his ability to order poignant and disarticulated fragments through memory, to Peter Eisenman, the incurable mystic of an Absence – the way in which, based on a certain religious and philosophical tradition, man is allowed to enter into contact with a Higher Being – rediscovered by emptying forms of their traditional meanings. Finally there are the writings of Jeffrey Kipnis on the 'Forms of Irrationality',[20] theorising the overlapping of universes of diverse discourses as escape routes from the banal rhetoric of building.

However, if the Jewish Museum is a masterpiece, this is not only a result of the esoteric correspondences

131    3.3 The Jewish Museum in Berlin by Daniel Libeskind

---

**Daniel Libeskind, Jewish Museum in Berlin, Germany, 1988–99: aerial view.**

The museum is composed of three interconnected elements, crossed by enclosed and open-air paths: the main volume, the Holocaust Tower (to the left) and the Garden of Exile (bottom centre).

19 Carl Gustav Jung (1875–1961), together with Sigmund Freud (1856–1939), is considered to be one of the fathers of modern psychoanalytical theory. His essays on synchronicity confront the theme of connections between events that are related by strictly causal laws, which take place simultaneously (they are, precisely, synchronic).

20 Jeffrey Kipnis, 'Forms of Irrationality', in John Whiteman, Jeffrey Kipnis and Richard Burdett, eds, *Strategies in Architectural Thinking*, The MIT Press (Cambridge, MA), 1992.

**Daniel Libeskind, Jewish Museum in Berlin, Germany, 1988–99: facade detail of the Garden of Exile.**

Filled with concrete piers, each of which is crowned with a tree, the Garden of Exile symbolises the contrast between constriction and freedom. The sloping floor of the garden creates a sense of vertigo as you walk between the piers.

with by Gehry in Bilbao, which hinges on the wrapping, though strident centrality of the atrium. Here space is a metaphor not of the city, but of the importance of a race of people: a symbolical allusion to the pilgrimage of mankind, of his very existential condition – that of being a part of history.

The *'raum'* (room), the space of rest and dwelling in the words of Heidegger,[21] no longer exists. It has given way to the *'mauer'* (the wall) that delimits a path, predetermining a trajectory and prefiguring a condition of nomadism.

between symbols and events; it is a masterpiece primarily for having synthesised the theme of the Holocaust in the unusual image of a building-fortress whose interior contains continuous paths, with no spaces of rest, forcing one to proceed without stopping, almost creating a labyrinth, where only the spaces-corridors of the upper floors actually display anything. This attitude differs greatly from that experimented

In Libeskind's museum these concepts are not accentuated or resolved through allegories. They are translated into a spatial experience that involves the senses – primarily sight, touch and hearing. They are forced, in the passage from light to dark, from hot to cold, from bustling noise to total silence, to confront our existential condition. In this way we experience what appears to be only a mental construction as a bodily experience.

21 Martin Heidegger (1889–1976) was a German philosopher involved with Naziism. His best-known work is *Being and Time* (1927), in which – after Edmund Husserl (1859–1938), of whom he was a disciple – he posed the basis of contemporary phenomenology. His traditionalist approach to architecture was expressed in the highly influential essay: 'Bauen Wohnen Denken' [Building Dwelling Thinking] (1951).

Jean Nouvel, KKL (Culture and Convention Centre), Lucerne, Switzerland, 1989–2000: view from the lake.

This building features a large steel roof that cantilevers out over the lake. The horizontal nature of the composition creates a relationship between the building and its natural surroundings.

# 3.4 The KKL in Lucerne by Jean Nouvel

In 2000, the year after the opening of Libeskind's Jewish Museum, Nouvel completed the Culture and Convention Centre (KKL) in Lucerne, Switzerland, a project that he won in a 1989 competition.

The building is characterised by its projecting roof of over 12,000 square metres, set some 23 metres above the lake which it overlooks. The roof, which cantilevers out over 45 metres on the lake side, has the primary function of underlining the landscape qualities of the building, placed along the horizon line. At the same time it creates a visual unity for the different volumes that contain the functional programme: a 1,840-seat concert hall, an auditorium, a museum and numerous spaces for dining. Built in copper, the underside of the roof is clad in aluminium panels; it is also a screen that reflects the lake, creating a dematerialising effect that vaguely recalls the Fondation Cartier in Paris while simultaneously perfectly defining a large space below, the Europlatz, populated by various open-air activities.

In fact the building, even while presenting itself as a collection of interior spaces, is conceived of as an exterior: an object so strongly rooted to its context that it should actually have been built atop the lake. Faced with a refusal of permission to proceed in this manner by Swiss authorities, Nouvel opted to bring water – and thus its luminous reflections – inside the building in channels designed to define its various functional parts that, based on a design that is as simple as possible, are placed one after the other, following the logic of addition theorised by Koolhaas on more than one occasion.

..............................................................

Jean Nouvel, KKL (Culture and Convention Centre), Lucerne, Switzerland, 1989–2000: view of the covered plaza.

The terraces on top of the building separate the large roof from the rest of the structure, further reinforcing its presence.

**Jean Nouvel, KKL (Culture and Convention Centre), Lucerne, Switzerland, 1989–2000: view of the covered plaza.**

The space beneath the large roof is used as a public plaza, the ideal meeting point between the natural landscape of the lake and the artificial landscape of the volumes containing the building programme: a concert hall and a museum.

What makes the building complex is not the functional programme, so much as the material differences of the spaces, with specific colours and patterns that vary from steel-grey grilles for service areas to blue and flame-red panels in the concert hall. Designed as a fragment of the ecological-metropolitan landscape – its form appears to have been devised to be observed from ad hoc points of view within the urban landscape of Lucerne – the interior of the building opens towards the lake with a large panoramic terrace that overlooks the entire region. A sign that, even in this era of the artificial, it is possible to creatively engage the natural world.

The digital house is to be composed of prefabricated, three-
dimensional modules that can
be increased over time. The
exterior facades feature large
screens.

## 3.5 The Un-Private House

In July 1999 the MoMA in in New York inaugurated the exhibition entitled 'The Un-Private House'.[22] The show presented 26 houses by 26 architects, some of whom were already famous (Rem Koolhaas, Bernard Tschumi, UNStudio, Herzog & de Meuron and Steven Holl), while others were already on their way (including MVRDV, Guthrie + Buresh,[23] Hariri & Hariri,[24] Preston Scott Cohen[25] and Shigeru Ban[26]). The exhibition focused on the theme of the private residence, a choice explained by the show's curator, Terence Riley, in the introductory essay to the catalogue: it is often individual owners who, when building their own home, entrust the work to innovative designers, anticipating and experimenting with changes that will later take place in society.[27]

It is thus easy to foresee that an analysis of 26 houses will reveal trends which, if nothing else, are in the phase of development. Which ones? Primarily the re-evaluation of the traditional idea of the house, understood as a private realm, an island of tranquillity, the antithesis of the chaotic nature of urban space. On the contrary, the projects presented appeared to focus on the creation of an organism that was permeable to the forces of the external world. This mixture, above all visual, is assisted by large glazed surfaces. Up to

22 The show 'The Un-Private House' was held at the Museum of Modern Art in New York from 1 July to 5 October 1999. It was organised by Terence Riley, Chief Curator of the Department of Architecture and Design.

23 Danelle Guthrie and Tom J Buresh established Guthrie + Buresh Architects in 1988 in Los Angeles.
24 Gisue Hariri (born 1956) and Mojgan Hariri (born 1958) opened their office in New York in 1986.
25 Preston Scott Cohen (born 1961) is based in Boston and teaches at Harvard's Graduate School of Design.

26 Shigeru Ban (born 1957) studied at the Southern California Institute of Architecture and later went on to Cooper Union's School of Architecture where he studied with John Hejduk, graduating in 1984. He gained fame during this period for his inventive use of cardboard to create emergency housing and for his elegant Japanese Pavilion at Expo 2000 in Hanover.
27 Terence Riley, 'The Un-Private House', in The Un-Private House, The Museum of Modern Art (New York), 1999, pp 9–38.

Hariri & Hariri, The Digital
House, 1997–8, Project for
the exhibition 'The Un-Private
House', 1999: rendering of the
kitchen.

Inside the digital house, virtual
space coexists with real space.
In this image the owner of the
house receives assistance via the
Internet.

this point, there is nothing really new: we need only mention the glasshouses of Pierre Chareau, Mies van der Rohe and Philip Johnson, or the evanescent apartment buildings by Connell, Ward and Lucas,[28] criticised by their inhabitants in the 1930s for being too transparent.

There was also a complex involvement of media elements that projected external events onto the interior walls of domestic spaces, transforming the building into a transmitter-receiver capable of producing events itself. This is the case in the work of Hariri & Hariri, who introduced virtual presences – whether they be chefs downloaded from the Internet who help prepare a meal, or guests for an evening – while cladding the exteriors of their buildings with liquid crystal display (LCD) panels to project computer-generated images. Or, in the work of Frank Lupo and Daniel Rowen,[29] television screens can be seen from any point in the

house, allowing its inhabitants, who work in the world of finance, constantly to monitor global markets. There is also the unsettling project by Diller + Scofidio where an external video camera captures a landscape that can be projected on virtual windows. Finally, Herzog & de Meuron presented a villa for a media art collector, in which almost all of the walls lost their materiality, becoming projection screens.

Together with the use of creative media, there was also an accentuated process of typological desegregation, with permeable and non-segmented environments. There was thus a reduction in the subdivision of internal spaces into separate rooms for specific functions, or for the clear distinction between private and public zones. In urban terms this represented a total abandonment of the monofunctional approach typical of the ideology of zoning, with the introduction within the dwelling of zones for work and production.

28 Amyas Connell (1901–80), Basil Ward (1902–76) and, from 1933, Colin Lucas (1906–88) were among the protagonists of Modern architecture in Great Britain.

29 Daniel Rowen and Frank Lupo were associates from the late 1980s to the early 1990s. In 1995 Rowen founded Daniel Rowen Architects.

30 George Orwell, the pseudonym
of the Englishman Eric Arthur Blair
(1903–50), was a journalist and the
author of *Nineteen Eighty-Four*, in
which he forecast a future where technology would be used by totalitarian
powers to control individuals.

31 Mack Scogin (born 1934) founded
Parker and Scogin Architects in 1984,
which later became Scogin Elam and
Bray and, finally, Mack Scogin Merrill
Elam Architects.

Four phenomena of social relevance led to the development of the un-private house:

One: a culture that was less worried about the idea
of transparency. While Frank Lloyd Wright – Terence
Riley states – never ceased to remind us of the
importance of privacy, George Orwell[30] warned of
the dangers of Big Brother and Edith Farnsworth
suffered in Mies van der Rohe's glasshouse, today
we inhabit a world where the presentation of one's
private existence is both accepted and in some cases
desired. We need only mention the tranquillity with
which we speak of private facts in public spaces
on the telephone, or the success of transmissions
that publicly present private, even intimate facts,
or the idea of observing and being observed as we
walk down the street, sit in a public square or visit
a shopping mall. Voyeurism and narcissism appear
to be new dimensions of metropolitan man and are
surely one aspect, not necessarily negative, to be
considered in the design of spaces, even residential
ones.

Two: the traditional family – two parents and
at least two children – was now a minority; the
number of singles and atypical families was on the
rise: couples without children, those with only one
child, common-law spouses, homosexual couples.
For these new social nuclei, with their increasingly
informal and often dynamic lifestyles, more projected towards the exterior world, it made little
sense to consider the hierarchical and cubicle-like
subdivision of space. In the words of one of the
26 designers, Mack Scogin:[31] 'There are no rooms,
just situations.' Consequently, the most appropriate typology appeared to be that of the loft, a
single environment separated by moveable partitions. Even in those cases when distribution was
still based on the identification of specific environ-

**Preston Scott Cohen, Torus
House, Old Chatham, New York,
USA, 1999–2002: project.**

The house is a union of a Modernist and, in many ways, Minimalist
space, with the complex forms of
blob architecture.

32 Herbert Muschamp, 'Living Boldly
on the Event Horizon', *The New York
Times*, 19 November 1998, p F7.

ments, they co-penetrated one another, creating a continuum: the watchwords of this new architecture were *blurring*, a term found elsewhere in this text, and *flexibility*.

Three: the introduction, at the vast scale and thanks to new technologies, of work-at-home situations. If the professional whose office was beside/inside their home was once a rarity, personal computers and Internet connections now made it possible to transform any desk into a branch office. This generated an interest in working from home and proposals whose objective, as demonstrated by some of the houses presented in the exhibition, was the improvement of the quality of one's microenvironment and the management, within the dwelling, of complex work-related activities.

Four: a reduced level of attention to the symbolic nature of the house, understood as a refuge that offers protection from the external world. There

was also a certain instability of the rhetoric of the hearth, which led architects to a programmatic brutalism that included a declared insensitivity to the psychological and functional aspects of the new concept of domesticity. For the critic Herbert Muschamp, it was now perhaps necessary to design 'a shelter from shelter',[32] a refuge that protected us from the idea of the house-shelter. This led to a return to a tradition that has its precedents in the sanitised formal ideology of a portion of the Modern Movement but which, as part of its exclusive snobbism, found an undeniable reference in Peter Eisenman's House VI in Cornwall, Connecticut (1972–5), where the sublime nature of the spaces is directly proportional to their scarce usability. This is also the case, for example, with the houses of Shigeru Ban, one of which was presented at the MoMA. Furnishings were almost entirely eliminated, walls disappeared and even the sanitary services were exposed, all in the name of the openness and freedom of contemporary dwelling.

**UNStudio, Möbius House, Het Gooi, The Netherlands, 1993–8: interior view.**

The intersection of volumes, other than responding to the functional programme, also renders the spaces very interesting.

## 3.6 The Möbius House

In formal terms, as affirmed by Riley in the introduction to 'The Un-Private House' catalogue, there is a face-off between two trends: one focuses on blobby forms, the other on boxes. If we wish to divide the group into two teams, on one side we could place Peter Eisenman, UNStudio, Greg Lynn, Stephen Perrella[33] and Foreign Office Architects;[34] the other team would be composed of Rem Koolhaas, Toyo Ito, Waro Kishy,[35] Kazuyo Sejima, Bernard Tschumi and Shigeru Ban.

The former work with plastic surfaces, managing structurally ambiguous forms in which it is difficult to separate the interior from the exterior, above from below, the volumes from the surfaces. Their work privileges interconnections, rather than clear spatial distinctions. For this group architecture is a continuous, wrapping and sensitive skin that will eventually be rendered intelligent using electronic sensors. It may also – and here we can mention the work of Greg Lynn[36] – be industrially produced, varying its form in relationship to the desires of the client, in the same way that it was now possible to purchase a custom-designed pair of Nike shoes in an interactive, online store.

The second trend moves within the box and is not extraneous to neo-Modernist and Minimalist trends, perhaps revisited by experimenting with new building materials.

The first trend can be found in the Möbius House (1993–8) by UNStudio, already mentioned in the previous chapter. It is a dwelling near Amsterdam, designed for a couple of professionals who also use the home for their work. Their requests were very specific: primarily the

33 Stephen Perrella investigates the complex spaces generated by the computer. He was the guest-editor of 'Hypersurface Architecture I', *Architectural Design*, vol 68, no 5–6 (1998) and 'Hypersurface Architecture II', *Architectural Design*, vol 69, no 9–10 (1999).

34 Alejandro Zaera Polo (born 1963) and Farshid Moussavi (born 1965) founded Foreign Office Architects (FOA) in 1995 after working for OMA. Zaera Polo, in addition to teaching in Europe and the United States, is also an active architectural critic. His writings have been published in *El Croquis*, *Quaderns* and *Architectural Design*.

35 Waro Kishi (born 1950) studied at the University of Kyoto. After collaborating with Masayuki Kurokawa (born 1937) in Tokyo, in 1981 he returned to Kyoto to found Waro Kishi, Architect & Associates.
36 Including the Embryological House, which will be discussed in paragraph 3.10.

UNStudio, Möbius House, Het Gooi, The Netherlands, 1993–8: diagram.

The sequence of functions takes place along the single surface of the Möbius strip.

37 This is the same process used in computer programming when, beginning with a scheme expressed as a block diagram, programmers seek to produce an efficient interface with the user, a spatial metaphor that is suitable for organising abstract relationships that would otherwise be difficult to express and manage: for example, the folders of a Mac and Windows environment as well as the windows, desktop and worksheets.

insertion of the house within the natural environment, of exceptional value above all in consideration of its proximity to a forest and a watercourse. Their request was for a home with a traditional nucleus composed of a living room and bedrooms; two separate offices, one for each member of the couple; a self-sufficient and fully independent apartment for guests; and finally, a two-car garage. Lastly, the office was asked to provide sufficient space for the couple's art collection, primarily paintings by the CoBrA group.

The working method adopted by UNStudio's Ben van Berkel and Caroline Bos to meet the client's needs was the same as that used in previous projects, a theory based on considerations of Gilles Deleuze's reflections on Abstract Machines. It consists of an a priori refusal of traditionally consolidated models or typologies. In-

stead, they proceeded by organising a rather complex diagram of the functions and interactions requested, creating an ad hoc form, with a highly metaphorical value, that spatially represented the particular nature of the problem being analysed.[37]

In this case it was the Möbius strip – a folded, figure-of-eight form. This is both an enclosed volume and an open surface, interior and exterior, a delimited object that is also a collection of spaces which almost follow one another in a sequence – immediately making clear, through its image, the desire for an interrelationship between domestic space and the natural environment, the autonomy of the couple and an ordering of the flows of functions that follow one another inside the house, throughout a 24-hour period.

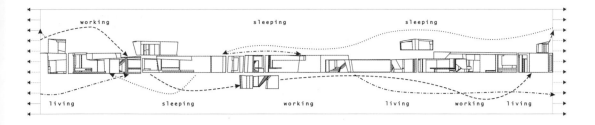

38 Bart Lootsma, 'Möbius One-Family
House, Het Gooi, The Netherlands', in
*Domus*, no 814 (April 1999), pp 40–9.

The Möbius House generated immediate interest. Bart Lootsma, writing for *Domus*,[38] was so impressed by the method used by van Berkel and Bos that he compared it to that of Koolhaas: the diagrammatic approach of the former would allow for the exposure of the particular qualities of each single case, while the typological approach of the latter would inevitably lead to the production of serial objects. *L'architecture d'aujourd'hui* presented the conceptual presuppositions in a lengthy article by Axel Sowa:[39] a sign that the diagrammatic method was looked at with growing interest, even by those outside of The Netherlands.[40]

However, it must be noted that, notwithstanding the novelty of such a complex geometry as the Möbius strip, in reality UNStudio simplified the curvilinear and continuous form into a sharp-edged design that moves away from the logic of hypersurfaces. The final result is closer to the fragmented forms of Deconstructivism. Connie Van Cleef, writing for *The Architectural Review*, picked up on this contradiction and expressed her perplexities: 'Although the interlocking edges of the Möbius strip suggest the formal organisation of the building, the mathematical model is not literally transferred to the architecture. The angular, jutting geometries bear little physical resemblance to the smooth Möbius curves ... Its complex, fragmented form has more in common with an inhabitable sculpture or Expressionist film set and its stark materiality and spatial perversions do not conform to conventional notions of gentle, informal domesticity.'[41]

Joseph Giovannini was of a different opinion. For him the house was a work of architecture of significant poetic intensity: 'Van Berkel & Bos simultaneously creates complexity and difference within a unifying gesture.' He continues: 'The firm is thus taking a philosophical stand at the edge of current theoretical debates: The world is complex, yes, and perhaps even beyond comprehension, but there is an underlying order.'[42]

**UNStudio, Möbius House, Het Gooi, The Netherlands, 1993–8: exterior view.**

The design of the house is the result of the transposition of a functional programme into the diagrammatic form of a Möbius strip, where the intersection of volumes resembles the form ∞.

39 Axel Sowa, 'UN-Studio: les outils de projétation', in *L'architecture d'aujord'hui*, no 321 (March 1999), pp 44–9.
40 Diagrammatic architecture was the object of significant interest, even in Anglo-American situations, primarily at the Architectural Association and Columbia University, due to the presence of Andrew Benjamin, a philosopher interested in architecture who taught at both schools. His published works include *What is Abstraction?*, Academy Editions (London), 1996, and *Architectural Philosophy*, Athlone Press (London), 2000. Of the many texts by other authors that deal with this issue, we mention Anthony Vidler, 'Diagrams of Diagrams: Architectural Abstraction and Modern Representation', *Representations*, no 72 (Autumn 2000), pp 1–20.
41 Connie Van Cleef, 'Radical Domesticity', *The Architectural Review*, no 1231 (September 1999), pp 48–50.
42 Joseph Giovannini, 'Infinite Space', *Architecture* (March 1999), p 102.

**Mecanoo, Delft Polytechnic Library, Delft, The Netherlands, 1993–8: exterior view.**

The sloping green roof is used, during the warmer months, as an outdoor study space.

## 3.7 A Dutchness in the State of Architecture

In 1998 the Architectural Association held a symposium entitled 'Is There a Dutchness in the State of Architecture?'.[43] The title is emblematic of the growing interest for what was by then being called the 'Dutch Phenomenon', a condition stimulated by a particularly favourable economic situation and the political desire to encourage new talent, creativity and youthful energy.[44] It was also a phenomenon that, since its initial presentation in 1996 in *L'architecture d'aujourd'hui*, could now boast a number of high-quality built works in The Netherlands that had a notable influence on international architectural debate, including, to mention a few: the Möbius House by UNStudio, which we have just discussed; the Minnaert Building in Utrecht (1994–7) by Neutelings Riedijk;[45] the Delft Polytechnic Library (1993–8) by Mecanoo;[46] the Police Station in Boxtel (1994–7) by Wiel Arets; the WOZOCO apartments for the elderly in Amsterdam (1994–7); and Villa VPRO in Hilversum (1993–7) by MVRDV.

43 Quoted in: Ton Verstegen, 'Perspectives of Crisis and Success', in Hans Ibelings, ed., *The Artificial Landscape: Contemporary Architecture, Urbanism, and Landscape Architecture in the Netherlands*, NAi Publishers (Rotterdam), 2000, p 244.

44 *The Artificial Landscape*, edited by Hans Ibelings, included a survey of over 65 architectural offices, and over 100 significant works, either recently completed or nearing completion. One of the institutions actively promoting the younger generation is the NAi, the Netherlands Architecture Institute. Located in Rotterdam, the building was designed by Jo Coenen (born 1949) and inaugurated in 1993.

45 Neutelings Riedijk Architecten was founded by Willem Jan Neutelings (born 1959) and Michiel Riedijk (born 1964) in 1992. Neutelings worked with OMA from 1981 to 1986.

46 Mecanoo was formed in 1984 in Delft. The office's founders, in addition to Henk Döll (born 1956) and Francine Houben (born 1955), were Roelf Steenhuis (born 1956; left in 1988), Erick van Egeraat (born 1956; left in 1995) and Chris de Weijer (born 1956; left in 1999).

47 The term is derived from the reflections found in the book: Ulrich Beck, Anthony Giddens and Scott Lash, *Reflexive Modernization: Politics, Tradition and Aesthetics in the Modern Social Order*, Oxford University Press (Oxford), 1994.

48 Bart Lootsma, 'Architecture for the Second Modernity', in *Space Design*, no 2 (1999), pp 83–5. It is interesting to note that idea of modernity was raised by Rem Koolhaas in 1990 during the convention 'Hoe modern is de Nederlandse architectuur?' held in Delft. The theme was heavily debated in Dutch circles.

49 Proof of this interest in this type of research, even transatlantic, can be found in the fact that Ben van Berkel and Caroline Bos edited an issue of the American magazine *ANY*: 'Diagram Work: Data Mechanics for a Topological Age', *ANY*, no 23 (December 1998).

**Mecanoo, Delft Polytechnic Library, Delft, The Netherlands, 1993–8: interior view.**

Those activities that require quieter spaces and concentration are located inside the cone, which is wrapped by spaces for other activities.

**Koen van Velsen, Media Authority Building, Hilversum, The Netherlands, 2002: exterior view.**

A brilliant example of Second Modernism, this building reveals the solid ties that join Dutch architectural research with the traditions of the Modern Movement.

For Bart Lootsma, the Dutch success was the result of an ability to operate in harmony with the *second modernity*[47] that resulted from the organisation of the world during the era of globalisation.[48] This meant, on the one hand, abandoning the romantic myth of the architect-genius who wishes to control the process from the first sketch to the last detail and, on the other, the introduction of flexible instruments that make it possible to provide a satisfying response to the requests made by the numerous subjects involved in the construction of a project: from politicians to builders, from clients to users.

Form, as per the precedent set by Koolhaas, is never the presupposition, but rather the final product that finds its justification only in the logical reasoning – as paradoxical as we wish – that substantiated it.

This is what we find in the diagrammatic architecture of UNStudio[49] or MVRDV, whose design process involves organising large amounts of data in two- and three-dimensional geometric figures called 'datascapes'.[50]

The resulting architecture produces innovative images that are often anything but banal in geometric terms and, while they make direct reference to the theory of complexity and systems, they are not always inspired by the aesthetic of the fold and the blob.[51]

On the contrary, in many cases the objective is a certain formal reduction that has more than a few points of contact with the new international style that was being delineated in many other Western situations, beginning with the rediscovery and re-elaboration of Minimalism in the early 1990s. This is the theory pro-

50 MVRDV present their design philosophy as follows: 'MVRDV pursues a fascination for radical methodical research: on density and on public realms. Through investigation and use of the complex amounts of data that accompany contemporary design processes, spaces are shaped methodically.

'Clients, users and specialists are intensively involved at an early stage of the design process. Reactions to the first designs can be processed quickly, creating a high degree of support for the design and encouraging the sort of new insights that can lead to specific innovative solutions. In this way our generalism and verve is linked with

the specialization and thoroughness of the other team members. The products of this approach can vary therefore completely. They range from buildings of all types and sizes, to urban designs, publications and installations, as well as the development of software programs.' (www.mvrdv.nl)
51 'In the thinking about second modernity, insights derived from systems theory like topology and dynamics, play an important role. Form is not seen as something static but as a condition of temporary equilibrium in a field of dynamic forces. The idea of French thinkers like René Thom, Gilles Deleuze/Felix Guattari, and Paul Virilio had a big

influence on Dutch architectural criticism, sometimes via a detour through the United States (Stan Allen, Greg Lynn, Manuel de Landa, Sanford Kwinter). In Dutch architecture, Derrida's deconstructivism has been smothered in what is sometimes known as "drunkard's style". Deleuze's notion of the fold appeared to undergo a similar fate. But his concepts of the diagram and framing, borrowed from film, continue to play a role.' Ton Verstegen, 'Perspectives of Crisis and Success', in: Hans Ibelings, ed., *The Artificial Landscape*, p 246.

**West 8, Borneo Sporenburg, Amsterdam, The Netherlands, 1996–2000.**

This contemporary project features a return to recurring motifs of Dutch urban planning. The result is a pleasant neighbourhood that unites the advantages of the consolidated city with the interesting forms of experimentation.

posed by, for example, Hans Ibelings, in the book in which he describes Supermodernism,[52] characterised by the overcoming of the symbolist romanticism of Post-Modernism and Deconstructivism. The architects who can be said to belong to this trend do not propose hidden meanings, using strong imagery to hide concepts that are extraneous to the world of architecture. Rather they seek to work with the existing, 'at the service of modernisation, which is currently most visible in the process of globalisation', and in this they resemble 'the last phase of Modernism, during the 1950s and '60s, when there was a strong tendency to accept prevailing conditions as inescapable facts'.[53] This leads to logical and effective forms and a realistic attitude that in turn leads to the acceptance of the complex metropolitan realities that define our era, no longer seen as stimuli for stylistic revolutions, but as concrete situations to be improved through specific interventions.

If the Dutch approach involved, on the one hand, what would later be defined by Ibelings using the term 'extreme logic',[54] on the other it represented a method of designing that led to the creation of an 'artificial landscape', cancelling the divisions between nature and artifice, between the object and the surrounding context. At the roots of this approach there is a culture that has always seen the landscape as the result of man's actions (design) and thus – unlike others, where construction is seen as act of violence towards nature – has never considered the two terms to be antithetical. There is also another condition by which the Dutch live within their landscape as if it were a single metropolitan reality, perceiving it as a fragmented space of sudden passages from the city to the countryside – in the words of Adriaan Geuze, 'as an addictive sequence of events'.[55] Finally, what generates the 'artificial landscape' is the logical method of designing, where form does not have an object-based, but rather a relational, value. It thus avoids self-referential sculptural objects, in order to join, as part of a single formal organism, all of the factors at play and connect, primarily, the building with its context. Of the most successful examples of artificial

52 Hans Ibelings, *Supermodernism: Architecture in the Age of Globalization*, NAi Publishers (Rotterdam), 1998. Enlarged edition, NAi Publishers (Rotterdam), 2002.
53 Hans Ibelings, *Supermodernism: Architecture in the Age of Globalization*, 2002, p 134.

54 'Extreme logic', in Hans Ibelings, ed., *The Artificial Landscape*, pp 104–34.
55 Adriaan Geuze, 'Accelerating Darwin', in Hans Ibelings, ed., *The Artificial Landscape*, p 254.

**West 8, Borneo Sporenburg, Amsterdam, The Netherlands, 1996–2000: view from the bridge.**

The exuberant form of the bridge reinforces the vital nature of this neighbourhood, in addition to making it a landmark in the city.

**Foreign Office Architects, International Port Terminal, Yokohama, Japan, 1995–2002: view from the sea.**

From the sea, the Yokohama Port Terminal appears to be a large, panoramic platform, similar to a ship, covered by a fragment of nature.

**Foreign Office Architects, International Port Terminal, Yokohama, Japan, 1995–2002: detail.**

The undulating surface, covered with wooden slats that alternate with insertions of natural elements, transform the roof of the building into a public space suspended between the earth and the sky.

landscape we can mention the Delft Polytechnic Library, the roof of which is a sloping, grass-covered surface where students can study outside; or the Dutch Pavilion for Expo 2000 in Hanover, Germany by MVRDV (2000), where trees and shrubs invade the various floors of the building; or the Secret Garden in Malmö, Sweden (1999–2001) by West 8, where vegetation is organised based on the principles of multistorey construction.

Another group that moves along the same lines of Dutch landscape architecture is Foreign Office Architects (FOA), run, as mentioned above, by Alejandro Zaera Polo and Farshid Moussavi. Their masterpiece, the International Port Terminal in Yokohama, Japan (1995–2002), is a more-than-100-metre-long, three-storey

**Foreign Office Architects, International Port Terminal, Yokohama, Japan, 1995–2002: view from the sea.**

The movement of the roof plane was obtained by progressively manipulating the sections of the structures below. The result is a building focused on the aesthetic results of varying a predetermined element.

**NOX, OffTheRoad_5speed, project for prefabricated housing near Eindhoven, The Netherlands, 1999: general view.**

This housing project is the result of the transformation, assisted by the computer, of traditional residential typologies, based on their reaction to external forces (similar to the evolution of living organisms in response to events).

**NOX, OfftheRoad_5speed, project for prefabricated housing near Eindhoven, The Netherlands, 1999: view of one of the building types.**

Balanced somewhere between the past and the future, the houses are similar to caves, though designed to be produced using sophisticated CAD-CAM techniques.

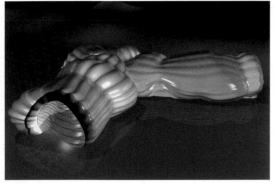

structure – roof, terminal and parking – that does not emerge from its context, but connects, almost without any interruption, to the urban fabric, offering the city, at the level of the roof, an enchanting artificial plane from which to observe the port. The interior, thanks to an obsessive study of the sections and structures (they designed over 100, each different from the next), is a welcoming and articulated space, with more than a few elements of Catalan inspiration.

# 3.8 New Landscapes, New Languages

In September 1997 Bruno Zevi investigated the formal implications of a renewed relationship with nature in a conference entitled 'Paesaggistica e linguaggio grado zero dell'architettura'.[56] For this Italian critic, when architecture becomes landscape it must free itself of the rhetoric of pre-codified artistic languages in order to draw upon what Roland Barthes,[57] since the 1950s, had been calling Degree Zero – a non-artificial and essential way of speaking, devoid of any unnecessary use of adjectives.

Whether this actually took place in the following years is difficult to judge. What is certain is that the late 1990s

**MVRDV, Dutch Pavilion, Expo 2000, Hanover, Germany: exterior view.**

For MVRDV everything is landscape. There is thus no difference in principle between nature and the built environment. In fact, the latter can capture the first, multiply it and organise it on various levels.

56 'Landscape and the Zero Degree of Architectural Language'. The proceedings of the conference, held in Modena, Italy, were published in *L'architettura: cronache e storia*, nos 503–6 (1999), in Italian and English.
57 Roland Barthes, *Le Degré zéro de l'écriture*, Editions du Seuil (Paris), 1953. English translation: *Writing Degree Zero*, Hill and Wang (New York), 1968.

58 Of those publications that have
analysed the variety of approaches
taken by contemporary architects
to the landscape, we mention: Paola
Gregory, *Territori della complessità: New
Scapes*, Testo&Immagine (Turin), 2003.
In English: *New Scapes: Territories of
Complexity*, Birkhäuser (Basel, Boston
and Berlin), 2003.

witnessed the emergence of a significant plurality of proposals for the construction of a new landscape, many of which led to the development of research that we have already seen arise in previous years,[58] and six of which appear to be of interest here.

## A: The Organic Landscape

For James Cutler[59] it was necessary to return to a traditional ecological attitude of 'first nature, then architecture'.[60] This approach generated horizontal buildings, covered by grass and built of natural materials, primarily wood, based on the indications provided earlier by architects such as Obie Bowman,[61] the designer of the Brunsell Residence in Sea Ranch, California (1987), a fascinating house that blends into its context.

Less mimetic, though no less organic, are the investigations into the integration between architecture and the landscape made by the Australians Glenn Murcutt[62] and Sean Godsell[63] and the American William Bruder.[64]

The designer of refined and lightweight single-family dwellings with a Modernist flavour, Murcutt was awarded the Pritzker Prize in 2002 for his essential structures, designed to enter into osmosis with the exuberant Australian landscape. When working on larger projects, such as the Arthur & Yvonne Boyd Education Centre in West Cambewarra, New South Wales, Australia (1999), he proceeds by ensuring the minimum impact on the local ecosystem, moving along the contour lines of the site, using natural materials, carefully controlling the building details and never losing the correct relationship with scale that unites the building, the user and the surrounding space. A similar approach is taken by Godsell who, to enable his projects to harmonise with their context, eliminates the rigid divisions between interior and exterior, using wood or rusted steel grates – as, for example, in the Kew House, Melbourne, Australia (1996–7) and the Carter/Tucker House in Breamlea, Victoria, Australia (1998–2000).

59 James Cutler (born 1949) founded James Cutler Architects (now Cutler Anderson Architects) in 1977.
60 The phrase can be found in James Wines (author) and Philip Jodidio (editor), *L'Architecture Verte*, Taschen (Cologne, London, Madrid, New York, Paris and Tokyo), 2000, p 178. English edition: *Green Architecture*.
61 Obie Bowman (born 1943) opened his office in Sea Ranch, California, in 1973.

62 Glenn Murcutt (born 1936) studied architecture between 1956 and 1960 at the University of New South Wales. He refers to his research as 'ecological functionalism'.
63 Sean Godsell (born 1960) graduated from the University of Melbourne in 1984. From 1986 to 1988 he worked with Sir Denys Lasdun (1914–2001). In 1994 he formed Godsell Associates Pty Ltd Architects.

64 William Bruder (born 1946) earned a Bachelor of Fine Arts degree in sculpture from the University of Wisconsin. After studying under Gunnar Birkerts (born 1925) and Paolo Soleri (born 1919), Bruder opened his own studio 64 kilometres north of Phoenix in New River, Arizona, in 1974.

66 Peter Buchanan, 'Pioneering a New Paradigm', from the catalogue of the exhibition held between 8 December 2001 and 3 March 2002 at the Deutsches Architektur Museum of Frankfurt am Main, Germany, and curated by Christian Niethammer: Ingeborg Flagge, Verena Herzog-Loibl and Anna Meseure, eds, *Thomas Herzog: Architektur + Technologie/Architecture + Technology*, Prestel (Munich and New York), 2001.

67 Thomas Herzog, *Solar Energy in Architecture and Urban Planning*, Prestel (Munich and New York), 1996.

Also the designer of refined, single-family dwellings, Bruder revives the organic tradition, using contemporary forms and materials. His Central Library in Phoenix, Arizona, completed in 1996, enters into a dialogue with the Monument Valley thanks to the giant, copper-clad walls that curve in one direction and undulate in the other. His other library, the Teton County Library in Jackson, Wyoming (completed in 1998) and the Museum of Contemporary Art in Scottsdale, Arizona (completed in 1999) are two projects that, without renouncing their presence, blend into the Western American landscape, partially as a result of their primarily horizontal appearance.

### B. The Post-Organic Landscape

There is another approach that results from organic and expressionist matrixes, drawing upon modern technologies and their formal image. Developed primarily in Germany, this movement, typified by the work of Thomas Herzog,[65] does not hesitate to use new build-ing materials and/or to re-engineer traditional building systems. The work of this Munich-based architect is characterised, as noted by Peter Buchanan, by the understanding that 'in sustainable architecture form owes more to architects who question accepted practices and reorient their work using scientific knowledge, than to the fireworks of self-appointed avantgardists who disguise old technology in spectacular new clothes'.[66] In 1996 Herzog published the book *Solar Energy in Architecture and Urban Planning*.[67]

Herzog's more interesting projects include the Expodach for Expo 2000 in Hanover (1999–2000), a roof structure supported by slender, organic columns that embody the principle of 'performance form' – a conformation that is not determined by preconceived notions, but which develops from the logical response to issues raised by design and context, above all when it is natural.

We can also mention the work of Günter Behnisch & Partner,[68] the other important German office

65 Thomas Herzog (born 1941) graduated with a degree in architecture from the Technical University of Munich in 1965. He opened his office, together with the sculptor Verena Herzog-Loibl, in 1972. In 1993 he won the gold medal from the German Society of Architects for his work as a 'solar architect'. He has worked in partnership with Hanns Jörg Schrade (born 1951) since 1994.

68 Günter Behnisch (born 1922) studied at the Technical University of Stuttgart. In 1952 he opened his own office in the city. In 1989, together with his son Stefan Behnisch (born 1958), he created a partner company to Günter Behnisch & Partner named Behnisch, Behnisch & Partner.

Peter Zumthor, Swiss Pavilion, Expo 2000, Hanover, Germany: detail.

The obsession with detail transforms the building into a sculpture with vague Japanese overtones, rather than the manifesto of environmental sustainability that it was to have been.

Catholic University in Eichstätt, Germany (1985–7). This approach led to what Behnisch calls 'situational architecture': a method of building that adheres to the task, time and site that, similar to the 'performance form' posited by Herzog, shares the need of protecting the design activity from the dangers of arbitrariness and formalism. This method was successfully applied in the New Bonn Parliament (completed in 1992) and the Geschwister-Scholl-Schule in Römerstadt, Germany (1992–4), together with numerous other projects begun by the office in the late 1990s, beginning with the Schleswig-Holstein Regional Insurance Centre in Lubecca, Germany (1992–7). All of these feature open structured plans that are inserted into the surrounding landscape, and large, glazed internal spaces that allow for micro-climatic conditioning and optimum environments, enabling them to compete, in terms of the quality of light and spatial variety, with the natural environment. Lastly we can mention the IBN Institute for Forestry and Nature Research in Wageningen, The Netherlands (1992–8) where the exterior landscape,

investigating themes of sustainability. Their work presents the logical development of an activity that, back in the 1970s – in the Olympiapark in Munich (1972), designed with Frei Otto[69] for the Olympic Games – led Behnisch to begin experimenting with lightweight and innovative structures. In the 1980s he anticipated, in order to better articulate his buildings within their natural context, the aesthetic of Deconstruction and Californian landform architecture in his library for the

69 Frei Otto (born 1925) studied architecture in Berlin before the Second World War. He began private practice in Germany in 1952. He is the world's leading authority on lightweight tensile and membrane structures, and has pioneered advances in structural mathematics and civil engineering. Otto founded the Institute for Lightweight Structures at the University of Stuttgart in 1964.

Baumschlager & Eberle, Bank of Tyrol and Vorarlberg, Wolfurt (Innsbruck), Austria, 1997–8: exterior view.

In order to render a building sustainable, it must not only be energy efficient, but must also have an aspect that is a more natural in appearance. This leads to the rediscovery, in a contemporary key, of wood cladding.

**Thomas Herzog, Expodach, Expo 2000, Hanover, Germany: view of the column.**

Contrary to Herzog's other projects, here the organic prevails over the technological. The result is a building with a very strong visual impact and symbolic value.

rendered more luxuriant by a well-managed plan for the planting of new species, enters into contact with the building's interior, also rich with natural vegetation, through the insertion of a large glass wall. 'We imagine,' the office stated when presenting the project, 'that over time the building will help the landscape become more intricate, varied and autonomous than that which presently exists.'

The buildings by the French duo Françoise-Hélène Jourda and Gilles Perraudin[70] are also focused on reconciling new technologies with the search for a new, sustainable landscape.

In 1998 they completed the Law Courts in Melun, France, a building endowed on its exterior with a canopy supported by tree-like columns. On the interior a garden helps to avoid the unpleasant and barracks-like aspect of legal buildings. Their Training Academy in Herne-Sodingen, Germany (1992–9) is a transparent greenhouse that contains various buildings and public spaces. A 'solar field' of over 1,000 square metres of photovoltaic cells transforms the complex into a power plant that produces 1 megawatt of energy.

After dissolving the partnership with Jourda, Perraudin continued his activity, focusing on the recovery of the quality of an ancient material such as stone – industrialising its extraction, transportation and installation in an attempt to reduce the costs of manual labour, based on the assumption that traditional construction methods have ecological potentials that it would be foolish to lose simply because we are now unable to insert them within the logic of contemporary building processes.

## C. The Technological Landscape

In Great Britain, the designers of High Tech – or Eco-Tech as we called it in the previous chapter – began to focus, with progressively more effort, on research into environmental topics, seeking to reconcile innovation with energy savings and definitively shaking off a label

70 Gilles Perraudin (born 1949) and Françoise-Hélène Jourda (born 1955) opened their office in 1989. In 1998 Perraudin moved on to found Gilles Perraudin Architecte.

**Norman Foster, City Hall, London, England, 1998–2002: interior view.**

The central space is occupied by two heliocoidal ramps designed with masterful technical skill, and apparently without any structural supports.

**Norman Foster, City Hall, London, England, 1998–2002: exterior view.**

The aerodynamic form is the result of the movement of the spirals inside the building.

**Norman Foster, Swiss Re Office Tower, London, England, 1997–2004: interior view.**

The interior features double-height spaces, some of which contain small gardens, making the building pleasant to use.

that referred to them as anti-ecological builders of steel and glass boxes which consumed great quantities of natural resources. One clear example is the project for the renovation of the Reichstag in Berlin by Foster & Partners (1992–9) where the destroyed dome of the German Parliament was reconstructed and transformed into a panoramic glazed structure with a shading mechanism that rotates 360 degrees, following the movement of the sun. The organic forms of nature become the inspiration for curved and wrapping shapes.

This is the case with two projects by Foster's office that changed the skyline of the city of London: the Swiss Re Office Tower (1997–2004) whose unusual shape, determined by bioclimatic studies, has led to its baptism as the 'Gherkin'; and the new City Hall (1998–2002), home to the offices of the Mayor of London and the Greater London Authority (GLA). The exterior of the latter has a complex curvilinear form, while the interior is filled with lightweight spiral ramps that rise up towards the sky without any apparent supports.

**Norman Foster, Swiss Re Office Tower, London, England, 1997–2004.**

The form of the building was determined by bioclimatic considerations and the desire to maximise solar exposure and reduce heat loss.

**Future Systems, House in Pembrokeshire, Wales, 1994–7: exterior view.**

This enchanting house recalls the technological imagination of the 1960s. It is integrated within its surroundings, without falling into the trap of a mimetic approach.

**Richard Rogers, Millennium Dome, London, England, 1996–2000: exterior detail.**

The Dome was one of the large projects designed to celebrate the new millennium. The inside of this gigantic tent was filled with display pavilions, designed by such architects as Zaha Hadid and Nigel Coates.

We must also mention the fascinating project by Nicholas Grimshaw, a revisitation of the truss structures of Buckminster Fuller, for the Eden Project in Cornwall, England (1995–2001). It is proof of the uninterrupted connection that joins research during this period, above all in the field of High Tech, with the intuitions of the radical culture of the 1960s and '70s.

There is also the house in Pembrokeshire, Wales (1994–7) designed by Future Systems,[71] which is rendered almost invisible within its stupendous natural context, without in any way renouncing a modern form. So much so that, as Marcus Field points out[72], the shell could have been entirely prefabricated in a shop – the fulfilment of a dream for Archigram.

71 Future Systems was founded in 1979 by Jan Kaplicky (born 1937) and Amanda Levete (born 1955) in London.

72 Marcus Field, *Future Systems*, Phaidon Press (London), 1999, p 105.

**Richard Rogers, Millennium Dome, London, England, 1996–2000: section.**

As can be seen in the section, the Dome was supported by cables suspended from slender steel poles. The latter were anchored to the ground by volumes containing service and support spaces.

Nicholas Grimshaw, Eden Project, Cornwall, England, 1995–2001: view of the interior of the dome.

Inspired by the geodesic structures of Buckminster Fuller, Grimshaw creates the conditions for an artificial Eden, with lush and dense natural growth.

### D. Soft-Tech Contextualism

Between 1997 and 2001 Renzo Piano completed four projects with a significant impact on the landscape, and was about to finish a fifth: the renovation of the historical port in Genoa, Italy (1988–2001); the Jean-Marie Tjibaou Cultural Center in Noumea, New Caledonia (1991–8); the reconstruction of the Potsdamer Platz in Berlin (1992–2000); the Aurora Place Office and Resi-

dential Buildings in Sydney, Australia (1996–2000); and the Parco della Musica Auditorium in Rome (1994–2002).

As proof of the fact that this Italian architect follows no single strategy, but rather an empirical and pragmatic method that allows him to calibrate his response in relationship to specific contextual conditions, the five works are very different from one another. In Genoa the technological choices make reference to the nautical world: a tensile structure reminiscent of the sails of a boat, and a panoramic elevator supported by steel spars. In New Caledonia, where nature remains uncontaminated and the traces of local culture can still be felt, Piano designed a complex of 10 wooden apses of differing heights, inspired by local, historical cabin structures. Built of wooden slats, they are inserted within their context, vibrating when hit by the ocean winds and producing a sound similar to that of wind in the trees. In Berlin, where the objective was that of creating a piece of the city, Piano proposed the construction of

Norman Foster, Reichstag, Berlin, Germany, 1992–9: view of the interior of the dome.

Foster rebuilt the dome of the Reichstag, destroyed during the Second World War, with a steel and glass structure with a panoramic viewing ramp open to the public. A system of mirrors captures natural light and brings it into the Parliament Hall below.

Michael Hopkins, Dynamic Earth, Edinburgh, Scotland, 1990–9: exterior view.

The construction of tents and mobile structures is a part of the High Tech tradition. In Hopkins' project they are characterised by their simplicity and elegance.

**Renzo Piano, Jean-Marie Tjibaou Cultural Center, Noumea, New Caledonia, 1991–8: aerial view.**

The project features large, wooden apses that recall and reinterpret, in a modern key, the forms of the cabins built by the local population. The wooden slats vibrate in the wind, emitting sounds when crossed by the wind.

an Italian-style neighbourhood, designed at the scale of man, with an articulated fabric of streets and public squares, flanked by terracotta-clad buildings. In Sydney, with its vertically developed downtown, Piano works to humanise the theme of the skyscraper, rendered energy-efficient by a natural ventilation system that also improves the urban landscape. Finally, in the Auditorium in Rome, the three shells of the concert halls, designed like the resonating cavity of a musical instrument, are clad with lead sheeting, creating a dialogue with the domes of the city's churches. They are organised around a central open-air theatre (the *cavea*). Their organic and blob-like forms ensure a contemporary presence that avoids being overpowering, within the Flaminio neighbourhood, a part of Rome in which residential structures alternate with parks.

## E. The Metaphorical and Metaphysical Landscape

A less pragmatic and more poetic and abstract approach is that taken by the Japanese architect Toyo Ito, who completed the Sendai Mediatheque in 2001. For Ito the new landscape is the result of the synthesis of nature and technology and has the force of a simple and effective image, both ancient and modern: that of running water. In fact, water has always been related to the idea of life and movement, so much so that it was evoked by the Greek philosopher Heracles in the image of the current of the river, always different and always the same. Furthermore, the liquid element, due to its ability to acquire almost any form, is highly suitable to representing the flows of the electronic society.

**Toyo Ito, Sendai Mediatheque, Japan, 1995–2001: exterior view.**

The light wells are surrounded by a cage of slender steel columns that define the structure of the building. If the media library resembles an aquarium, the pilasters are reminiscent of a bamboo thicket.

The patterns etched onto the glass facade modulate sunlight, while the varying floor-to-floor heights, designed with a studied and Oriental imbalance, give rhythm to what would otherwise be a simple glass box.

During this period even Herzog & de Meuron began to demonstrate, and to a growing degree, a sensitivity towards the theme of the landscape. This was achieved by questioning the very concepts of nature and artifice. On the one hand they demonstrated the artificiality of that which appears to be natural: for example, the use of stone or wood in unusual ways that exalt their geometric and abstract qualities. Or, vice versa, the naturalness of what seems to be artificial: for example the patterns of thermal insulating materials, in some cases exposed behind exterior glazing panels. The result is a physical world that is simultaneously metaphysical, made up of continuous surprises that leave us amazed at the richness of the infinite and unexpected relationships that exist between things, their forms and their structures. This can be seen, for

As a result, the Mediatheque is designed like an aquarium, the floors of which are connected by circular wells: they allow light to filter in from above, contain the vertical connections and the fibreoptic cables that carry flows of information. The wells are transformed into focal points of the composition by steel columns that recall bamboo stands along the river banks, while artificial lighting is used to create the effects of water: for example, the garage is lit with an azure that recalls the ocean.

**Toyo Ito, Sendai Mediatheque, Japan, 1995–2001: exterior view.**

The glass walls reveal the wells of light that cut through the building and contain the elements of vertical circulation and building services.

**Toyo Ito, Sendai Mediatheque, Japan, 1995–2001: view of the one of the light wells.**

The ceiling heights inside the media library vary from one storey to another and each light well contains a different function. The result is a building with a significant variety of spatial conditions.

**Herzog & de Meuron, Pharmaceutical Research Centre for the Basel Hospital, Switzerland, 1995–9: view of an exterior detail.**

The choice to subdivide the wall into a natural and more artificial wall increases the visual appeal of this building.

Herzog & de Meuron, Tate
Modern, London, England,
1994–2000: view of the large
interior hall.

Herzog & de Meuron's renovation
is made up of only a few moves.
For example, they leave the large
turbine hall as the space of access
to the museum, adding only a few,
transparent longitudinal volumes
that overlook it.

Herzog & de Meuron, Dominus
Winery, Yountville, California,
USA, 1995–7: exterior view.

The building is clad with stone-
filled steel cages (gabion baskets). This choice, in addition
to guaranteeing optimal micro-
climatic conditions for the conservation of wine, also produces
suggestive lighting effects inside
the space.

example, in the Dominus Winery in Yountville, California
(1995–7) where the walls of the building are made of
gabion baskets. The building simultaneously appears to
be fragile and massive, ancient and contemporary. On
the interior light filters between the stones, filling the
space with suggestive contrasts of chiaroscuro. In the
Pharmaceutical Research Centre for the Basel Hospital,
Switzerland (1995–9), what from a distance appears as
an elegant, though cold and anonymous, building with
a glass facade, reveals itself, up close, and thanks to the
skilful use of transparencies, to be a universe composed
of complex fractal geometries, the basic element that
organises the most fragmented natural landscapes.

Less successful, on the other hand, is the project for
the creation of the Tate Modern in London (1994–2000).
However it was this project – consisting of the reuse of
a gigantic industrial building by Sir Giles Gilbert Scott –
which, due to the importance and visibility of the commission, launched the duo on the international scene.

## F. Dis-Architecture

If for Ito nature is to be sublimated, through metaphorical re-elaboration, in the abstract forms of architecture, for Emilio Ambasz[73] and James Wines the problem
is the inverse: it is architecture that must bend to meet
the whims of nature, return to a natural state, even at
the cost of losing its artificial aspect.

For some time both architects, who can boast a
militant role in the Radical movements of the 1960s

Herzog & de Meuron,
Pharmaceutical Research
Centre for the Basel Hospital
Switzerland, 1995–9: exterior
view.

The building appears to be a simple, glass-clad volume. However,
seen from up close the etched
glass and the insulating material
behind give the building finish
depth and interest.

73 Emilio Ambasz (born 1943) was
born in Argentina and studied at
Princeton University, from which he
graduated in 1970. From that year
until 1976 he was curator of the Architecture and Design Department at the
Museum of Modern Art in New York.

**Emilio Ambasz, ACROS Building, Fukuoka, Japan, 1990–5: exterior view.**

This building presents itself to the city in a twofold manner. On the street side it has a modern facade, while the park side is designed like a ziggurat whose terraces are covered with rich vegetation, making the building disappear.

and '70s, had been developing and presenting their post-architectural theories under the headings of 'dis-architecture' or 'an-architecture'. However, it is only during the period in question – also the result of the experiments being made by younger architects working on the theme, such as Edouard François[74] and, for certain aspects, François Roche[75] – that their work, previously snubbed or scarcely considered by critics, was re-evaluated.

The ACROS Building in Fukuoka, Japan (1990–5) by Ambasz is a conference centre designed to disappear, transforming itself, as its vegetal covering grows, into a sequence of hanging gardens. The only emerging element is the cut that marks the entrance, whose form alludes to the symbolism of archaic architecture and, simultaneously, the inhabitation of a grotto.

After completing the promenade and the Arabian Pavilion at the Seville Expo in Spain (1992) and a park in Chattanooga, Tennessee, the same year,

James Wines went on to complete numerous other projects of significant environmental interest, though they remained on paper: particularly notable are the Museum of Islamic Arts in Doha, Qatar (1997) and the United States' Pavilion for Expo '98 in Hanover. In 2000 he published *Green Architecture*[76] and was busy working on two projects in Italy, one of which – the sculpture garden in Carate, Brianza – was completed in 2006. Both projects demonstrate a progressively more decisive ecological approach, where the construction of architecture becomes an integral part of the organisation of the landscape – so much so that, in the end, the two elements are almost indistinguishable from one another. It would not be out of place to state that nature is the new building material, also because, as Wines himself states, 'glass curtain walls are hardly avant-garde icons any more – in fact they have become the ultimate right wing symbol'.[77]

74 Edouard François (born 1957) graduated in 1983. The work of his office, located in Paris, is notable for the ample use of natural elements, even as cladding, to hide the masonry mass of buildings.

75 François Roche (born 1961) graduated from the École Nationale Supérieure d'Architecture de Paris-Belleville. In 1989, together with Stéfanie Lavaux (born 1966), he founded the office now known as R&Sie(n), located in Paris. Their work is characterised by metamorphic forms that break the distinction between built space and the natural environment.

76 James Wines (author), Philip Jodidio (editor), *Green Architecture*, Taschen (Cologne, London, Madrid, New York, Paris and Tokyo), 2000.
77 Luigi Prestinenza Puglisi, 'Entretien avec James Wines, Président de SITE', in *James Wines & SITE: Architecture dans le contexte/Architecture in Context*, Éditions HYX (Orléans), 2002, p 52. The interview was previously published in *Il Progetto*, no 4 (December 1998).

## G. A Sculptural Approach and Landform Architecture

Moving in an opposite direction with respect to that proposed by Ambasz and Wines, we find those architects who wish to create a new landscape, beginning with the construction of sculptural objects or, as in the case of landform architecture, by materialising in one work, with strong lines of plastic energy, the flows and forms of the surrounding context.

The projects of the Spanish architect and engineer Santiago Calatrava, as we have mentioned elsewhere, are the result of an observation of structural principles that generate natural forms. During this period he completed the elegant Ponte Bianco, a pedestrian bridge over the Nervión River, near the Guggenheim Museum in Bilbao (1991–7); the City of the Arts and Sciences in Valencia, also in Spain (completed in 2006); and the addition to the Milwaukee Art Museum in Wisconsin (1994–2001). These buildings and spaces are reminiscent of gothic forests or living hybrid structures, suspended between the distant and Palaeolithic past and an imaginary future worthy of science fiction. However, there is an excess of invention that never leads to a simplification of the structural forms – for example removing material and weight – but rather a process that makes them much more complex. The result is that – and this can be seen above all in Valencia – the works capture attention and generate curiosity, while tiring one's eyes with a continual play of references, with the end result that they are perceived as being redundant.

The year 2000 was witness to the tragic death of Enric Miralles, an architect destined to become – as demonstrated in the previous chapters – one of the protagonists of the new millennium. His best projects, balanced between an organic Expressionism and Deconstructivism, were posthumously completed by Benedetta Tagliabue. They are characterised by a formidable tension with the landscape, the creative use of rough materials and a decidedly chromatic approach. Examples include the new Scottish Parliament in

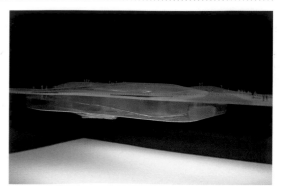

**UFO, Sarajevo Concert Hall, Sarajevo, Bosnia-Herzegovina, 1999: competition.**

The concert hall is buried below ground, freeing up the space above for use as a park. The soft curves that model the terrain hide the entrance to the building.

Zaha Hadid, Landesgartenschau, Weil am Rhein, Germany, 1999: aerial view.

The pedestrian path that crosses the building helps to articulate it volumetrically and, at the same time, to tie it to the site, transforming it into an element of the landscape.

Frank O Gehry, DZ Bank Building, Berlin, Germany, 1995–2001: interior view.

Obliged to follow Berlin's rigid planning regulations, which called for the maintenance of alignments with neighbouring buildings, Gehry created a pavilion on the interior whose form recalls a horse's head that, together with the form of the fish, are recurring themes in his work.

Edinburgh (1998–2004) or the renovation of the Santa Caterina Market in Barcelona, Spain (1997–2005), the latter of which features a striking ceramic tile-clad roof whose coloured surface transforms what is usually a forgotten part of any building into a fascinating artificial landscape.

The Landesgartenschau, a pavilion designed by Zaha Hadid in Weil am Rhein and completed in 1999 to host events related to a gardening show, represents a decisive shift, one could even say naturalistic and environmentalist, towards the construction of new landscapes. The building is tied to its site by curving lines that hint at both the paths that cross the park and the fluid lines of nature. At the same time, through the dynamic architectural decomposition of the building, Hadid charges the site with a plastic energy that was

otherwise lacking. A similar method is also employed in her successful 1998 competition-winning entry for the new Contemporary Arts Centre in Rome. This time the theme is that of a cultural machine, located on a 3-hectare site in the Flaminio neighbourhood (the same that hosts Renzo Piano's Auditorium) that will be home to a museum for temporary exhibitions, experimental multimedia spaces, an educational wing and independent and extra-institutional activities. Hadid proposed a building whose form is the result of different generating lines, this time tied to existing urban realties. The objective was that of creating a living system, conceived of as a field of forces, navigated by visitors attracted by the varying distribution of points of density inside the structure. The elements of vertical circulation and oblique volumes are located at points of confluence, interference and turbulence. The building is a system with multiple directions, filled by an uninterrupted flow of energy, where architecture loses it consistency as an object, becoming a piece of the urban landscape.

Miralles Tagliabue, Santa Caterina Market, Barcelona, Spain, 1997–2005: exterior view.

The building interprets the vital spirit of Spanish artistic traditions. The roof is brightly coloured, creating a pleasant view from the balconies of the buildings that surround the market square.

161 3.8 New Landscapes, New Languages

78 Seattle's James Marshall Hendrix (1942–70) was a rock musician and one of the most important innovators of the sound of the electric guitar.

## 3.9 New Landscape: The West and East Coast

A similar sensitivity, sculptural and vital to the relationships between architecture and the environment, was developed, in particular, by architects working in Los Angeles.

Frank Gehry's Experience Music Project in Seattle, Washington (1995–2000) demonstrates a new, and surprising, declination of the theme of the building-landscape. The museum further develops the design principles employed in Bilbao, consisting of the creation of sculptural masses clad with metal panels. However, here Gehry complicates the process by introducing colour and abandoning the contextualism of a Baroque matrix (the two wings embracing the city, the obelisk-like tower, etc) that characterises the Guggenheim. The museum, returning to the pop imagery of the building-icon tested in the entrance to the Chiat/Day offices, is reminiscent of Jimi Hendrix's[78] broken guitar, to whom the museum is dedicated. It is precisely this clearly declared extraneousness to the urban context, and the involving energy of its masses, somewhat strident and blobby, that creates a project that was immediately accepted by the city. The public was attracted by the digital instruments that transform the environment into an interactive experience, complemented by the fluid flow of the building's interior spaces.

Though obliged to follow the rigid rules imposed by the head architect of the city of Berlin, Hans Stimmann – the alignment of the street and the use of the same materials as in other buildings in the city – Gehry managed to create another surprising work with the DZ Bank Building (1995–2001). The closed exterior volume, ordered by a sequence of openings that are plastically carved into the facade, is juxtaposed against the fascinating interior spaces, illuminated by a glass skylight and enlivened by the presence of pavilion-sculpture, the form

**Frank O Gehry, Experience Music Project, Seattle, Washington, USA, 1995–2000: view from the street.**

The Seattle project further complicates the game begun in Bilbao and used in the Walt Disney Concert Hall in Los Angeles, introducing a greater variety of chromatic effects. The project is inspired by Jimi Hendrix's famous broken guitars.

**79** The Getty Center (1984–97) creates a dialogue between the numerous buildings of the museum complex and the hill on top of which they sit. However, despite a number of brilliant solutions, the project demonstrates the limits of an approach based on an attempt to create a coexistence between a contemporary language and traditional criteria used to organise the exterior spaces – in this case those of Hadrian's Villa in Tivoli (AD 117–33). These limits are also made evident by the use of a material – Roman travertine – that was intended to produce a warmer effect than Meier's usual enamel-finished steel panels, but which ended up compromising the purist language used by him in his most successful recent works.

of which vaguely recalls a horse's head – a motif that, together with the fish, belongs to the architect's figurative imagery.

No less fascinating is the approach to landform architecture pursued by Morphosis. In Los Angeles, at the time home to the recently completed and imposing complex of the Getty Center designed by Richard Meier, Morphosis were demonstrating that it was possible to develop a more decisive and energetic attitude.[79] As mentioned previously, the work of Morphosis is based on two recurring aspects: a gestural approach and relations. The first produces dynamic volumes that are both intense and almost violent, as if generated more by nature than by the ordered composition of masses. The second questions the categories of interior and exterior, and the relationship between the body and architecture. In 2000 Thom Mayne completed two works that resulted in his receiving the Pritzker Prize in 2005: the Diamond Ranch High School in Pomona, California (1993–2000) and the Hypo Alpe Adria Centre in Klagenfurt, Austria (1996–2000). The horizontality

**Peter Eisenman, City of Culture of Galicia, Santiago de Compostela, Spain, 1999–: project.**

The project disappears under the earth, modifying the form of the land. Axes and cuts are generated by the surrounding context.

of the former enables it to blend into the landscape, which is further enhanced by the open-air space-path where 'cantilevered volumes project dramatically into space, roofscapes fold and bend like shifting geological plates'.[80] The second project 'gives voice to ... conflicting forces, harnessing the dynamism of global connectivity and anchoring it to an activated land surface; its charged forms break the earth's crust, while they also maintain a dialogue with the rural countryscape'.[81]

Even more intense is the work of Eric Owen Moss, the third protagonist of the Los Angeles architectural scene, who pushes the limits of research in projects such as the parking structure and offices of the Wedgewood Holly Complex in Culver City, Los Angeles (1999) or the Mariinsky Cultural Centre in St Petersburg, Russia (2001). In both projects the architectural image appears to slip away, assuming the precarious aspect of natural forms when they are subjected to intense, dynamic tensions, for example during an earthquake.

One architect who inspired by the work of Mayne and Moss is Michele Saee.[82] In his work the lessons of Deconstructivism and landform architecture coexist with formal exuberances and plays of light and matter deriving from his Iranian origins, together with a refined spatiality resulting from a period of study in Italy, where he came into contact with the Florentine avant-garde.

Less sculptural and more intellectual is the approach taken by the architects of the East Coast, spearheaded by Philip Johnson.[83]

After working with Gehry on the design of the Lewis House in Cleveland, Ohio (1989–95), a villa where kitsch and pop come together, Johnson sought to develop his own brand of postmodern Deconstructivism that was not extraneous to his passion for curved forms and new digital trends. The results, as demonstrated by the project completed with Alan Ritchie[84] for the Children's Museum in Guadalajara, Mexico (1999) are

164

80 Thom Mayne, 'Not Neutral', in *Morphosis*, Phaidon Press (London), 2003, p 272.
81 ibid, p 271.

82 Michele Saee (born 1956) graduated in Florence in 1981, where he began working with Superstudio. In 1982 he worked with Morphosis. He opened his own office in Los Angeles in 1985.
83 Through his work with the MoMA – he was Director of the Architectural Department – Philip Johnson, during his lengthy and fruitful lifetime (1906–2005), was a sponsor of every possible style: from the International Style to Post-Modernism, through to Deconstructivism and Blobitecture. In the 1990s he was also a point of refer-

ence for innovative architects such as Gehry, Eisenman, Hadid and Koolhaas.
84 In 1994, Philip Johnson joined forces with his previous associate Alan Ritchie (born 1938) and established the new architectural firm of Philip Johnson/Alan Ritchie Architects.

85 The Virtual House Competition
was sponsored by *ANY* magazine and
Franz Schneider Brakel GmbH + Co.
The jury was composed of Kurt W
Forster, Akira Asada, Rebecca Horn
and the philosophers Gilles Deleuze,
John Rajchman, Eric Alliez, Erik Oger,
Elizabeth Grosz, Paul Virilio and Gilles
Châtelet. Competition participants
included Jean Nouvel, Toyo Ito, Peter
Eisenman, Daniel Libeskind, Herzog &
de Meuron and Alejandro Zaera Polo.
The results of the competition and the
proceedings of the conference held in
Berlin in March 1999 were published
in *ANY*, no 19/20 (September 1997).

refined sculptures that have little to do with the digital experiments being made by the latest generation for whom complex forms are not preconceived – as if they were Platonic forms – but the result of interrelations involving the user and context.

During this period Peter Eisenman, undoubtedly influenced by the work of Greg Lynn, was attempting to identify new techniques of design based on a reflection on the instruments offered by the digital revolution. In his projects for the United Nations Library in Geneva (1995) and the Virtual House (1997),[85] Eisenman defined a method in which the architect does not act directly to create form, but manipulates the parameters that determine it. To this end, using a grid that is later deformed, he activated a fixed number of external forces, or attractors, each of which, in turn, can be related to context – for example the force of the wind, the importance of a certain exposure or a line of communication. By varying the influence of the attractors – it does not matter if this is based on

scientific reasoning, symbolism or an entirely arbitrary approach – he modifies the form of the building that is thus determined completely by these external factors and no longer by internal principles of function.

What is more, by using an approach that makes little distinction between the natural and metropolitan landscape, Eisenman continues to experiment with techniques of composition borrowed from digital culture, such as layering (working in overlapping layers), scaling (working with shifts in scale), folding, warping and morphing (the deformation of surfaces and volumes). This process led to the design of numerous interesting projects, one of the most significant being the cultural centre in Santiago de Compostela, Spain, begun in 1999. The building is designed at the scale of the landscape, almost mixing with the contour lines based on an articulation of geometries that result from a reading of the site.

**Steven Holl, Sarphatistraat
Offices, Amsterdam, The
Netherlands, 1996–2000:
exterior view.**

The building is clad in perforated steel. The different – though consistently blurred – colours of the wall and the lights behind the facade give the building a vague and variable luminosity, similar to an Impressionist painting.

**Steven Holl, Kiasma Museum, Helsinki, Finland, 1993–8: exterior view.**

The form of the museum is the result of the inversion of circulation paths, based on the same processes used by the optical nerves that connect the right eye with the left hemisphere of the brain, and vice versa.

Finally, this line of research is flanked by the neo-phenomenological work of Steven Holl who, during this period, began to move in a clearly naturalistic direction. After the Kiasma Museum in Helsinki (1993–8), whose form is based on a metaphor suggested by the human body – the inversion of optical nerves that overlap one another to reach the opposite hemisphere of the brain – in the Sarphatistraat Offices in Amsterdam (1996–2000) he uses a perforated metal screen to cover the concrete finish, which is also treated with blocks of different colours and chromatic intensity. The resulting building shimmers in the light and produces a sensation of visual instability, reminiscent of Impressionist paintings from the second half of the 19th century and the early 20th century, in particular the *Waterlilies* by Claude Monet.[86] The use of light and colour ensures that the building becomes an integral part of its surrounding environment.

## 3.10 A New Avant-Garde

Thanks to the projects completed at the end of the last century, the research of more innovative architects began to respond to the perplexities of conservative critics, meeting with an almost unlimited success, reinforced by the growing attention of magazines.[87]

It is the realm of digital and blob architecture – or, in the acute irony of Kurt Andersen, 'post-Bilbao blobitecture'[88] – that appears to generate the most important novelties, in particular the experiments of Greg Lynn who, unlike so many other architects fascinated by new forms, independently of their structural coherence, attempted to use the computer to retrace the dynamic forms of living organisms.

Despite the disappointing results of the Presbyterian

86 Claude Monet (1840–1926), after initiating Impressionism in 1872 with his painting *Impression: Sunrise* (shown at the first group show of the Impressionists in 1874), painted the *Waterlilies* series between 1909 and 1926.

87 In December 1999 *L'architecture d'aujourd'hui* published five ways to be or not to be modern. In the same month *The Architectural Review* published a similar issue, entitled 'Emerging Architecture'. In the US, *Architectural Record* entitled its issue 'The Millennium. Future to Come'; while the Italian *Casabella*, for decades cautious of the avant-garde, dedicated its end-of-the-millennium issue to the 'USA, architettura come spettacolo' [Architecture as Spectacle]. Its essays took a step back from the so-called

world of images, while presenting the research of Gehry, Douglas Garofalo (born 1958), Lynn, Michael Mcinturf, NBBJ, Diller + Scofidio and Asymptote – reinforcing, if not exalting this idea. The monthly *Domus* dedicated its January 2000 issue to blob architecture, publishing projects by Greg Lynn, Kolatan/MacDonald, dECOi, OCEAN NORTH, NOX and Karl S Chu.

88 Kurt Andersen, 'The Future', in *Architectural Record*, no 12 (December 1999), p 86.

89 The three offices worked from three different cities: Greg Lynn FORM in New York, Michael Mcinturf Architects in Cincinnati and Garofalo Architects in Chicago.
90 Including: *Folds, Bodies and Blobs: Collected Essays*, La Lettre volée (Brussels), 1998, and *Animate Form*, Princeton Architectural Press (New York), 1999.
91 From 'Greg Lynn: Manufactured Houses', in *Architectural Record*, no 12 (December 1999), p 105.
92 ibid, p 108.

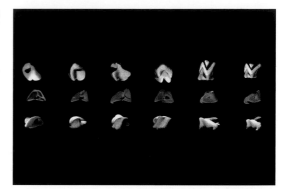

Church of New York (1995–9), a building he designed in long-distance collaboration with Michael Mcinturf and Douglas Garofalo,[89] the approach taken by Lynn appeared fertile enough that a 2000 issue of *Time* magazine listed him as one of 100 possible innovators of the future. To support his design hypotheses he produced numerous fascinating installations and publications,[90] illustrated by his captivating renderings.

In 2000 Lynn, together with Asymptote, was invited to represent the United States at the Venice Biennale. For the occasion he proposed a laboratory involving students from Columbia University, to define what he called the Embryological House. The idea was that of creating a dwelling based on the same criteria used to produce Nike shoes or Ford automobiles: 'The trend in many industries,' Lynn explained, 'is to use *flexible manufacturing* in which computerised machines can make a range of components.'[91] The house was constructed using double-curved aluminium panels, supported by a steel and aluminium structure. The fact that the panels could vary in terms of form and dimensions made it possible for the house to assume different shapes, as if it were a moving or growing organism. Lynn went on to say: 'If you design a seed, you can grow endless variations from it. But all of the information needed for any variation is encoded in the original.'[92] However, the objective revealed itself to be too complicated and the house, based on the prototype and planned for 2003, was never put into production.

The work of Asymptote can be placed along a cyber-platonic line, focused on the creation of forms in which the virtual and the real come together. We can mention, as an example, the Virtual Guggenheim Project (1999), where the information available online is rendered concrete, spatially represented in the form of architectural images while, vice versa, the real spaces of the museums managed by the Foundation were converted into virtual, online models. The group also designed the Technology Culture Museum located on the East River's Piers 9 and 11 in Manhattan, a project

**Asymptote, The Advanced Trading Floor Operations Centre in the New York Stock Exchange, USA, 1999.**

One of the many possibilities offered by the digital revolution is that of blurring the boundaries between real and virtual space. In this project the information from the Stock Exchange is materialised into spatial forms.

**Greg Lynn, Embryological House, 1998–2000: project.**

The Embryological House was designed to evolve based on a programme similar to the genetics that allow living beings to modify themselves in relation to their environment. Though production was planned for 2003, the houses have yet to become a reality.

**Reiser+Umemoto, West Side Masterplan, New York, USA, 1999: project.**

The forms obtained by the use of complex geometries can be adapted, better than their Euclidian counterparts, to the complex morphologies of urban space.

with wrapping forms and an interior filled with ramps that offer views of the works on display from unusual vantage points. Unlike a traditional structure, this museum is interactive and spatially flexible, both in plan and elevation: the floor of the exhibition area, for example, can disappear, revealing a large pool of water, while the ramp above can be reconfigured.

Other American protagonists, both native and by adoption, who began to work with the blob or, in any case, with complex geometries, include Kolatan/MacDonald, Karl S Chu,[93] Nonchi Wang,[94] Reiser + Umemoto,[95] Preston Scott Cohen and Ammar Eloueini.[96] The latter produced projects enlivened by a play of light filtered through subtle screens. Given that these installations were located in protected environments, such as theatres, commercial spaces or museums, they were built of lightweight and ephemeral materials that well describe, in figurative terms, the tension between the immateriality – of light, design and movement in space – and the concrete qualities of the body.

93 Karl S Chu (born 1950) completed his Master studies at the Cranbrook Academy of Art in 1984. He is a professor at the Southern California Institute of Architecture and founder of X Kavya, based in Los Angeles.
94 Nonchi Wang, after graduating from the Tunghai University in Taichung, Taiwan in 1981, went on to complete his Master studies at Yale University, graduating in 1987. He founded amphibian Arc in 1993.

95 Jesse Reiser (born 1958) and Nanako Umemoto founded the New York-based office Reiser + Umemoto in 1986.
96 Ammar Eloueini (born 1968) founded AEDS (Ammar Eloueini Digit–all Studio) in 1997.

**Greg Lynn, Douglas Garofalo, Michael Mcinturf, Presbyterian Church, New York, USA, 1995–9: exterior view.**

Designed in three different cities by three different architects researching blob forms, this church demonstrates the difficulties encountered when ideas must be converted into practice.

**Alsop & Stormer, Peckham Library, London, England, 1995–2000: exterior view.**

The building is supported on slender pilotis, freeing up the ground plane for public activities. The playful and unusual forms and the uninhibited use of colour are part of Will Alsop's strategy of producing vibrant objects with rich and vital energy.

**SHoP, Dunescape Installation at PS1, New York, USA, 2000.**

This project, a temporary installation at PS1 of an artificial landscape, was designed using the computer, and constructed of wooden slats. It belongs to a branch of research pursued by those who build complex forms using simple and economic systems of production and assembly.

To complete the panorama, we can briefly mention the work of the transnational offices OCEAN NORTH[97] and UFO.[98] They represent a new and interesting phenomenon that is the result of the aggregation of young professionals who met their partners while attending foreign study programmes at such schools as the Architectural Association in London, the Berlage Institute in Rotterdam or New York's Columbia University. UFO, with its offices in London, Korea and Italy, gained attention with its competition-winning entry for the new Sarajevo Concert Hall in Bosnia-Herzegovina (1999). The fluid interiors of the project are almost entirely below ground, in order to respect the morphology of the site.

97 OCEAN NORTH has offices in Frankfurt, London, Oslo and Rome. Its members include Achim Menges (born 1975), Michael Hensel (born 1965), Birger Sevaldson (born 1953), Steinar Killi, Andrea Di Stefano and Aleksandra Jaeschke. Kivi Sotamaa (born 1971) and Tuuli Sotamaa (born 1974), Finnish architects whose work varies between the search for new geometries and the organic inheritances of Alvar Aalto, were also founding members of OCEAN NORTH, but have practised independently as Sotamaa Design since 2005–6.

98 Urban Future Organization (UFO) was founded in London in 1996 as a collective of self-organised architectural practices who share common design strategies. Its members are: Andrew Wai-Tat Yau (born 1970), Claudio Lucchesi (born 1966), Denis Balent (born 1970), Steve Hardy (born 1970), Jonas Lundberg (born 1970), Kia Larsdotter (born 1974), Andrei Martin (born 1975), Eduardo de Oliveira Barata (born 1977), Dirk Anderson (born 1977), Jung Mook Moon (born 1968), Theodoros Kanellopoulos (born 1975), Francesco Giordano (born 1964), Zlatko Haban (born 1978) and Jackie Yan (born 1974).

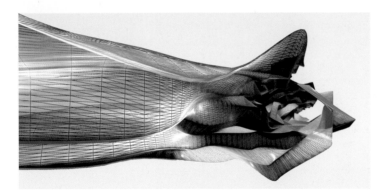

**Karl S Chu, X_Phylox project, 1999: drawing.**

Chu uses the computer to investigate spaces that are beyond our normal understanding. His complex drawings, accompanied by often-hermetic writings, are dense with scientific and philosophical references.

## 3.11 Landscapes or Aesthetic Objects?

For many architects a reflection on the theme of the landscape does not necessarily lead to a new aesthetic of innovative and complex forms. In reality, many architects, who still feel strong ties to the Modern Movement and a distance from the experiments of the avant-garde, see the research into the integration between architecture and the landscape, urban or rural, as the antidote to an excessive aestheticisation of the practice of architecture and, above all, as the means to avoiding the creation of sculptural objects that are extraneous to their context.

This, for example, is the critical view taken by Kenneth Frampton who, in an interview with Günther Uhlig, says: 'I think perhaps that landscape is of greater importance than architecture. I personally think that the landscape should be given greater emphasis in architecture schools. Architecture as the cultivation of the landscape seems to me what ought to be about at the end of the century and not the creation of endless aesthetics objects.'[99] When asked about the success of the 'Un-Private House', he juxtaposes the issues faced by the architects invited to participate in the MoMA exhibition against 'the concerns of critical architects such as Alvaro Siza or Tadao Ando who are by no means deluded about continuing the project of the Enlightenment but who at the same time assume a certain responsibility for the cultivation of the landscape and the integration of their works to the ground.'[100]

The relationship pursued by Álvaro Siza with the landscape is the result of a decomposition resulting from a plastic reflection on Cubism – Siza is also a

99 Kenneth Frampton in conversation with Günther Uhlig, 'Towards a Second Modernity', in *Domus*, no 821 (December 1999), p 21.
100 ibid, p 20.

**Rafael Moneo, Kursaal Auditorium, San Sebastian, Spain, 1990–9: exterior view.**

In this project, characterised by the use of lightweight and transparent materials, Moneo appears to be testing a new approach that brings him closer to more experimental contemporary research.

101 Relative to this theme, William
JK Curtis states: 'The fragmentations
and erosions in Siza's buildings have
a poignant aspect that has to do with
the passage of time and the sense
that all buildings are but temporary
traces on an old landscape.' William
Curtis, 'An Architecture of Edges', in *El
Croquis*, no 68–9 (1994), p 33.

sculptor – and a reflection on the necessity of offering sites a lasting and non-ephemeral sign[101] and, finally, a rereading of the organic tradition, in particular the work of Alvar Aalto. The difference is that while the latter refers to the Nordic atmosphere and its materials, first and foremost wood, Siza seeks instead to capture that of the Mediterranean. This results in a prevalence of white plaster and a more defensive approach to sunlight – which, in Southern Europe, is decidedly more intense. Siza's University Library in Aveiro, Portugal (1988–94) hints at the lessons of the Finnish master in the slight curve of the volume and the spatial qualities of the multistorey reading room, lit from above by skylights. Traces can also be found in two other important works – the Serralves Foundation in Porto, Portugal (1991–9) and the Faculty of Science and Information in Santiago de Compostela, Spain (1993–9), both of which play with a plastic articulation of the exterior volumes and the dynamic qualities of the interior spaces: the former with a compact plan that frays at the edges, opening towards a complex internal patio, while the latter

is based on a comb-like plan that opens towards the surrounding landscape. The Portuguese Pavilion at Expo '98 in Lisbon, with its monumental forms that recall the architecture of the Fascist period, is partially offset by the lightness of the roof that covers the open-air plaza. The significant engineering issues raised by its 60 x 85-metre span were resolved in collaboration with Arup Engineering (the interiors of the pavilion were entrusted to Eduardo Souto de Moura[102]). An openness towards the landscape can also be found in the Santa Maria Church in the Marco de Canavezes district of Porto, Portugal (1990–7), where the long window creates a relationship between the external and natural world and the interior space dedicated to prayer. We can also mention the anachronistic – for its forms that recall colonial architecture – University Rectorate in Alicante, Spain (1995–8), with its courtyard of porticoes reminiscent of some historical parade ground.

Even the Japanese architect Tadao Ando raises some opposition to the kaleidoscope of images of new

102 Eduardo Souto de Moura (born
1952), after working from 1974 to
1979, went on to graduate in 1980
from the School of Fine Arts in Porto.

**103** In all his buildings, Louis Kahn (1901–74) allowed void spaces to predominate. In the Salk Institute in La Jolla, California (1959–65), for example, it is the space of the central plaza that initiates a silent dialogue with the ocean it overlooks.

architecture and metropolitan chaos by proposing a cold, though intense, Minimalism based on the contrast between nature, matter (with a preference for concrete) and light that very closely resembles the poetics of silence of Louis Kahn.[103] The resulting works of architecture are not very welcoming or inhabitable and comfort is replaced by contemplation. The projects play, by creating a precarious equilibrium, with couples of opposites, such as the relationship between interior and exterior, between abstraction and figuration, part and whole, and simplicity and complexity. Ando has stated that his primary sources of inspiration are Piranesi and Albers,[104] citing two antithetical figures: the first was attracted by the glories and remnants of history, inspiring a concept of the landscape obsessed with the memory of classicism, while the second extends towards geometric abstraction and simplification.

This Minimalist rigour is clearly displayed in the new headquarters for Giorgio Armani, the Teatro Armani in Milan, Italy, completed in 2001.

The landscape dimension of Piranesi can be found, instead, in the Benetton Research Centre in Treviso, also in Italy (1992–2000), where Ando is overtaken by a nostalgia for classicism, demonstrated in sequential rows of columns in reinforced concrete, evocative of archaeological remains.

The neo-Piranesian search for geometries that decompose as part of a convulsive dialectic which oscillates between order and disorder can be found in the Awaji-Yumebutai International Conference Center in Tsuna-gun, Hyogo, Japan, completed in 2001. This modern Hadrian's Villa hangs in the balance between the abstraction of forms and the citation of exotic works of architecture, with its fascinating play of terraces topped by flowers that vaguely recall the atmospheres of India.

Working along lines similar to those pursued by Álvaro Siza we find the work of Rafael Moneo, the designer of the National Museum of Roman Art in Mérida, Spain

**104** Tadao Ando, 'Représentation et abstraction', in *L'architecture d'aujourd'hui*, no 255 (February 1988).

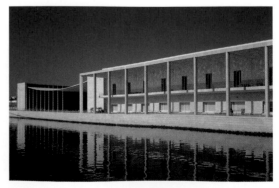

**Álvaro Siza, Portuguese Pavilion for Expo '98, Lisbon, Portugal: exterior view.**

The Portuguese Pavilion for Expo '98 is composed of two monumental volumes, similar to Italian neo-Rationalist buildings constructed during the Fascist period. The two volumes are connected by a lightweight concrete roof that is similar to a tent.

**Tod Williams, Billie Tsien, Williams Natatorium, Cranbrook, Bloomfield Hills, Michigan, USA, 1995–2000: interior view.**

An attention to materials and light characterises the work of Tod Williams and Billie Tsien. This can be seen, for example, in the treatment of the walls and roof in the pool.

(1980–6) mentioned elsewhere in this text, a building that does not hesitate to refer to themes of Roman spatiality, wrapping them with flat, brick-clad arches. The master of many contemporary Spanish architects, with whom he shared a golden era in late-1980s Spain, and professor at many important universities – from Lausanne to Harvard, where he was Chairman of the Architecture Department from 1985 to 1990 – Moneo has always managed to avoid the opposition between experimentation and tradition. He has done this in the name of an aesthetic tied to the inheritances of Modernism, though open to and accepting of new input.

This leads to the denial of any personal approach and the search for a design quality that goes beyond the power of the image. There is also a certain eclecticism, not without its nostalgia for the architecture of the past, that leads him to design very different buildings. His more contextual works include the block that contains the House of Culture in Don Benito (1991–7) and the Murcia City Hall (1991–8), both in Spain. The first features a brilliant corner resolution, the play of openings and changes in colour. The second is notable for its elevations: the main facade is clad in rhythmically perforated local stone, vaguely reminiscent of the

Italian constructions of the Fascist period. A more contemporary image can be found in the Auditorium and Conference Centre in San Sebastian, Spain (1990–9), two irregular and transparent sloping volumes, which perhaps owe something to the work of Herzog & de Meuron. His Moderna Museet (Museum for Modern Art) in Stockholm (1990–8) is a successful insertion within a landscape marked by the presence of natural and historical elements, and the Gregorio Marañón Hospital in Madrid (1996–2003), a block dropped into the urban structure of the Spanish capital, likewise demonstrates Moneo's ability to work with context. His Museum of Fine Arts in Houston, Texas (1992–2000), a box enlivened by a few well-placed cuts, and the Cathedral of Our Lady of the Angels in Los Angeles (1996–2002), a rhetorical and out-of-scale structure, demonstrate the limits of an attitude that often approaches the urban landscape in a monumental and classicist manner.

# 3.12 Aesthetics, Ethics and Mutations

The direction of the seventh Venice Architecture Biennale was entrusted to Massimiliano Fuksas,[105] who chose the provocative title 'Less Aesthetics, More Ethics'. To underline the marginal role played by architecture in contemporary urban phenomena, as well as the danger of its definitive shelving, he prepared a giant megascreen[106] for the event that displayed, in a sequence of images as chaotic as it was effective, the countless problems faced by a global metropolis. For Fuksas: 'Self-referential works of architecture, with their gaze permanently on the past, are no longer of any interest:

105 The decision to nominate Massimiliano Fuksas also contributed to the rejuvenation of Italian architecture that, at the time, was suffering from a heavy inheritance of Post-Modernism and historicism. I attempted to reconstruct the architectural climate in Italy during this period in: Luigi Prestinenza Puglisi, 'Complexity and Contradiction: The Italian Architectural Landscape', in 'Italy: A New Architectural Landscape', *Architectural Design*, no 187 (May/June 2007), pp 6–18.

106 The screen, designed by Massimiliano Fuksas and Doriana Mandrelli in collaboration with RaiSat and Studio Azzurro, was over 280 metres long, occupying the entire wall of the Corderie, one of the buildings that host the Biennale.

**107** Massimiliano Fuksas, 'Less Aesthetics, More Ethics', from the exhibition catalogue *Less Aesthetics, More
Ethics*, Marsilio (Padua), 2000, p 13.

we all live along a borderline, with continuous crossings and incursions.'[107] In such a difficult and contradictory world, it no longer made any sense to imagine a resolution to problems that made recourse to formalisms, attractive styles or sophisticated architectural languages.

What was necessary, instead, was a new aesthetic that, overcoming nostalgias and classicisms, is capable of looking at phenomena as they are, capturing their energy and unexpressed potential, and accepting their contradictions. 'The URBAN MILITARY MODEL, with its plan and planning, cannot resist against the energy of a magma in continuous mutation. Any rigid structure will explode into a thousand pieces: only those who have the intelligence to change together will survive. Drawing energy, and emitting it.'[108] This results in the acceptance of experimentation and innovation, against tradition and the academic approach. Using this key,

we can examine the exclusion of numerous architects from the exhibition and the euphoria of those invited to participate, above all the younger generation; a euphoria that could also be found in the national pavilions of those countries that shared the choices made by the exhibition's Italian director. First and foremost there were the Americans who, as we have seen, called upon two young professors from Columbia University, Hani Rashid and Greg Lynn, entrusting them with the responsibility of running an experimental workshop to examine new technologies.

By highlighting the contradictions and, together, the opportunities offered by metropolitan realities, Fuksas focused attention on a theme that had been interesting a growing number of critics and architects for some time. If it is true, as Kurt Andersen observed, that many architects from the newest generation proved themselves to be allergic to social and political involvement,[109] it is also true that during this time, and in many places, we acquired an understanding of the

**108** ibid, p 16.

**109** 'We are Reaganites now – we all pretty much accept the ultra capitalist circumstance, and any kind of squishy socialist utopian notion is off the table right now.' Kurt Andersen, 'The Future', in *Architectural Record*, no 12 (December 1999), p 86.

fact that the city had been transformed and that if we wished to act within it, it must be studied and analysed from new and more effective points of view.

On 24 November 2000, the Arc en rêve centre d'architecture in Bordeaux inaugurated an exhibition emblematically entitled 'Mutations'.[110] The show was curated by, amongst others, Rem Koolhaas, Stefano Boeri[111] and Sanford Kwinter.[112] The first presented the work that he had been carrying out for some years with his students at the Harvard Design School, focusing on urban realties in China and Nigeria, in addition to the impact of shopping on the contemporary city. Stefano Boeri presented the work of the Multiplicity in USE (Uncertain States of Europe) research group, investigating the profound changes that globalisation is causing in cities as different as Mazara del Vallo, Belgrade, Pristina and San Marino. Stanford Kwinter dealt with changes to American cities and, in particular, Houston, a metropolis that was historically averse to constrictions of urban planning.

The images that accompanied the exhibition were primarily statistics, diagrams and a significant number of photographs by well-known photographers, including the Italian Francesco Jodice. The objective was that of demonstrating that the world – as stated on the last page of the exhibition catalogue, covered with the large text WORLD=CITY – will tend more and more to resemble a city. Numerous clichés keep us from seeing it as it really is and understanding its development. This results in the necessity of organising alternative and targeted strategies, even if they are programmatically partial, focused on substituting the traditional urban masterplan with bigness, the urban landscape, diagrammatic techniques and other instruments defined by recent architectural research.

........................................................................................................................................

**110** The show closed in March 2001. The catalogue, published in English, French and Spanish, is: Rem Koolhaas, Stefano Boeri, Sanford Kwinter, Daniela Fabricius, Hans Ulrich Obrist and Nadia Tazi, *Mutations*, Actar and Arc en rêve centre d'architecture (Barcelona), 2000.

**111** Stefano Boeri (born 1956) runs the Milan design firm Boeri Studio and co-founded the interdisciplinary research group Multiplicity, which explores issues of urban transformation. He was editor-in-chief of *Domus* from 2004 to March 2007, since which time he has been editor of *Abitare*.

**112** Sanford Kwinter is a writer and editor based in New York and is associate professor at the School of Architecture at Rice University. He was a cofounder of Zone Books, with Jonathan Crary and Bruce Mau, and also founded the content and communications design firm Studio !KASAM.

## 3.13 The Eleventh of September Two Thousand and One

Both 'Less Aesthetics, More Ethics' and 'Mutations', even if still far from the hyper-problematic and often pessimistic attitude that would plague the years to come, marked an inversion in the trend with respect to the first and second halves of the 1990s, when the complexity of the world was counterbalanced by an almost unlimited faith in the liberating powers of art, science and the digital revolution. It was still a time when the experience of Bilbao[113] – a city on the verge of bankruptcy saved by the regenerative powers of cultural innovation in the name of globalisation – appeared to be the exemplification of a method that could be easily copied.

This cycle ended with an economic crisis, following the collapse of the bubble created on the stock market by the listing of shares in new economies – companies that bet everything on the Internet – many of which lost over 90 per cent of their listed value. This was the end of a golden era that, supported by financial markets in the midst of a speculative boom, pushed along the economies of the western world and stimulated, with levels of growth in the double digits, those of emerging countries – India and China in particular.

A series of scandals shook the world's faith in the system when it was discovered that many companies had falsified their budgets, listing, with the complicity of banking institutions, junk titles that fooled many investors. At the same time journalistic investigations began to reveal that globalisation concealed new and intolerable forms of slavery, implemented through the

113 There were many who spoke of the Bilbao effect, including John Rajchman, 'Effetto Bilbao', in *Casabella*, no 673/674 (December 1999/January 2000), pp 10–11.

114 The first books of warning included: Naomi Klein, *No Logo: Taking Aim at the Brand Bullies*, Picador (New York) and Flamingo (London), 2000 – a journalistic investigation translated into numerous languages that obtained an extraordinary success in terms of sales.

delocalisation of manufacturing to parts of the world whose labour forces were not governed by any union rules.[114]

Technology – fostered by the Internet, low-cost flights and real-time communications, one of the primary motors of development and change[115] – was now looked upon with fear. The warnings of a growing climate of suspicion towards the digital world was the panic – which turned out to be unfounded – of a collapse of the information system caused by the so-called Millennium Bug (the anticipated failure of a computer's internal clock to process the number 2000). There was also a call for the 'slow', required by the senses to mitigate against the 'fast', imposed by electronic interaction. Finally, there was the success of apocalyptic writers and thinkers, such as the architect and philosopher Paul Virilio,[116] who looked at progress in catastrophic terms.

The definitive blow to the entire system of values came on 11 September 2001 when two aeroplanes were hijacked and piloted by Islamic terrorists in a suicide attack against the Twin Towers in New York, which were completely destroyed. A third aeroplane hit another building-symbol: The Pentagon.

Markets around the globe, for months on the downturn, had such a violent reaction that the entire world, only a few days after the attacks, held its breath and waited for the reopening of the New York Stock Exchange, fearing that, together with a collapse in shares, they would be witnessing the collapse of the entire Western economy.

Faith in globalisation, in the creative and problem-solving power of innovation seemed to have definitively disappeared. We discovered, after years of hope and optimism, that not only was the world a complex place, but it was also impervious to reason, or at least this is how it appeared. It also became clear that Western culture was not so easy to export and that, while the tools of the digital revolution were capable of reducing

115 Of the many books that, with a great deal of clarity, sought to analyse the relationships between new technologies and new forms of dwelling, I mention: William J Mitchell, *City of Bits: Space, Place, and the Infobahn*, The MIT Press (Cambridge, MA and London), 1995; and William J Mitchell, *e-topia: 'Urban Life, Jim – But Not As We Know It'*, The MIT Press (Cambridge, MA and London), 1999

116 Paul Virilio (born 1932) has been studying the relationship between architecture, technology and power since 1958 when he completed an investigation of the Atlantic Wall, the 15,000 German bunkers located along the Atlantic shoreline. With the development of information technologies, he became interested in the ties between vision, aesthetics, speed, politics and catastrophic events. His books include *The Aesthetics of Disappearance*, Semiotext(e) (New York), 1991, and *The Vision Machine*, British Film Institute (London), 1994 and Indiana University Press (Bloomington and Indianapolis), 1995.

the number of problems, by speeding up processes they generated new ones, multiplying them and creating, above all, immense levels of resentment in those who were excluded. Further complicating this situation was the extreme reaction of the Americans, who declared war on terrorism in Afghanistan and, successively, in Iraq. A phase of expansion was replaced by a phase of implosion, where the new technologies that were to have liberated mankind were progressively used for military and repressive functions. This could not help but provoke reconsiderations and new questions, even in the field of architectural research. The warnings – not without a certain aesthetic self-indulgence – launched by 'Less Aesthetics, More Ethics' and 'Mutations', now appeared to be prophetic, if for nothing else, for having indicated the need for a radical change in direction.

## 3.14 Starting Over

The years between 1998 and 2001 present an interesting parallel with those between 1926 and 1932. Both can be referred to as heroic periods in the history of architecture that produced works of extraordinary interest, not to mention a considerable number of true masterpieces.[117] Each of these periods was directed by architects working within avant-garde movements, crowning over a decade of research and investigation. Their creativity was stimulated by a fervid social and cultural context, in burning acceleration and driven, in one case, by the mechanical revolution and, in the other, by its digital counterpart.

117 Of the masterpieces from the period between 1926 and 1932, here we mention: the Bauhaus Building in Dessau (1925–6) by Gropius and Meyer; Le Corbusier's Villa Savoye in Poissy (1928–31); the Weissenhofsiedlung in Stuttgart (1927), directed by Mies van der Rohe; the German Pavilion at Barcelona (1929) and the Tugendhat House in Brno (1929–30), both designed by Mies; the Zonnestraal Sanatorium in Hilversum (1926–8) by Jan Duiker (1890–1935); and the Maison de Verre in Paris (1927–31) by Chareau and Bijvoet.

In short, the imperative of the standard and that of the individual.

The completion, during both periods, of formally mature and technically convincing works contributed to the success not only of their authors, who became the recognised protagonists of an international movement, but of the very movement that they represented. This had immediate repercussions, in terms of emulation, on the younger generations, resulting in the diffusion of a new aesthetic approach. However, this success also marked the end of the heroic period, and the beginnings of a stylistic routine that did not hesitate to make use of a-critical repetition and pre-packaged formulas. In fact, the baptism of the International Style in 1932 finds a parallel in the beginning of the Star System in 2001. In both cases the aesthetic certainties acquired were placed in a state of crisis by historical events – for the former by the rise and/or consolidation of important dictatorships (Hitler, Stalin and Mussolini), and for the latter by the global turbulence (the wars in Afghanistan and Iraq) that followed in the wake of the attacks on 11 September 2001. Euphoria was replaced by anxiety, exposing the contradictions, retreats and setbacks. At the same time we were witness to the discovery of original and unexplored fields of research.

How should we start over? Undoubtedly – as we will see in the next chapter – we can refer to the new ethical awareness that emerged from the ruins of the attacks and wars, together with a new relationship with nature, convincingly defined between 1998 and 2001, from an important plurality of viewpoints and within the most vital fields of research.

**Daniel Libeskind, Project for Ground Zero, New York, USA, 2002: rendering of the view from the harbour.**

Libeskind's Freedom Tower represents an ideal connection with the Statue of Liberty, becoming its modern transposition. The height of 1,776 feet (541 metres) recalls the date of American Independence.

## 4.1 The World Trade Center

'Let me put my cards on the table. It's important to me that the spire is shaped in a way that recalls the Statue of Liberty. And I want the tower to be 1,776 feet high, so the building stands for something substantive, the Declaration of Independence. In the end, this is what matters to me.'[1]

With these words, as he tells us in his biography, Daniel Libeskind, recently named the winner of the competition for the masterplan for the World Trade Center, defended his project in front of David M Childs,[2] the director of SOM, that architect selected by the developer Larry Silverstein, and the figure responsible for Libeskind's removal from the job. It is interesting to note that by underlining the symbolic aspects of his architectural design, Libeskind manages to expose Childs' simpler, and more commercial, concerns.

The symbolic nature of the terrorist attack on the Twin Towers must be countered with an equally symbolic, though less forceful, gesture, something that can be achieved only by focusing on the higher values of American civilisation: its openness towards foreigners in search of a better future and the culture of freedom.

Of the various participants in the competition for the reconstruction of the World Trade Center, Libeskind was most successful in translating this concept into form, as demonstrated in a rendering of the new Freedom Tower, a twin sister for the Statue of Liberty, the first image encountered by immigrants arriving in America.

The competition, held in September 2002, was anything but simple, due to the complexity of the related themes: an emotional and symbolic component, significant economic interests, the intricacy of such a delicate urban area in the heart of Manhattan, and con-

1 Daniel Libeskind, *Breaking Ground: Adventures in Life and Architecture*, John Murray Publishers (London) and Riverhead Books (New York), 2004, p 248.
2 David M Childs (born 1941) is a Consulting Design Partner in Skidmore, Owings & Merrill, having joined the firm in 1971. He was appointed Chairman of the Commission of Fine Arts by George W Bush in 2003.

3 Composed of: Shigeru Ban (Tokyo, Japan), Frederic Schwartz (New York), Ken Smith (New York), Rafael Viñoly (New York) with ARUP (New York), Buro Happold Engineers (Bath, England), Jörg Schlaich (Stuttgart, Germany; born 1934), William Moorish (Charlottesville, VA; born 1948), David Rockwell (New York) and Janet Marie Smith (Baltimore, MD).

4 The United Architects group brought together six architectural offices known for their avant-garde work: Foreign Office Architects (London); Imaginary Forces (New York and Los Angeles); Kevin Kennon Architects (New York); Reiser + Umemoto (New York); UNStudio, Ben van Berkel and Caroline Bos (Amsterdam) ; and Greg Lynn FORM (Los Angeles).

5 Composed of: SOM (Chicago; New York; San Francisco; Los Angeles; Washington DC; Hong Kong; Shanghai; and Brussels); Field Operations (New York); Tom Leader (Berkeley, CA); Michael Maltzan (Los Angeles); Neutelings Riedijk (Rotterdam, The Netherlands); and SANAA (Tokyo, Japan) – together with artists Iñigo Manglano-Ovalle, Rita McBride, Jessica Stockholder and Elyn Zimmerman.

siderations related to the future and issues of security. Of the over 400 aspiring participants, the other selected participants were: Foster & Partners; THINK group, directed by Rafael Viñoly;[3] United Architects;[4] Peterson/Littenberg Architecture; a consortium led by Roger Duffy of Skidmore, Owings & Merrill (SOM);[5] and, finally, an association between Richard Meier, Peter Eisenman, Charles Gwathmey and Steven Holl, baptised by some as the Dream Team, and by others as the New York 4.

The choice of the seven design teams – made by New Visions, a group of 21 architects, engineers, urban planners and landscape experts – was a very balanced representation of architectural trends: one exponent of Deconstructivism (Libeskind) and one of High Tech (Foster); top architects from the New York scene (the Dream Team); representatives of the new 'blob' generation (United Architects); two important professional groups (SOM and THINK); and, finally, architects sensitive to New Urbanism and the theories of Leon Krier and Prince Charles (Peterson/Littenberg).

The projects were presented to the public from December 2002 to February 2003 in the Winter Garden of the World Financial Center, drawing over 80,000 visitors, who left over 10,000 comments. The website set up by the Lower Manhattan Development Corporation (LMDC) received over 8 million hits. The popular imagination went into overdrive in attempting to give each project a nickname: 'The Kissing One' (Foster), 'Tic-Tac-Toe' (the Dream Team), 'The Skeletons' (THINK) and 'The One with the Circle' (Libeskind).[6] This resulted in an unintentional and pitiless level of rhetoric, combined with a certain formal self-indulgence that the competing architects should have been careful to avoid. The greatest weakness was to be found in the projects by the groups pursuing a more linguistic research: United Architects and the Dream Team.

The project submitted by United Architects featured a semicircle of towers, joined on five floors, separating as they moved upwards. One of them was to have become the world's tallest building. The point of union,

6 Libeskind, *Breaking Ground: Adventures in Life and Architecture*, p 156.

**Daniel Libeskind, Project for Ground Zero, New York, USA, 2002: rendering.**

Alongside the Freedom Tower, Libeskind's project includes smaller towers, located around pools containing the foundations of the collapsed Twin Towers, transforming them into a memorial.

**THINK (Rafael Viñoly and others), Project for Ground Zero, New York, USA, 2002: rendering of the view from the harbour.**

Two empty steel towers house a memorial and spaces dedicated to cultural activities, while the other buildings contain office and commercial spaces.

which began at the 60th floor, created a 'City in the Sky', destined to host commercial activities, cultural and recreational spaces and parks. However, the final result was excessive, oversized and cumbersome, in addition to being difficult to build because it could not be separated into phases.

The Dream Team proposed five towers, each 339 metres high, connected by a series of horizontal structures: a monumental grid that, dense with symbolism and references – first and foremost the grid of Manhattan – was, with a great deal of irony, interpreted by many as a net for capturing aircraft.

A more successful project is that submitted by Foster, who chose to make reference to the Twin Towers by proposing two structures, each 538 metres high, which came together at three points, creating panoramic public spaces to be used for exhibitions and recreational activities. The spaces were to have been planted with trees, making them suspended parks used to purify the

air and provide natural ventilation. To justify his courageous decision to concentrate the building volume in only two structures, Foster cited the possibility of freeing up space at ground level for public use.

Of the three proposals presented by THINK, the most successful was that composed of two empty cages – the Towers of Culture – that recalled the Twin Towers. These void structures contained free-floating spaces for cultural activities: the memorial, the museum, the open-air amphitheatre, the conference centre and a panoramic viewing platform. The building programme was located in nine lower buildings.

The project submitted by Daniel Libeskind, as mentioned, focused on the metaphorical values of the soaring Freedom Tower, in addition to the impact of the overall project, created by introducing four smaller towers: 'This wasn't a stand-alone tower singing solo,' he stated, 'but part of a symphony with the four other towers.'[7] This is partially the result of their placement,

7 ibid, p 248.

The Dream Team (Richard Meier, Peter Eisenman, Charles Gwathmey and Steven Holl), Project for Ground Zero, New York, USA, 2002: rendering of the view from the harbour.

The project is composed of five towers connected by horizontal elements. The result is a grid that recalls the pattern of Manhattan's streets.

designed to allow the passage of light to create a suggestive effect that would commemorate the tragic event every year on 11 September.

Setting aside the project by Foster – the most innovative in urban planning and environmental terms, though difficult to build because it could not be broken down into various phases – we are left with the projects by THINK and Libeskind. In fact, the jury selected these two projects on 1 February 2003. This was followed by two weeks of burning controversy, the taking up of positions, below-the-belt strikes and the unexplainable turncoat actions of a few critics.[8] However, in the end, partially assisted by an event that should not have had any bearing on a purely architectural decision, the project was awarded to Libeskind, who had successfully obtained the support of Governor George Pataki. The jury's decision is a recognition of the clearest project, undoubtedly the most effective in terms of its ability to communicate. There was no shortage of disgruntlement amongst architectural intellectuals, whose primary grudge had to do with the fact that the winning architect was considered, for many reasons, to be an outsider. This, as Paul Goldberger was quick to point out, led to a paradoxical situation: 'Although Libeskind has spent most of his career as an academic, he was now positioned as a populist figure. This may be why, despite his background as an avant-garde architect, he didn't get as much support among the city's artistic and intellectual community as Viñoly did, even though Viñoly, paradoxically, has always been much more a corporate architect.'[9]

Without the support of his most authoritative colleagues[10] and faced with the diktats of the developer Larry Silverstein – who favoured, over the intellectual with little experience, an office with proven operative skills, such as SOM – the project was almost immediately compromised. The new Freedom Tower, designed jointly and not without conflict by the members of the new 'team', was presented in December 2003. Visibly heavier in its proportions, it progressively resembled

8 Including Herbert Muschamp, the *New York Times* critic who, after supporting Libeskind's project ('Studio Libeskind. If you are looking for the marvellous, here's where you can find it.' Herbert Muschamp, 'A Goal for Ground Zero: Finding an Urban Poetry', *The New York Times*, 28 January) during the qualifying phase, went on to attack it ferociously ('aggressive tour de force, a war memorial to a looming conflict that has scarcely begun.' Herbert Muschamp, 'Balancing Reason and Emotion in Twin Towers Void', *The New York Times*, 6 February).
9 Paul Goldberger, 'Eyes On The Prize: The amazing design competition for the World Trade Center site', *The New Yorker*, 10 March 2003.

10 Decisive support, even if bipartisan, was offered to Libeskind by the director of the *Architectural Record*, Robert Ivy, who invited David M Childs and Libeskind to maintain the original force of the winning project, while accepting what was perceived as a 'forced marriage' by the architectural community. Robert Ivy 'Editorial: An Open Letter to David Childs and Daniel Libeskind', *Architectural Record*, no 8 (August 2003).

the corporate buildings designed by large, professional offices around the globe. The myth of the American dream, already found in the rhetoric of the original project, was reinforced by the date chosen for the laying of the cornerstone: 4 July 2004, the feast day of American Independence.

## 4.2 Clouds and Monoliths

Of the numerous pavilions built for the Swiss Expo in 2002,[11] three particular buildings stand out as result of their ability to bring new issues of discussion to the sphere of architecture. They are: the Blur Building, designed by the American duo Diller + Scofidio; the Monolith by Jean Nouvel; and the steel towers by the Austrian architects Coop Himmelb(l)au.

The Blur Building undoubtedly captured the majority of the public and press attention, becoming the symbol of the Expo. This steel structure was placed some 20 metres above the level of the lake, and was composed of a 100-metre-long by 60-metre-wide platform with no function other than that of producing vapour, using a system of 29,000 nozzles that atomised the lake water. The result was a giant cloud, a pure piece of scenography that could be admired from the river's edge, as well as from the inside, by raincoat-clad visitors. 'It's incredible,' Ricardo Scofidio exclaimed, 'the structure that's required to make this nothing.' To build the platform, which cantilevers out from four slender columns, it was necessary to create a steel skeleton based on the principles of 'tensegrity' (tensional integrity) defined by Buckminster Fuller; to realise the cloud and the lighting effects it was necessary to employ complex electronic programs capable of calibrating the emission of water vapour in relation to climatic conditions and the desired effect.

11 The 2002 Swiss Expo was held simultaneously in Biel, Murten, Neuchatel and Yverdon-les-Bains, from 15 May to 15 October.

It would be easy to dismiss this project as a one-off event: 'a building that represents nothing, but a spectacular nothing'.[12] However, this was not the case for many critics, who interpreted this sui generis work as an anticipation of the potential of a form of research that combined nature and technology, interaction and the scale of the landscape, and the poetics of dematerialisation – blurring – that, for some time, was being pursued by many young architects of the digital generation, as well as others, such as Toyo Ito, Peter Eisenman and Coop Himmelb(l)au.[13] At the same time the project also explored new dimensions in the relationship between the body and space: 'entering Blur will be like walking into a habitable medium – one that is featureless, depthless, scaleless, spaceless, massless, surfaceless and contextless. Disorientation is structured into the experience.'[14]

If Diller + Scofidio focused on sensorial disorientation and the dematerialisation of space, or what Ned Cramer un-ironically referred to as 'Gas Architecture',[15] Jean Nouvel, on the other hand, was more interested in the Monolith: a gigantic cube clad in cor-ten steel set in the middle of the lake.

12 Interview between Antonello Marotta and Diller + Scofidio in Antonello Marotta, *Diller + Scofidio: Il teatro della dissolvenza*, Edilstampa (Rome), 2005, p 79.
13 The exhibition 'Blurring Architecture' by Toyo Ito held at the Suermondt-Ludwig-Museum in Aachen, Germany, was later presented, between 1999 and 2001, in Tokyo, Antwerp, and Auckland and Wellington, Australia. The word 'blur' can be found repeatedly in the writings of Peter Eisenman, for

example: Peter Eisenman, *Blurred Zones: Investigations of the Interstitial: Eisenman Architects 1988–1998*, The Monacelli Press (New York), 2003. In 1995 Coop Himmelb(l)au designed a project known as Cloud no 5 for the plaza in front of the UN Headquarters in Geneva, Switzerland.

14 In Ned Cramer, 'Diller + Scofidio's Blur Building for the Swiss Expo '02 in Yverdon-les-Bains', *Architecture* (July 2002), p 58.
15 ibid, p 59: 'And just as Paxton invented Glass Architecture, Diller + Scofidio have given humanity Gas Architecture.'

The monolith designed by Jean
Nouvel is the antithesis of the
Blur: a cube clad in cor-ten steel
that contrasts with the liquid
forms of the surrounding lake
landscape.

It would not be risky to state that the choice made by this French architect – beyond the simple expedient of juxtaposing a monolith and a cloud – represents a precise declaration: an attention to the physical world, the concrete, the tactile, and a distancing from digital interaction and transparency, themes that, furthermore, Nouvel himself had already explored in the Institut du Monde Arabe and the Fondation Cartier. This also required a certain distancing from the research of the avant-garde, coupled with an attitude that, rather than creating problems for the sciences of complexity and non-Euclidian geometries, listened to the ways in which man interacts with the world of objects: using the senses, as part of a physical relationship that is both instinctive and tied to the natural world. In this way Nouvel opposes technological advancement against the inexorable richness of matter, and the impossibility of translating it into binary code.

The towers designed by Coop Himmelb(l)au for the Arteplage in Biel demonstrated the extraordinary plastic skill that had become their hallmark, though without the force – even obtuse and unattractive – that characterised the previous work of this Austrian duo, such as the attic on the Falkestrasse (1983–9). On the one hand this change led to a growing acceptance by the public of architectural compositions once judged unacceptable and, on the other, to the progressive reduction of what was once avant-garde research, to mere formal play.

## 4.3 The Star System

While Kenneth Frampton had already noticed, back in 1993, that 'today there exist *media* architects who divide the most interesting share of projects',[16] from 1997 onwards many governments, in the wake of the success of the Bilbao Guggenheim, made increasingly frequent recourse to

16 From: Gabriella Lo Ricco and Silvia Micheli, *Lo spettacolo dell'architettura*, Bruno Mondadori (Milan), 2003, p 1.

Diller + Scofidio, Blur Building, Swiss Expo, Yverdon-les-Bains, Switzerland, 2002: exterior view.

The Blur is a slender steel structure based on the principles of tensegrity, which produces water vapour. The result is a giant cloud that represents the will of architecture to shed its weight and solidity.

the Star System, aware of the significant benefits, in terms of popularity, of the construction of a building by a famous, brand-name architect.

In truth, their highly iconic buildings have become magnets for tourism and the regeneration of urban areas in serious states of decay, such as abandoned industrial areas, docklands and port areas. We need only mention three examples: Libeskind's Imperial War Museum North (1997–2001) and Michael Wilford's[17] The Lowry (1992–2000), both in Salford Quays, near Manchester, Great Britain; the numerous projects for the requalification of waterfronts in Barcelona, Spain; and, finally, Zaha Hadid's new maritime station and David Chipperfield's judicial buildings in Salerno, Italy (under construction).

This led to the creation of an elite group of architects competing for progressively more important projects.

As with all elite groups and new markets, it also generated numerous conflicts and cheap shots, for those trying to enter the market, and those trying to remain part of it.

For the disenchanted, it is not difficult to imagine that the production of numerous theoretical texts, critical declarations and philosophical references simply concealed brilliant strategies employed by young, and not-so-young, architects who wished to gain access to this restricted circle of professionals, now constantly in the public eye.

Furthermore, the competition for increasingly more important commissions was responsible for the super-production of 'effect-generating' projects and works of architecture-sculpture that tended to stand out from the contexts in which they were built. As Peter Davey pointed out: 'We live in a world permeated by the cult of celebrity and dominated by the electronic media, which demand constant novelty. The more unusual the

17 Michael Wilford (born 1938) joined the London practice of James Stirling in 1960 and was taken into partnership in 1971. He continued the practice as Michael Wilford & Partners after Stirling's death in 1993.

18 Peter Davey, 'Bling, Blobs, Bur-
geoning: Problems of Figure', *The
Architectural Review*, no 1297 (March
2005), p 74.

gesture, the more enhanced an architect's brand. The cult of celebrity has been so successful that most of the limited international competitions are open only to a small group of celebrated architects – perhaps no more than 100 – who are almost forced to become increasingly demonstrative and outré to ensure that they retain their place in the hierarchy of the celebrated.'[18]

The result – similar to that which takes place in the world of automotive design or fashion, where it is becoming more and more difficult to distinguish between an entry-level Fiat or Renault, or a pair of jeans by Dolce & Gabbana or Armani – is that the Star System is responsible for the growing similarity between products. For example, the addition to the Mariinsky Theatre in St Petersburg, Russia (2003), designed by the Minimalist architect Dominique Perrault, recalls previous experiments with complex geometries made by others. Renzo Piano's KPN Telecom Tower in Rotterdam, The Netherlands (1997–2000) experiments with electronic pixels. Herzog & de Meuron's Laban Centre in Deptford, London (1997–2003) integrates their research into materials with an investigation of space that owes much to Rem Koolhaas; while the tectonic Rafael Moneo, in his Kursaal in San Sebastian, Spain (1990–9), explores transparent architecture.

The similarity between the final products, other than being imposed by a market that tends to reiterate a repertoire held to be successful, is also the result of the growing role played by the back office. The stars,

**Renzo Piano, New York Times
Building, New York, USA,
2000–7: view from the street.**

This skyscraper is notable for the dematerialising effect of the ceramic slats used as brises-soleil. To increase the vertical effect they continue beyond the top of the building's volume.

**Renzo Piano, Zentrum Paul Klee, Bern, Switzerland, 1999–2005: exterior view.**

The undulating profile creates a relationship between the museum and the surrounding landscape. As in all Piano's museums, a great deal of attention is given to lighting.

manner of …'. The final works, even those of the highest quality, cannot help but suffer from this growing de-personalisation.

The popularity of the stars, furthermore, inevitably leads to an ambiguous and, in some cases, elusive attitude towards experimentation. The protagonists of architectural debate, in fact, are well aware that without innovation they will soon be superseded by new trends. However, at the same time, they also know that innovation, in order to be commercially successful, must be more form than substance, more spoken than real. In short, it must find space within the general rhetoric of novelty that renders a product commercially viable. Thus their projects tend to express, using a concept, a lifestyle philosophy that is often more aesthetic than concretely pursuable. It becomes a metaphorical projection, a dream, wishful thinking. Their work focuses on the aspects of communication rather than – as in the Modern Movement – on aspects of technique, function and social value.

pressed by obligations of publicity and promotion, dedicate less and less time to designing: in some cases limiting themselves to the development of the concept, carrying out only the most generic control. The resulting projects are, in reality, the work of partners or, even more often, young assistants trained in university and post-university faculties, imbibed with an eclectic sprit and invited to come and design 'in the

This dynamic not only applies to architecture but, as highlighted by Yves Michaud in his book *L'art à l'état gazeux*,[19] also affects the other arts. So much so that today it is difficult to distinguish between performances by different artists – for example Maurizio Cattelan, Vanessa Beecroft, Damien Hirst or Pipilotti Rist – and television advertising. This is also part of a more general process in which various disciplines abandon the traditional know-how that tended to generate well-defined objects, in order to access a universe of reciprocal contaminations, predominated by pure relational values and guided by techniques of communication that, in turn, base their effectiveness on special effects and surprises. In short: fashion.

What led the world of architecture towards these dynamics was the progressively closer ties between architects and fashion designers: the latter often invited the former to design their showrooms or head offices,[20] to prepare marketing strategies and, if we look at Koolhaas and Prada, to develop alternative ways of conceiving of the relationship between shopping and urban space.

In fact, Miuccia Prada presented her new stores as an opportunity to redefine contemporary culture and interpret the idea of shopping in an innovative and experimental way. This was echoed by Koolhaas who affirmed that the new spaces offered people the possibility not to shop and to access private spaces designed for the public, in order to balance the ever more aggressive appropriation of a city's public space by stores and shopping malls.

What is more, the fact that fashion designers and architects do not focus their marketing strategies on the intrinsic nature of the quality of their products, but on lifestyle philosophies suggested by them, renders the historical separations of commodity economics obsolete. Fendi and Armani design kitchens and lines of furniture, opening stores that sell books and food; while Piano, Meier, Rogers and Lynn have no trouble

19 Yves Michaud, *L'art à l état gazeux: Essai sur le triomphe de l'esthétique*, Éditions Stock (Paris), 2003.

20 Pawson for Yves Klein; Sejima for Dior; Ito for Tod's; Chipperfield for Dolce & Gabbana; Tadao Ando for Armani and Benetton; Citterio for Bulgari; Herzog & de Meuron for Prada; Fuksas for Armani; Gehry for Issey Miyake; Future Systems for Comme des Garçons.

**Renzo Piano, High Museum of Art, Atlanta, Georgia, USA, 1999–2005: exterior view.**

Built alongside an important building by Richard Meier, the new building makes reference to the white panels of its neighbour, whilst setting itself apart through the increased simplicity of the plan and its laconic nature.

21 The phrase is taken from the OMA-AMO website: www.oma.eu

designing door handles, household appliances, watches, tea sets and coffee makers, or lending their faces and names to advertising, for example Fuksas for Renault and Foster for Rolex.

However, if an architect sells a lifestyle model, within which the public manages to recognise itself – no more or no less than that which takes place with a brand of jeans or a luxury automobile – the very organisation of an architectural office's production must change, focusing less on objects and more on the market: building designers are suddenly flanked by marketing and image specialists. Or, based on Koolhaas' intuitions when he founded AMO, it is necessary to create a new structure to accompany the existing technical one. Thus, 'while OMA remains dedicated to the realisation of architectural projects, AMO applies architectural thinking in its pure form, to questions of organisation, identity, culture and program, and defines ways – from the conceptual to the operative – to address the full potential of the contemporary condition.'[21] Consequently the architect is no longer, as he once was, the technician who gives form to a programme, dictated by a potentially public client, but – as part of the same system used by those who produce consumer goods for the general market – he is now the figure who, beginning with the input resulting from his own analyses, creates new needs, in order to satisfy them.

## 4.4 The Crisis of the Star System

For the eighth Venice Architecture Biennale, held in 2002, Deyan Sudjic,[22] the show's director, avoided taking sides. Rather than siding with one or another of current architectural trends, he asked leading

22 Deyan Sudjic (born 1952) is an influential writer, curator and teacher. Having trained as an architect at Edinburgh University, he founded *Blueprint* magazine in 1983 and went on to edit *Domus* between 2000 and 2004.

architectural offices to simply present their current projects, based on the hypothesis that many years pass between the phase of design and construction and that, undoubtedly, of the many projects being designed at the time, two or three would be important for the future of architecture. 'If the next five years reveal a project with the popular impact of the Bilbao Guggenheim, we can be sure that the drawings have already been completed, or that there is a virtual representation or one or two models. Obviously it is not yet complete. Perhaps construction has not yet begun. Perhaps its designers are still evaluating the possibility of building it out of steel or concrete. In any case, the project already exists as an idea. If there is to be another debut building with the impact of the Jewish Museum in Berlin, its architect has surely already been awarded the commission.'[23]

As a result, Sudjic chose to organise the exhibition according to typological containers: the dwelling, work, stores, religious buildings and spaces of representation.

His intention was to let the public select the masterpieces from amongst the works presented – should they so wish, and if they were truly to be found. This apparently neutral choice actually raises two relevant questions. In the first instance it denounces the difficulty faced by critics in carrying out their work, that of orienting the future through theoretical choices. The destiny of a project, Sudjic appears to imply, is increasingly more difficult to grasp and guided by extra-disciplinary factors – fashion, communication, public impact and large, commercial strategies – that are no longer the object of reflection. Secondly, the show presents, almost becoming its apotheosis, the conspicuous production of high-quality work by the Star System. This work undoubtedly meets with public approval – so much so that the number of visitors to Sudjic's Biennale far exceeded previous editions – even though it is increasingly difficult to identify a true ability to affect social phenomena. There were many museums, many luxurious single-family residences, though only a few programmes capable of changing cities, above

23 Deyan Sudjic, 'Next', in Next, Marsilio (Venice), 2002, p 15.

24 Kurt W Forster, 'Crossroads
– Around 1980', *Metamorph: Trajectories*, Marsilio (Venice), 2004, p 125.

all the poorer and more degraded ones. However, that Sudjic's Biennale, by ignoring them, raised relevant issues, was made clear in the two successive Biennales: 2004, directed by the historian Kurt Forster, and 2006, directed by Richard Burdett. The former can be read as a response to the role of the critic, the latter to the effects of the Star System within the more complex metropolitan phenomena that define the current century.

For Forster, who entitled his Biennale 'Metamorph', it was essential to rediscover, within new works of architecture, those trajectories that considered the transformations taking place. He chose to identify them by returning to the 1980s, a period of four approaches: two successful approaches focused on the future, and two failures, attracted by the past. The first were employed by Frank O Gehry and Peter Eisenman, the latter by Aldo Rossi and James Stirling: 'Aldo Rossi's melancholy isolation of buildings beyond scale and site stands in contrast to James Stirling's uninhibited

contamination of Modernist and Constructivist ideas. Eisenman and Gehry deliberately looked beyond building as we know it, in order to develop architecture *ex machina* by the former, or, with the bold introduction of fish (among other creatures) *ex natura* by the latter. At these crossroads of 1980, the trap was set, but it snared only the Postmodernists.'[24]

In order to orient visitors within contemporary processes of metamorphosis, Forster abandoned the typological containers adopted by his predecessor, organising others structured according to keywords: Transformations, Topography, The Nature of Artifice, Surfaces, Atmosphere and Hyper-Projects. However, the show was confusing, primarily because the projects presented in one category could easily have belonged to others: for example, the number of works that, as Forster himself admitted, 'appear to draw on virtually all our previous categories: they conjoin site and structural frameworks into new topographies, creating variegated atmospheres by means of spaces and conduits which are

25 Kurt W Forster, 'Hyper-Projects', *Metamorph: Trajectories*, p 339.

fashioned from materials that unfold the impression of cyclical time.'[25]

What emerged, in any case, was a growing interest in the territorial and geographic dimension that Bruno Zevi had already identified as nodal conditions during his 'Landscape and the Zero Degree Of Architectural Language' conference, held in September 1997.

This is the direction that may lead to a new key to interpretation, reconstructing scales of values capable of orienting critical research. However, the choice made by Richard Burdett in 2006 was that of cancelling any discussions of form to focus on an analysis of urban problems. The exhibition, entitled *'Città: Architettura e società'* [Cities: Architecture and Society] highlighted the transformations of contemporary metropolitan realties: primarily those of the Third and Fourth World. However, by doing so, Burdett also highlighted precisely what Sudjic sought to ignore: faced with the impetuous changes of social and economic forces, brand-name architecture – which fills the pages of architectural magazines and about which critics write such a great deal – is, in the end, entirely insignificant.

## 4.5 The Crisis of Architectural Criticism

Suspicious, on the one hand, of the optimism of the Star System, which steps back from more structurally relevant problems, and shaken, on the other, by sociological reflections that highlighted the limits of this aestheticising approach, critics had trouble identifying new operative hypotheses. Evidence of this can be found in the reduced production of relevant theoretical texts from 2001 onwards, and their even scarcer effects on the market, above all if compared to those published during the

26 We can mention, for example, the success of critical publications written during this period by architects such as Koolhaas, Tschumi, MVRDV, Toyo Ito, Libeskind etc.

27 Including the progressively more diffuse Taschen books, published simultaneously in multiple languages, invading the market thanks to attractive packaging and competitive pricing.

previous decade.[26] What made this separation even harder to swallow was, finally, the growing number of coffee-table books, where images take precedence over words and the critical aspect is intentionally ignored, in favour of a more apologetic[27] approach. This crisis also affected architectural magazines, one of the privileged instruments during the 1980s and '90s for the communication of architectural ideas.

The slow agony of *Architecture* – a magazine with a glorious past, partially the result of its having absorbed *Progressive Architecture* in 1996 – is emblematic of a more general condition of distress.[28]

For many the cause was to be attributed to the Internet which, through the rapid and free diffusion of information and images, robbed traditional publishing of its role as the privileged instrument for the diffusion of architectural ideas and, as a result, readers and publicity. However, beyond the Internet, there was also a growing difficulty in defining and characterising an authoritative voice. The choice ranged between avoiding the pitfalls of becoming refined publications, useful only for the promotion of things that are already public knowledge and filled with magnificent photographs selected and paid for by the protagonists of the architectural scene, or falling back into generic sociological, cultural or political reflections. This is what happened, for example, with *Domus* magazine. In September 2000 it passed under the direction of Deyan Sudjic, who turned it into a brilliant instrument for the presentation of the new. In a sudden and drastic shift, in January 2004 the magazine was placed in the hands of Stefano Boeri, who drastically reduced the number of architectural projects presented in each issue to make way for surveys, philosophical writings, geopolitical interventions and investigations of the status of the contemporary metropolis.

28 The July 2002 issue of *Architecture*, in a state of crisis for some time after ceasing to be the official publication of the American Institute of Architects (AIA), was signed by CC Sullivan, Reed Kroloff's successor as editor-in-chief. However, despite the new management, the magazine continued to lose readers and content. After a lengthy period of agony, the decision was made to cease publication to make way, in October 2006, for a new magazine entitled *Architect* and directed by Ned Cramer, that privileged technical issues over critical ones.

29 *Volume*, no 12 (2007), '*Al Manakh*': a special issue of *Volume* on occasion of the International Design Forum Dubai, 27 to 29 May 2007. The issue was edited by Ole Bouman, Mitra Khoubrou and Rem Koolhaas, and was co-produced by Archis, AMO, C-Lab and Moutamarat.

30 Amongst the stories of the succession of famous and long-term directors, there are two that stand out: the direction of *The Architectural Review* (from Peter Davey to Paul Finch) in 2005, and *Abitare* (from Italo Lupi to Stefano Boeri), in 2007. A summary of the cultural approach of the British magazine can be found in: *The Architectural Review*, no 1297 (March 2005), a monographic issue entitled: 'Davey Reflects on a Quarter of a Century'.

One example of a radical rethinking of the role and function of the architectural magazine can be found in the metamorphosis of *Archis*. In 2005 the magazine's director, Ole Bouman, changed the title of the magazine to *Volume*. He enlarged the editorial board – devising the slogan 'To Beyond or not to Be' – to include AMO, the research half of OMA, and C-LAB, the Columbia Laboratory for Architectural Broadcasting, directed by Mark Wigley. *Archis*, even more drastically than Boeri's *Domus*, abolished the presentation of projects in order to confront the themes that determine the physical form of the planet: wars and catastrophes included. In 2007 the magazine published a special issue dedicated to Dubai,[29] the Disneyland-city that is home to some of the most emblematic transformations of the new way of building the contemporary city. It is a city that attracts Rem Koolhaas who, together with Bouman and Wigley, is one of the magazine's Project Founders. However, the sensation is that *Volume* is more suited to a restricted minority of intellectuals, and subscriptions – primarily amongst architects interested in the real production of buildings – are on the wane. This fluctuating market also affects magazines with a more traditional approach, such that some have had to cease publication, including *L'architettura: cronache e storia*, which published its last issue in 2005, five years after the death of its founder, Bruno Zevi.

Others – despite the lack of official data – manage to survive with reduced editorial staff, less pages, and economies of any nature. Many attempt to renew themselves by changing directors.[30]

Equally, in the wake of the intelligent decision made by *Architectural Design*, some have chosen to offer a monographic approach that allows the magazine to preserve its interest, long after its date of publication.[31] Two other examples that, while following different approaches, manage to go against the grain are *The Architect's Newspaper* and *A10*.[32] By using new methods of communication,[33] both magazines lay claim to an interest in what takes place outside the sphere of the

31 It is interesting to note that issues such as 'Folding in Architecture' (1993), guest-edited by Greg Lynn, have been republished about 10 years later.
32 The first issue of the bimonthly *The Architect's Newspaper*, directed by William Menking, was published in 2003. The first issue of the bimonthly *A10*, directed by Hans Ibelings, was published in late 2004/early 2005. The two magazines are both economi-

cally priced – in fact, *The Architect's Newspaper* is free for architects living in the New York area.
33 Both focus on information and critical commentary, written with a journalistic bent. *The Architect's Newspaper* is directed at the community of architects who work, primarily, in and around New York. *A10* is aimed at the new audience of the enlarged European Union, including the nations created after the fall of the USSR in 1991.

These countries are now home to a new generation of designers, stimulated by a growing construction market. *A10* has also decided to focus on a transnational editing board, undoubtedly more attentive to what takes place in each specific nation.

34 In the wake of its success, the decision has been announced to publish an issue that deals with the Los Angeles area.

35 The acceptance, and later the assimilation, of avant-garde architectural trends naturally took place at different speeds, depending on the country of reference. In more traditional countries, such as Italy, the process was particularly lengthy and complicated. See: Luigi Prestinenza Puglisi, 'Complexity and Contradiction: The Italian Architectural Landscape', in 'Italy: A New Architectural Landscape', *Architectural Design*, no 187 (May/June 2007), pp 6–18.

Star System – the former by investigating the problems of the metropolitan area of New York in journalistic and theoretical terms;[34] the latter by seeking to understand what actually takes place in Europe and, in particular, in its peripheries, spaces that are now – thanks to new forms of communication – part of an interesting dimension that allows for the mixing, generating new syntheses, of local and global issues.

## 4.6 The End of the Star System?

The generation of innovative architects that emerged from the crisis of Post-Modernism and found a moment of coagulation in the 'Deconstructivist Architecture' show later went on to give life, in the 1990s, to a new season of creativity – a season that, however, as of the symbolic date of 11 September 2001, seems to have exhausted itself in the Star System.

This led to a cycle that, in as much as it is marked by peculiar characteristics, is also a recurrence in the history of architecture: the birth of a movement, initially a minority and viewed with suspicion, if not contested,[35] that, later, is accepted to the point that it becomes dominant. However, this acceptance also brings with it a loss of originality and innovative force.

The consequence is a growing fatigue in finding new working hypotheses. Not only because – as we have already seen – it is the same architects who standardise themselves by becoming eclectic, but also because the system, assimilating them and rendering them banal, tempers the more innovative positions, above all those that more vigorously placed themselves in explicitly antagonistic positions with respect to dominant culture.

In this light we can read the book by Rafael Moneo, *Inquietud teórica y estrategia proyectual en la obra de ocho arquitectos contemporáneos*, perhaps one of the

**Herzog & de Meuron, Laban Dance Centre, Deptford, London, England, 1997–2003: detail.**

The windows reflect light in a different manner than the metal-acrylic cladding panels into which they are inserted. They thus become evident insertions within the overall design of the building.

The ethereal colours of the facade cladding in metal-acrylic
panels change in the sunlight,
often merging with the sky.

36 The book was published simulta-
neously in Spanish (Actar), Italian
(Electa) and English: *Theoretical Anxi-
ety and Design Strategies in the Work of
Eight Contemporary Architects*, The MIT
Press (Cambridge, MA), 2005.

more important works of architectural publishing in recent years.[36] The book examines works by Venturi, Scott Brown & Associates, Stirling, Rossi, Eisenman, Siza, Gehry, Koolhaas and Herzog & de Meuron. However, the analysis avoids going beyond form and arriving at the deep-seated differences that are at the foundations, touching on an ideological aspect. Seeing these differences as simple alternative strategies to confronting the problem of form, Moneo runs the risk of endorsing the misunderstanding that created the Star System: the hypothesis that architects are nothing other than brilliant creators of unusual and refined images and that, precisely for this reason, they are substantially interchangeable, exactly like fashion designers – Armani or Versace, Siza or Gehry.

Fortunately, as much as the Star System tends to homogenise, it still contains significant differentiations not only related to style, but also more relevant cultural and existential aspects. While it is not difficult to find architects who adopt formalist or rearguard positions, and others whose works clearly demonstrate creative fatigue, it is not rare to find some who continue to operate with theoretical intelligence, asking new questions. Of the numerous projects of notable interest realised from 2002 onwards, the following section presents 10 works, which will be used to discuss two other phenomena, in a certain sense lateral to the Star System: super-creativity and ultra-minimalism.

# 4.7 Ten Projects

### Herzog & de Meuron, Laban Dance Centre, Deptford, London, 1997–2003

After initial experiments, oriented towards a more rigorist approach, we have seen how the work of Herzog & de Meuron began to focus on a more active use of space, though not always with convincing results. The Laban Dance Centre in Deptford, London (1997–2003) marks a decisive turning point, immediately evident

The interior circulation routes are
characterised by irregular forms,
strong chromatic contrasts and
the insertion of glazed surfaces
that open the building to its surroundings.

Herzog & de Meuron, Laban
Dance Centre, Deptford,
London, England, 1997–2003:
view of the entrance.

This project is clearly different
from Herzog & de Meuron's previous work. This can be seen in the
complexity of the interior spaces,
beginning with the entrance,
freely inspired by the work of
Koolhaas.

in the entrance, the arrival point of two ramps and a theatrical circular stair. Organised on two floors, the building is conceived, *alla* Koolhaas, as a *promenade architecturale* that winds, uninterrupted, along slightly irregularly shaped corridors. These spaces overlook others used for various activities, as well as offering views of the exterior panorama and glimpses of interior courtyards, guaranteeing natural interior lighting and a view of the sky overhead. There is also an attractive use of colours and materials. What dominates is the contrast between the shocking pink and pea green, perhaps a homage to the last works of James Stirling. There is also no shortage of black, with the tar-like effects used by Koolhaas in Fukuoka or Euralille. Many materials have been left exposed, for example the concrete of

the ceilings and the ductwork, part of an approach that is a little bit Calvinist and a little bit radical chic, the duo's claim to fame. On the exterior, thanks to the use of polycarbonate panels with a rainbow finish that ranges from yellow to pink to light green, the building assumes reflections of colour that vary throughout the day. This generates an evanescence that contrasts with the concrete materiality of the lawn, with its geometric designs.

The Laban demonstrates all the possibilities of an experimentation that involves space, envelope, colours and materials. Herzog & de Meuron continue to pursue this approach in an ever-growing number of commissions. Here we can briefly mention – for the

Herzog & de Meuron, Prada
Aoyama Epicentre, Tokyo,
Japan, 2000–3: exterior view.

Crisscrossed by reinforcing elements, the skin of this building
plays a structural role. Structure,
cladding and interior spaces
thus come together to work in
synergy.

**Toyo Ito, Grin Grin, I-Project, Fukuoka, Japan, 2002–5: aerial view.**

The green roof is an integral part of the exhibits in this museum dedicated to natural vegetation. Reflecting the theme of the museum, the building infringes as little as possible upon its natural context.

37 Wakato Onishi, 'New Century Modern', *Domus*, no 878 (February 2005), pp 14–27.

creative use of perforated metal, producing a vaguely Wrightian work of architecture – the De Young Museum in San Francisco, California (1999–2005); and – for the close correspondence between skin, structure, use of materials and interior spatiality – the Prada Aoyama Epicentre in Tokyo (2000–3). There are also the projects for the Allianz Arena in Munich, Germany (2000–5), which transforms into a giant and colourful light sculpture, and the new Olympic Stadium in Beijing (2002–8), designed like a giant concrete basket. While the latter is not without its formal self-indulgences, it undoubtedly represents an abandonment of the dichotomy between skin and structure.

### Toyo Ito, Tod's Omotesando Building, Tokyo, 2002–4

Toyo Ito's Tod's Omotesando Building in Tokyo (2002–4) is a building in which structure and skin coincide. Coherent with his organic approach, Ito interweaves columns and beams as if they were the branches of a tree. However, in order to subtract concrete of its weight,

he places the glass flush with the facade, exposing the concrete only on the exterior while painting the rest of the facades white. In this way, when seen from the street, the structure appears like a thin, grey-silver sheet that dialogues with the lights of the metropolis. Even concrete – Ito seems to say – can vibrate, losing the monumental weight that characterises the work of his rival, Tadao Ando. However, as Wakato Onishi[37] was quick to point out, the Omotesando lacks a sufficient interior spatiality – something that can be found in Herzog & de Meuron's Prada building, only a few blocks away. This is most probably the result of commercial decisions made by Tod's, who imposed the division of the building into a lower part, to be used as a store, and an upper part, which contains the offices.

Other projects completed by Ito in this period are based on a more convincing spatial dynamic. The Grin Grin, I-Project in Fukuoka, Japan (2002–5), for example, is a pleasant promenade through interior spaces and of discovery, wandering along undulated roofs covered with

**Herzog & de Meuron, Allianz Arena, Munich, Germany, 2000–5: exterior view.**

Each of the rhomboidal elements into which the exterior cladding is divided can be illuminated with a different colour of light. This system, managed by a computer, makes it possible to illuminate the stadium with the colours of the soccer teams who take the field.

**Toyo Ito, Mikimoto, Ginza 2, Tokyo, Japan, 2004–7: exterior view.**

The openings follow no apparent logic, communicating the idea of an object that lies in the balance between artifice and nature. The building finish is similar to that of a pearl, a reference to its occupants: a famous pearl-trading company.

Toyo Ito, Tod's Omotesando
Building, Tokyo, Japan, 2002–4:
exterior view.

The structure is inspired by the
design of the branches of a tree.
In the lower part of the building,
in order to insert the entrance,
the design is broader, though
less dense, while towards the
top its slenderness and density
increase.

natural vegetation. Finally, there are works that experiment with new directions of research, such as the Mikimoto, Ginza 2 in Tokyo (2004–7), a tower whose pearl finish (Mikimoto specialises in the sale of pearls) and openings in its non-geometric facade make it resemble a toy, found by chance in one of the most competitive and efficient cities in the world.

### Rem Koolhaas/OMA, Seattle Central Library, Washington, USA, 1999–2004

The Seattle Central Library in Washington (1999–2004) attempts to answer two questions: what is the role of public space today? and how can a library function in a society that now has so many other media, besides the printed page?

To respond to both questions, Koolhaas avoids pursuing the approaches experimented with in the unexecuted competition designs for the Bibliothèque Nationale de France, Paris (1989) and the Jussieu Library, Paris (1992) – the 'Swiss cheese' building, where the mass that contained the books was perforated by the spaces containing other activities; and the project with the continuous ramp that connected the floors of the building. In this case he opts for an intermediate approach. On the one hand the specialised platforms that satisfy the library's technical functions: the offices, the storage spaces, the classrooms and parking. On the other, the *in-between* spaces that become public plazas: a living room on the first floor (a covered plaza that recalls the famous Centre Pompidou in Paris), a 'mixing chamber' where users are placed in contact with other media and, finally, the reading rooms on the upper levels. The entire structure of platforms and public plazas is wrapped by a net-like envelope that defines a volume, unlike many of the other building blocks in Seattle, with a decisively non-prismatic form. In fact,

Rem Koolhaas/OMA, Casa
da Música, Porto, Portugal,
1999–2005: exterior view.

The exterior of the building is a
monolithic block, almost devoid
of any relationship with its urban
context. The interior is characterised by an articulated *promenade architecturale*.

**Rem Koolhaas/OMA, Seattle Central Library, Washington, USA, 1999–2004: exterior view.**

A series of technical platforms, offset in relation to one another, are fragmented by spaces open to the public. A mesh skin wraps the entire building, offering views of the various internal functions.

the platforms are not placed in precise correspondence with one another, but are slightly offset to guarantee the possibility of interesting connections, even visual, between one platform and another, and between one public space and another. This dynamic articulation can be appreciated from the exterior through the transparent mesh skin that envelopes the building – above all at night.

Coherent with his paranoid/functionalist approach, Koolhaas' project also presents a perfect correspond-

ence between form and function, even if the result is an unsettling and unusual object. Similarly unsettling and unusual, though once again the result of coherent design strategies, are the Casa da Música in Porto, Portugal (1999–2005) and the China Central Television (CCTV) Headquarters in Beijing, China (begun in 2002). The first is a monolithic building, whose interior is carved out by a sequence of interconnected spaces; the second is composed of a pair of skyscrapers joined at the base and the summit to create a unitary, ring-like form.

**Rem Koolhaas/OMA, Casa da Música, Porto, Portugal, 1999–2005: interior detail.**

Traditional elements of Portuguese decoration are decontextualised and transformed into contemporary super-graphic insertions.

**Rem Koolhaas, CCTV Headquarters, Beijing, China, begun 2002 (under construction): rendering.**

The building is composed of two towers connected at the base and summit. The result is a monumental form whose atypical appearance ensures that it stands out, even in the chaotic skyline of Beijing.

**Thom Mayne/Morphosis, Caltrans Offices,
Los Angeles, USA, 2002–4**

In this case, the investigation of public space – located outside the building – is undertaken by Thom Mayne in the new Caltrans offices in Los Angeles, California (2004). The building, located in the heart of the downtown, is clearly different from two others located in the same area: the Walt Disney Concert Hall by Gehry and Rafael Moneo's Roman Catholic Cathedral. Unlike the first, Mayne's building is square; unlike the second, it is rich with invention. The *parti* chosen by Mayne is, in reality, very simple: a tall, linear volume, to which a lower building is perpendicularly attached, forming an L and leaving a quadrant open for use as public space. Mayne stated: 'We are not making an object, but a space.'[38] This objective also underlies the choice of operating by making grand gestures.

**Thom Mayne/Morphosis,
Caltrans Offices, Los Angeles,
USA, 2002–4: view of the public
square.**

A video installation by the artist Keith Sonnier ensures the vitality of the public square that Mayne has created in front of the building entrance. Perforated sheet steel cladding improves the thermal performance of the main facade.

38 From: Joseph Giovannini, 'Caltrans Building', *Architectural Record*, no 1 (January 2005), p 122.

**Steven Holl, School of Art and Art History, Iowa City, Iowa, USA, 2000–6: exterior view.**

The building is inspired by a work of Cubist art. This reference is a pretext for the decomposition of the volumes and the opening of the building towards its natural surroundings.

The main building is clad on the long sides with steel sheeting, similar to that used for the Sun Tower in Seoul and the Hypo Alpe Adria Centre in Austria, which – other than guaranteeing a vibrant visual and metallic effect, typical of the work of Morphosis – also helps to reduce solar heat gain. The northern facade is fully glazed, while the south facade is covered with photovoltaic panels. The result is a building that is fragmented into horizontal planes. The vitality of the public square is guaranteed by commercial activities, macro-graphics (for example the building number written in large, block numbers) and a neon light installation by the artist Keith Sonnier, the primary function of which is to highlight the joint between the two volumes. Finally, the interior spaces feature an elevator lobby every three floors, lit by natural light wells and visible from the various departments.

Morphosis demonstrates a reduced interest in the creation of the precious, Deconstructivist details that were present in their early work, in favour of a new operative strategy that combines art, public space, ecology and light. This strategy was also pursued in the Science Center School in Los Angeles (1989–2004) and the US Federal Building in San Francisco (1999–2006), both in California.

**Massimiliano Fuksas, Milan Trade Fair, Milan, Italy, 2002–5: exterior detail.**

The buildings that flank the elevated main axis are placed on the site like plastic objects. Water and a careful landscaping project multiply the visual surprises and the play of reflections.

Massimiliano Fuksas, Milan Trade Fair, Milan, Italy, 2002–5

Built in record time – 24 months of construction – with respect to endless Italian schedules, the Milan Trade Fair complex in Milan, Italy (2002–5) is undoubtedly Massimiliano Fuksas' most important project: over 210,000 square metres of space, with 2,000 parking spaces. The structure features a giant, elevated walkway that is more than 1.5 kilometres in length. The overall effect is one of great complexity and simple and clear rationality. The initial impression is given by the glazed roof that covers the walkway, a clear investigation of blob

**Massimiliano Fuksas, Milan Trade Fair, Milan, Italy, 2002–5: aerial view.**

The roof that covers the central axis of circulation is managed as if it were a single, mile-long sculpture. It is supported by round columns with branch-like extensions.

**39** In fact, it was designed using Rhino, a software program used to calculate complex, three-dimensional forms.

geometries.[39] This element is, in turn, counterbalanced by the fact that the spatial organisation of the complex's interior spaces is very simple: a central, rectilinear axis flanked perpendicularly by eight, almost identical, functional 'blocks', each of which contains four types of buildings: the large display pavilions; restaurants; conference rooms; and, finally, office space. There is also one atypical block that contains the Service Centre and the Auditorium.

On more than one occasion Fuksas has referred to the idea of a cinematic sequence. This is particularly true in this complex, where the visitor, carried along by moving walkways that lead from one end of the circulation axis to the other, watches as the various images of architectural space unfold before his/her eyes, like scenes in a film. What renders this experience even more captivating is the studied intervals that separate the points of primary formal interest of the roof structure, the rhythmic alternation of the blocks and, on their interior, the choice of the buildings' forms – opaque or transparent

**Massimiliano Fuksas, Ferrari Headquarters, Maranello, Italy, 2000–3: exterior view.**

For the new Ferrari head offices, Fuksas separates the various volumes to obtain perspectival views that pass through and beyond the building.

boxes, mixed with lightweight 'flying saucers'. Finally there is the use of colour, the choice of materials and the scenic effects of landscaping, which – through the use of water and plantings – soften the impact of the architecture, all of which is further enhanced by the decision to separate the various building volumes by inserting a series of voids.

### Richard Rogers, Terminal 4, Madrid Barajas Airport, Madrid, Spain, 1997–2006

If the Milan Trade Fair complex demonstrates that even blob structures can, without a great deal of problems, be inserted within high-quality building projects located in the world's major metropolises, the fourth terminal at Madrid Barajas Airport in Spain (1997–2006), designed by Richard Rogers, attempts a synthesis between what

were, up until this time, the three branches of High Tech: technology, perception and symbolism. The objective here is to produce a building with rigour, humanity and narrative ability.

To achieve this synthesis, Rogers uses a structural module of significant formal interest, with a roof, crowned by a gentle curve, alluding to images typical of local traditions: from the hills of the Spanish landscape to the image of the bull's head, synthetically represented by Picasso's gestural sketch. The imposing and efficient technological image of the slender, inclined and brightly coloured steel columns is balanced by the cladding of the ceiling vaults in thin strips of bamboo. This choice, in addition to improving acoustic performance, also renders the interiors warm and welcoming, tempering the artificial aspect by inserting a hint of nature.

**Richard Rogers, Terminal 4, Madrid Barajas Airport, Madrid, Spain, 1997–2006: interior view.**

The undulating ceiling in bamboo slats creates a pleasant contrast with the concrete and steel structures. Light filters in from the sides though oculi inserted in the design of the roof.

Zaha Hadid, Phaeno Science Centre, Wolfsburg, Germany, 2000–6

The Phaeno Science Centre in Wolfsburg, Germany (2000–6), a commission awarded to Zaha Hadid in an international competition, is the first large project completed by this Anglo-Iraqi architect, after a series of smaller projects such as the Vitra Fire Station or the Landesgartenschau. The project is notable for its inventive structural system: upside-down pylon cones in reinforced concrete that contain specific functions. This allows for an open plane below the building, while the upper storeys are progressively occupied by the conical elements that pass through them and function as enclaves. Thus, while the ground floor is used as a public plaza that, thanks to the design of its undulating surface, can be referred to as an 'artificial topography', the upper levels are organised into thematic areas, located inside the enclaves. The result is a complex whose organisation in clusters makes it both polycentric and dynamic, enlivened by the relations that even manage to connect various levels inside the building.

What unites the entire organism – the interior of which recalls the complex geography of an urban space, or a multi-polar system for the production of energy – is the compact concrete walls, whose impact is lightened by the insertion of windows and inclined cuts. The choice of exposed concrete, as we have seen in the fire station in Vitra, was probably dictated by the desire to

Zaha Hadid, Phaeno Science Centre, Wolfsburg, Germany, 2000–6: exterior view.

The project is created by combining a series of upside-down, conical structural piers. These elements free up the ground plane for public use and come together at the upper floors to create a defined and continuous space.

Diller Scofidio + Renfro, Institute of Contemporary Art, Boston, Massachusetts, USA, 2000–6: exterior view.

The building is cantilevered out over the harbour. A media library protrudes from the underside of the cantilever, framing the water like a telescope. The space below is designed as an extension of the public space of the Boston Harbourwalk.

40 Further proof of the critical attention to the work of Diller + Scofidio
can be found in the retrospective show
held at the Whitney Museum in New
York in 2003: 'Scanning: The Aberrant
Architectures of Diller + Scofidio'.

41 Charles Renfro has been working
with Diller + Scofidio since 1997, and
has been a partner since 2004, when
the firm became Diller Scofidio +
Renfro.

avoid any further complications – for example using chromatic effects – of what is already a complex spatial machine. It is also the result of the desire to confront the city by inserting a unitary mass. This sculptural, and in many ways monumental, sign can be compared to Herzog & de Meuron's Forum 2004 building in Barcelona (2000–4) or the monoliths of Rem Koolhaas.

in the Seagram Building in New York (2000) and the Slither Housing in Gifu, Japan (2000). All the same, the office does boast a significant level of international recognition, the result of both their Blur project for the 2002 Swiss Expo and their performances that investigate the relationship between physical and virtual space, between the body and the mind, between perception and new technologies.[40]

### Diller Scofidio + Renfro, Institute of Contemporary Art, Boston, Massachusetts, 2000–6

Diller + Scofidio, although active since 1978, are unable to boast a relevant list of built works; in fact their only built projects are the Brasserie Restaurant

The Institute of Contemporary Art in Boston, Massachusetts (2000–6), designed together with Charles Renfro,[41] is the first non-ephemeral project of a certain importance produced by the office. Designed to overlook the body of water in the port, it does so with

**Frank O Gehry, IAC/
InterActiveCorp Building, New
York, USA, 2007.**

This office complex represents a
formal simplification of Gehry's
previous work. It is also a return
to his research into the twisting
of volumes that generated such
positive results in the 'Fred &
Ginger' building in Prague.

a courageous cantilever that allows for the positioning of display spaces on the upper levels, freeing up the ground plane for use as a public platform facing the water. The auditorium and media library also face in this direction. The latter is perhaps the most distinctive element of the exterior of the museum: it protrudes from the cantilever like a downward-sloping telescope. In fact, the interior space concludes with a glass wall-screen that frames the sea, transforming it into an immense, abstract image. The same framing is repeated by the computer screensavers located in rows on long tables. The result is a space, suspended between reality and artificiality, in which images multiply in a play of reflections, where boundaries between spaces are lost. This is the same effect generated by Blur, demonstrating that the difference between ephemeral architecture and that which is not considered architecture at all, is much more flexible than we may care to admit.

### Gehry Partners, IAC/InterActiveCorp Building, New York, 2007

Of the various archi-stars, Gehry is undoubtedly the most internationally well known. So much so that – and this is a singular example in the history of cinema – he is the only living protagonist of a commercially

**Jean Nouvel. Agbar Tower,
Barcelona, Spain, 2000–5: view
from the city.**

The unusual form of the tower
makes it a landmark in the city.
The facade is subdivided into tiny
coloured squares, like pixels on a
computer screen.

**Jean Nouvel, Musée du Quai Branly, Paris, France, 1999–2007: exterior view.**

The garden, designed by the landscape architect Gilles Clément, assumes a figurative role that is no less important than that of the building. The objective is to demonstrate that architecture is now a landscape composed of built and natural spaces.

**42** *Sketches of Frank Gehry* (2005), directed by Sydney Pollack.

released film dedicated entirely to his work.[42] After completing the Walt Disney Concert Hall in 2003, Gehry demonstrated that his strategy of relating to context was more solid than a traditionalist approach, such that the building quickly became a landmark in downtown Los Angeles. All the same, the many projects that followed, spread across the globe, reveal a level of creative fatigue. The use of metal scales appears self-referential and the Marqués de Riscal Winery in Elciego, Spain, completed in 2006, is shocking for its decorative excesses and almost mannerist auto-celebration. A more convincing project is the IAC/InterActiveCorp Building in New York, completed in 2007. Here Gehry abandons the research that tended towards the composition of various articulated volumes – the line that connects the Vitra Design Museum to the Walt Disney Concert Hall to the Bilbao Guggenheim – in order to return, stripping it of its Baroque excesses, to the research into torsion defined with the 'Fred & Ginger' building in Prague. The result is a building complex that confronts the themes imposed by the New York City block, and a rediscovery of the pleasure of a game that balances simplicity and complexity.

## Jean Nouvel, Musée du Quai Branly, Paris, 1999–2007

With his Musée du Quai Branly in Paris (1999–2007), Jean Nouvel erases the traditional relationship that exists between the street and the building. Instead of being aligned, as one would have expected, along the street front, the building pulls back, leaving space at the centre of the site for a garden designed by the landscape architect Gilles Clément.[43] It would appear that Nouvel wishes to tell us that it is nature that must reclaim space from architecture. This position is further underlined by the choice to cover some of the museum's walls with natural growth, in homage to the French tradition of green walls, and the dis-architecture of Ambasz. However, unlike the latter, who submerges his buildings in nature, Nouvel does not abandon the compact masses, the coloured metal panels, or the no

**Jean Nouvel. Agbar Tower, Barcelona, Spain, 2000–5: interior view.**

The varying degrees of transparency and the different colourations of the pixel-treated surfaces that define the design of the facade create atmospheric lighting conditions on the interior.

**43** Gilles Clément (born 1943) is a landscape architect and author of the theory of the *jardin planétaire* and the concept of the garden in movement, according to which it is necessary to give time and natural processes an important role in the design of urban green spaces.

Jean Nouvel, Musée du
Quai Branly, Paris, France,
1999–2007: view from the
Seine River.

The mass of the building is set
back from the street edge; the
facade along the street is covered
with grass and plants.

less colourful boxes that protrude from the facade (the few spaces that, requiring a moment of concentration and rest, are physically removed from the circulation through the museum).

The interior spaces are less successful. Here Nouvel's idea was to create a 'fictional map' that reproduces the continuity of the surface of the Earth, represented by a sloping and continuous path. It is a brilliant concept – something that we have already seen, for example, in the work of Koolhaas – but it transforms the exposition of some 3,500 objects from the world's primitive cultures into a bazaar of chaotic relics, in many cases creating confusion.

## 4.8 Super-Creativity and Ultra-Minimalism

The phenomenon of Super-Creativity runs parallel to that of the Star System. It consists of the production of architectural objects with a significant level of scenographic impact. For example, Future Systems' project in Birmingham, Great Britain, for the new Selfridges department store, completed in 2003: a large amoeba-like form, covered with circular aluminium discs. The building generated no shortage of perplexities, above all for its insertion into the surrounding context.

A no less decisive impact was generated by the Mediacentre in Hilversum, The Netherlands (1999–2006) by Neutelings Riedijk. In this case the strangeness

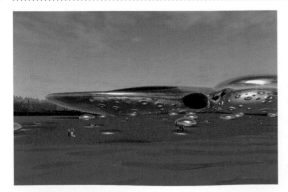

Vito Acconci, Seoul Performing
Arts Centre, Seoul, Korea, 2005:
project.

This blobby building was designed
to be a large sculpture related to
its environmental surroundings
but has trouble creating a
pleasing space for public use
around it.

Future System, Selfridges, Birmingham, England, 1999–2003.

This large department store is clad with a skin of round discs. The object, undoubtedly unusual, is intentionally separated from its urban surroundings.

of the building is justified by the transposition, obtained using the diagrammatic method, of a complex programme.

By following a more instinctive strategy, the artist Vito Acconci[44] tends to produce out-of-scale sculptural objects, though not without some form of environmental value – such as, for example, the Performing Arts Centre in Seoul, Korea (2005).

One of the most notable demonstrations of Super-Creativity can be found in the Kunsthaus in Graz, Austria

(2000–3), designed by Peter Cook and Colin Fournier. The object, another blob, is happily inserted within its Baroque context, both an ectoplasmic 'friendly alien' reminiscent of 1960s pop culture – of which Cook, one of the members of Archigram, was a protagonist – and, at the same time, belonging to the most recent season of blob architecture. The exterior is covered by electronically controlled round fluorescent lights. The friendly alien is thus transformed into a low-resolution screen for the projection of messages. Inside the building moving walkways allow visitors to cross the spaces, enjoying them, as in Fuksas' fairgrounds, as if they were part of a cinematographic sequence.

Another work of significant impact is the addition to the Ontario College of Art & Design in Toronto, Canada, by Will Alsop, completed in 2004. The building, over 6,000 square metres of study space and classrooms, is suspended in mid-air to avoid compromising the unbuilt space and existing buildings below. Resting on twelve 25-metre-high slender steel columns, each

44 Vito Acconci (born 1940) is one of the most relevant avant-garde artists from the late 1960s, known for his body art performances. In recent years he has been increasingly involved in the world of architecture.

Neutelings Riedijk, Mediacentre, Hilversum, The Netherlands, 1999–2006: interior view.

The unusual exterior, with its multicoloured glass facade, contains highly successful interior spaces that develop below ground level.

**Peter Cook and Colin Fournier (Spacelab), New Kunsthaus, Graz, Austria, 2000–3: night view.**

A system of computer-controlled circular neon lights transforms the building into a large, low-resolution display screen capable of projecting messages.

**Peter Cook and Colin Fournier (Spacelab), New Kunsthaus, Graz, Austria, 2000–3: exterior view.**

The project is composed of a blob-like structure, a panoramic observatory and the volume of the existing historical building. The entrance is located at ground level and defined by a glass wall.

45 Kazuyo Sejima (born 1956) and Ryue Nishizawa (born 1966) work separately and together, since 1995, as SANAA.

is aseptic, abstract, immaterial, anti-hierarchical, monochrome and inflexible. The primary exponent of this trend is the Japanese architect Kazuyo Sejima who, together with her partner Ryue Nishizawa,[45] has for many years been pursuing, with more rigour, the diagrammatic Minimalism that defined her early work, which we have discussed in a previous chapter.

painted a different colour, the building is an aluminium box-sculpture, whose white background is covered by numerous randomly placed black squares and windows that are transformed into a motif which is more pictorial than architectural.

In opposition to Super-Creativity we find Ultra-Minimalism. The chaos and formal exuberance of modern society is opposed by an ordered aesthetic, which

Sejima and Nishizawa's most important work from this period is the 21st Century Museum of Contemporary Art in Kanazawa, Japan (1999–2004). The building is a circular space, defined by transparent glass walls, which wrap boxes of varying heights, widths and lengths. With its highly refined proportions and absolutely simple organisation – the boxes are placed according to the most banal orthogonal grid – the museum allows for no flexibility, the exact antithesis of the complex

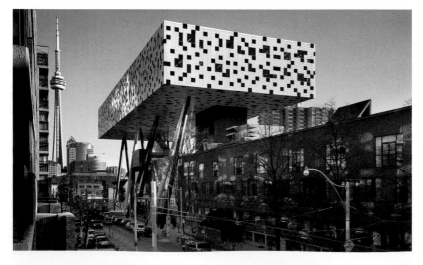

**Will Alsop, Sharp Centre, Ontario College of Art & Design, Toronto, Canada, 2000–4: exterior view.**

The building is suspended in the air, in order not to occupy the space below. The lively decoration of the box transforms it into a multicoloured sculpture.

**Ábalos & Herreros, Multifunctional Building in Las Palmas de Gran Canaria, 2001–3: exterior view.**

Ábalos & Herreros focus on aspects that were relatively ignored during the 20th century. Their Minimalist and Modernist re-reading sets them apart from the neo-traditionalist approach favoured by the majority of Spanish projects in recent decades.

display machines of the High Tech movement. The tiny steel columns, barely 10 centimetres in diameter, communicate the idea of dematerialised perfection: beyond the Platonic, beyond Minimalism, beyond Calvinism, and close to anorexia.

When asked about her design method, Sejima stated: 'We never start from a simple base, even in the schematic design phase. We seem to start from very complicated things that gradually become simple.'[46] In this case 'simple' is to be understood as 'elementary' because, in the end, what resists the process of reduction is only those units that cannot be subdivided any further.

This can be seen in the House in a Plum Grove, Tokyo (2003), designed by Sejima (on her own), where the reduced building volume is subdivided into primary residential functions: eating, studying, sleeping, entertaining, washing. This generates the thickness, little more than a centimetre, of the steel dividing partitions; the extremely reduced space of the rooms, some

little over a metre; and the decision, to keep them from becoming too narrow and suffocating, that they be placed in communication with one another via internal perforations. The consequence is that the inhabitants of the house, from any point inside it, have the sensation of living in a grid that is the result of a pure and, simultaneously, sophisticated conceptional operation.

Obviously an architecture of this type, in order that it maintain its ideal aspect, leaves little room for the realities and disorder of everyday life, including dirt and time. Perhaps its success is to be found precisely in this abstraction of the materiality of the body and a laic asceticism that refutes the values of consumerist society, even if at the same time it pursues them by searching for an extreme level of refinement. This can be compared to the proposals being made by new Japanese design, for example the Muji chain of stores, theorising a return to a few elementary objects of basic needs but which are sold at prices that reflect their 'designer' status.

46 Cristina Díaz Moreno and Efrén García Grinda, 'Fragment from a conversation', *El Croquis*, no 121–2 (2004), p 13.

**Mansilla+Tuñón Arquitectos, Regional Documentary Centre, Madrid, Spain, 1994–2002.**

Formalists from the school of Moneo, this architectural couple demonstrate its stylistic eclecticism, together with an ability to propose convincing and cautiously experimental buildings, capable of dialoguing with their urban context.

**NOX, Maison Folie de Wazemmes, Lille, France, 2001–4: exterior view.**

NOX's objective in the design of this arts centre is the creation of an interactive structure that uses audio and lighting effects, even at the cost of generating a theatrical experience.

**Mathias Klotz, Faculty of Economy, Diego Portales University, Santiago, Chile, 2004–6: exterior view.**

Klotz is one of the most interesting of South America's younger generation of architects. His approach involves the mixture of contemporary forms and the use of techniques and materials that are consciously unsophisticated.

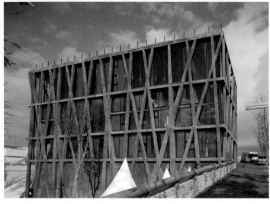

In fact, as can easily be observed by the failure of the low-cost housing projects designed by Sejima herself – for example the Gifu Kitagata Apartment Building in Motosu, Gifu Prefecture, Japan (1994–8) – ultra-Minimalist asceticism functions perfectly in luxurious single-family dwellings and the spaces of intellect and culture, though to a lesser degree when dealing with simpler and less researched activities.

...........................................................

**Rudy Ricciotti, Centre Chorégraphique Nationale, Aix-en-Provence, France, 1999–2006: exterior view.**

The exposed structure differs from others of the same period for its wilful hardness, in harmony with the neo-Brutalist aesthetic pursued by Ricciotti.

**Kengo Kuma, LVMH Headquarters, Omotesando, Tokyo, Japan, 2001–3.**

Kuma's buildings stand out from their chaotic Japanese context for their balanced and measured proportions and a skilful use of light, shadow and shading, obtained by brises-soleil composed of slender wooden elements.

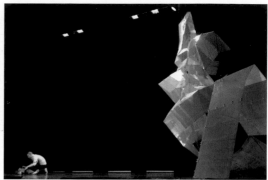

## 4.9 Back to Basics

Even though they do not come close to the ultra-Minimalism of Sejima and Nishizawa, there are numerous other architects, mostly Japanese, who have focused on a return to the essential: this 'back to basics' approach, a term used by The Architectural Review,[47] is pursued by, amongst others, Kengo Kuma[48] and Shigeru Ban. Kuma focuses his research on primary relationships and nature: through the tactile qualities of materials, the relationship with light, water and the landscape. This can be seen, for example, in the LVMH Headquarters in Omotesando, Tokyo, Japan (2001–3) and the Z58 Offices and Showroom in Shanghai, China (2006). Despite the fact that both are located in difficult metropolitan contexts, Kuma has designed enchanting spaces, suspended between nature and artifice. He has managed to obtain vibrant effects of chiaroscuro using vertical and horizontal diaphragms, constructed of slender fins or, as in Shanghai, with a wall of horizontally separated planting boxes.

**Shigeru Ban, Travelling Museum, 2006: exterior view.**

Constructed by uniting 152 shipping containers, the building is a warning against waste and a means of promoting recycling. The entrance columns are made of cardboard and the roof of waterproof sheeting.

47 The monographic issue of *The Architectural Review*, no 1326 (August 2007) was entitled 'Japan: Back to Basics'.
48 Kengo Kuma (born 1954) graduated from the University of Tokyo. Between 1985 and 1986 he studied at Columbia University. In 1987 he opened Spatial Design Studio and, in 1990, Kengo Kuma & Associates.

**Ammar Eloueini Digit-all Studio (AEDS), Stage Set Design for John Jasperse Company, California, USA, 2003: interior view.**

Eloueini uses the computer and the art of origami to design spatially innovative structures that are based on the logic of complex geometries and blob structures.

Oliviero Godi & Dorit Mizrahi (Exposure Architects), Octospider Cafeteria, Satin Textile Co Ltd, Bangkok, Thailand, 2000–4: exterior view.

The form of the cafeteria is the result of the desire to provide each table with a view of the landscape. The building was also raised above an artificial lake, created by recycling water used in the making of fabric.

David Chipperfield, Des Moines Public Library, Des Moines, Iowa, USA, 2001–6: day and night views.

The building, with its rigorously Minimal appearance, loses its metallic finish at night – opening itself up before one's eyes.

49 The competition was awarded to Ban in 2003.
50 Jean de Gastines (born 1957) has been associated with Shigeru Ban since 2000 for all of his projects built on French soil.

Of a more experimental temperament, Shigeru Ban earned his fame in the 1990s for his inventive cardboard structures, put to the test after the Kobe earthquake of 1995 in the construction of a 170-square-metre church that was built using tubes measuring 5 metres in height, with a thickness of 16 millimetres. Ban also designed 21 shelters, once again in cardboard, that can be assembled in six hours. The shelters are covered with a Teflon fabric and tied to the ground by sand-filled plastic crates. The project raised the interest of the United Nations High Commission for Refugees; a great deal of interest was also expressed by the world of architecture and Ban's clients, such that he was awarded the design of the Japanese Pavilion for Expo 2000 in Hanover and a demonstrative pavilion in the MoMA gardens (2000). Both structures were built using thin, recycled and recyclable cardboard cartons. The former – designed and calculated with Frei Otto and Buro Happold – was composed of three domes tied together to create a 72 x 35 metre space, with a height of over 15 metres.

Stimulated by the objective of designing a more ingenious and simpler life, Ban is also the author of numerous experiments in the field of residential design, of which we mention here the House in Kawagoe, Japan (2001), known as the 'Naked House', a large, indifferent interior space filled with wooden boxes on wheels used as bedrooms. This design choice allows for the simplest flexibility of living space.

Of Ban's most recent work, other than the new Pompidou Centre in Metz[49] – designed in collaboration with Jean de Gastines[50] and employing the tensile technologies normally used for circus tents – we can mention the Nomadic Museum, a prefabricated, itinerant gallery for exhibitions of the naturalist documents of Gregory Colbert. It was designed by uniting 152 shipping containers, stacked to create four floors and set in four rows. Other materials employed include cardboard columns, standard hollow-core panels and plastic sheeting for the roof that, however, is to be substituted by a solar cloth, to increase energy efficiency. The museum

SANAA (Kazuyo Sejima + Ryue Nishizawa), 21st Century Museum of Contemporary Art, Kanazawa, Japan, 1999–2004.

The different display spaces, with rigorously prismatic forms, are enclosed inside a circular structure. The project is dematerialised by the large, continuous glass wall that wraps around the building.

Sarah Wigglesworth Architects, Eco-House, Islington, London, England, 1998–2002: exterior view.

This ecological house, located in the suburbs of London, was built by recycling materials and using historical building techniques – for example, hay insulation.

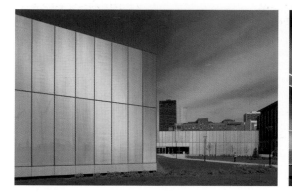

can be 'built' in 10 weeks, and has already stopped in numerous cities, including New York and Santa Monica.

The work of Shigeru Ban raises the issue of an architecture that focuses on invention, creativity and an economy of means, rather than the creation of figurative icons. As Paul Finch points out: 'In a world with the same distinctive icons everywhere, none of them will be distinctive in any meaningful way, instead becoming icons in the old sense of the word, that is to say similar representations of the same thing, the same thing being architecture itself.'[51]

A champion of the art of frugality is represented by Rural Studio, a programme launched by Samuel Mockbee[52] with the Auburn University and, after his

death, taken over by Andrew Freear. The programme consists of letting final-year architectural students work in pilot programmes in poor parts of the country, using recycled materials and equipment donated by sponsors. For the students it represents a chance to learn how to set aside the stylistic and formalist fixations that they have learned in previous years at school. For the local population it is an important assistance that, since 1994, has led to the realisation of some 60 projects, including Lucy's House in Mason Bend, Alabama (2001–2), where, instead of using traditional techniques, the walls were built by overlapping carpet tiles donated by a sponsor to create a neo-Expressionist red tower. Another assisted project was the Fire Station in Newbern, Alabama (2003–5), built entirely in wood and polycarbonate.

In England, of the recent works that unite creativity with cheap and/or recycled materials, the Eco-House in Islington, London (1998–2002) designed by Sarah Wigglesworth is particularly worthy of note. The project

51 Paul Finch, 'Spanning Cultural Difference', *The Architectural Review*, no 1326 (August 2007), p 19.
52 Samuel Mockbee (1944–2001), after working as an architect attentive to regionalism, was the driving force behind the Auburn University Rural Studio Program, begun in 1992.

**53** Peter Davey, 'And the Future?', *The Architectural Review*, no 1297 (March 2005), p 88.

**54** NL Architects is based in Amsterdam and composed of four associates: Pieter Bannenberg (born 1959), Walter Van Dijk (born 1962), Kamiel Klaasse (born 1967) and Mark Linnemann (born 1962). While officially founded in 1997, their collaboration dates back to the early 1990s, when they were students in Delft.

**55** SeARCH, an acronym for Stedenbouw en ARCHitectuur (Urban Planning & Architecture) was formed in 2002 by Bjarne Mastenbroek (born 1964), Uda Visser and David Gianotten.

**56** Julien De Smedt (born 1975) and Bjarke Ingels (born 1974) created PLOT in Copenhagen in 2001. In 2006 the group split into JDS Architects and BIG (Bjarke Ingels Group).

**57** Exposure Architects comprises Oliviero Godi (born 1960) and Dorit Mizrahi (born 1971).

**Kazuyo Sejima + Associates, Asahi Shimbun Yamagata Building, Japan, 2003: exterior view.**

The purity of the volumes and the almost total absence of any thickness render this building an abstract and almost unreal project.

uses numerous materials with a great deal of fantasy: from sandbags to hay, used as insulating materials. For Peter Davey it is 'the most sexy and witty building I have seen for years: fetishist, full of clever inventions, happy with overlapping story telling, wild yet tender, ever open to change … We all live in houses like that in our imaginations.'[53]

In The Netherlands, NL Architects[54] designed the Basket Bar in Utrecht (2002–3), where the playing field is intelligently realised to make space at ground level for public functions, including a cafeteria and an open square, used for social activities.

SeARCH's[55] Theehuis Pavilion in Veluwezoom National Park in Rheden, The Netherlands (1998–2002) is a very refined project that combines natural and artificial materials to re-invent the anything-but-simple typology of the display pavilion.

In Denmark, PLOT[56] were responsible for the Maritime Youth House in Copenhagen (2004). The project demonstrates that it is possible to create continuous spaces, rendering them attractive through the use of wood.

Finally, we can look at the Octospider Cafeteria in Bangkok, Thailand (2001–4) by Exposure Architects.[57] Designed to improve the labour conditions of workers in the adjacent textile factory, the cafeteria is raised above ground, creating a pleasant relationship with the surrounding landscape. Even the form, which recalls the open fingers of a hand, is the result of the desire

**SeARCH, Theehuis Pavilion, Veluwezoom National Park, Rheden, The Netherlands, 1998–2002: exterior view.**

One of the more interesting groups from the younger generation of Dutch architects, SeARCH propose works of architecture in which the themes of Modernism mix with a new ecological sensitivity and a taste for natural materials.

**Edouard François, Housing, Louviers, France, 2006: exterior view.**

The unfinished tree trunks that clad the entire building give it a rustic appearance, in line with the aspirations of a growing segment of the population for more ecological forms of dwelling.

to allow a decent view from each table. The pond over which the structure is built was created by recycling the water used in the washing of the fabrics. The circular ramp transforms the passage along the route that unites the spaces of work and the cafeteria into a daily event.

## 4.10 The Next Stop

What direction will architecture take in the near future?

It would not be out of line to imagine that the Star System will continue to dominate, reinforced by new commissions, above all from emerging countries: China, India and the Persian Gulf, primarily Dubai, now the centre of significant economic and financial interest. Of these new projects,

**NL Architects, Basket Bar, Utrecht, The Netherlands, 2002–3: exterior view.**

A raised basketball court frees up space for a bar and public square used as a meeting point.

In this project PLOT use inclined planes to connect exterior spaces, enhancing the relationship between the building and the sea. The large glazed surfaces, the slender steel handrails and the use of wood make the building agreeably modern.

many will undoubtedly be of great poetic and formal interest. In fact, it is difficult to imagine that creative figures such as Gehry, Hadid and Koolhaas will continue tirelessly to repeat themselves, accepting the banal and easy success that celebrity can generate.

On the other hand, what we can expect from emerging architects is undoubtedly an ambivalent approach. Some will seek to become part of the Star System, while others will choose to set themselves apart. In the first case this will generate the diffusion of what will, sooner or later, develop into a style, not unlike what took place with the International Style.[58] In the second case, we will be witness to the emergence of new tensions, restlessness and design ideas that are no less interesting than those that, some 20 years ago, provoked the important changes in the world of architecture whose fruits we now enjoy.

There is no doubt that many of these changes are already under way, and it is only as a result of far-sightedness that we critics, who know how best to read the past with respect to what we now observe, are unable to identify and decipher them. This is the same mistake made by those of the previous generation who, back in 1980, ignored the eccentric contributions of such architects as Gehry and Koolhaas to the otherwise Post-Modern Strada Nuovissima presented at the Venice Biennale or, even earlier, in 1978, when they were unable to forecast the novelties announced by the addition to a house in Santa Monica, once again by Gehry.

At present we are witness to the development of three new directions.

The first consists of the growing importance of context, to the detriment of the object. Architecture continues more and more to deal with the territorial dimension and, given that there no longer exist any clear lines of demarcation, nature enters into it with progressively

58 The International Style, launched in 1932 by the exhibition of the same name held at the MoMA, simultaneously spread and standardised the ideas of the Modern Movement. It was also responsible for the creation of a number of very important and defining works of architecture in the 1950s.

**UNStudio, Mercedes-Benz Museum, Stuttgart, Germany, 2001–6: interior view.**

The scenographic complexity of the interior spaces is further enhanced by the play of transparent surfaces, created by the application of perforated panels.

Mario Cucinella, Sino Italian
Ecological and Energy Efficient
Building (SIEEB), Beijing,
China, 2003–6: exterior view.

The south-facing terraced hanging garden is home to rich vegetation and over 1,000 square
metres of photovoltaic panels
that fulfil the majority of the
building's energy requirements.

more force, in many cases as a building material.
Other than energy savings and sustainability, the next
frontier will be the new relationship with that which
surrounds us. This is what has led to the refusal of a-
contextual works of architecture-sculpture, in addition
to the scarce interest in well-proportioned tectonic
compositions – in the end, also designed as sculptural
objects, autonomous with respect to the landscape.

The second direction will tend to re-examine the
relationship between High Tech and Low Tech,
overcoming the excessive enthusiasm of the 1990s for
the digital, as well as the fear, after the collapse of
the Twin Towers, of all things technological. Obviously
this is not to be read as a banal balance, defined by
middle-of-the-road choices, but rather as passionate
encounters and confrontations – between the simple
and the complex, the slow and the fast, the digital
and the mechanical, automatic and manual, light and
heavy, transparent and opaque, abstract and concrete,
etc – many of which, as we have already seen, are

already being defined in the projects designed by the
younger generation of architects.

The third direction places architecture in the realm of
desires. This means overcoming the phase of elementary
needs and standards, and facing up to complex
requirements, new lifestyles. Communication and
rhetoric are predominant here: as with fashion and art,
both less and less involved in object-oriented research,
and progressively more in relational dynamics. At this
point it will be up to architects to decide whether they
wish to use the mystifying techniques of the former, or
the much less acquiescent ones of the latter.

Mario Cucinella, Sino Italian
Ecological and Energy Efficient
Building (SIEEB), Beijing,
China, 2003–6: view of the
interior courtyard.

The waterfall located in the
interior courtyard is both visually
pleasing and an active part of
the control of the building's
microclimate.

UNStudio, Mercedes-Benz
Museum, Stuttgart, Germany,
2001–6: exterior view.

The building appears to be a single, compact mass. However, a
series of cuts and shifts in the
surfaces of the volume reveal the
complex articulation of its interior spaces.

# TIMELINE:
# 1988–2007

## 1988

### Buildings completed

- K Kada, Glasmuseum, Bärnbach, Austria, 1987–8
- Herzog & de Meuron, Apartments in Hebelstrasse, Basel, Switzerland, 1984–8
- IM Pei, Javits Convention Center, New York, USA, 1979–88
- P Rudolph, Bond Center, Hong Kong, 1984–8

### Architecture: other important events

- 'Deconstructivist Architecture' opens at the MoMA in New York
- Pritzker Prize awarded to G Bunshaft and O Niemeyer
- † R Banham, English critic

### The arts, literature, criticism, science, fashion and trends

- I Calvino: *Lezioni americane*
- M Yourcenar: *Quoi? L'Eternité*
- S Rushdie: *The Satanic Verses*
- P Almódovar: *Women on the Verge of a Nervous Breakdown*
- B Levinson: *Rain Man*
- † R Feynman, American physician
- Mandela 70th Birthday Tribute Concert, London, Wembley Stadium, 11 June
- Nobel Prize for Literature awarded to N Mahfouz

### Historical events

- *perestroika* in the Soviet Union
- Separatist tensions in Estonia, Lithuania, Armenia and Georgia
- France: re-election of the Socialist François Mitterrand
- USA: George HW Bush becomes the 41st President
- Poland: official recognition of the Solidarity movement

## 1989

### Buildings completed

- FO Gehry, Vitra Design Museum, Weil am Rhein, Germany, 1987–9
- Coop Himmelb(l)au, Rooftop Remodelling, Falkestrasse 6, Vienna, Austria, 1983–9
- A Rossi, Il Palazzo Hotel, Fukuoka, Japan, 1987–9
- IM Pei, Bank of China, Hong Kong, 1982–9

### Architecture: other important events

- Pritzker Prize awarded to FO Gehry

### The arts, literature, criticism, science, fashion and trends

- K Ishiguro: *The Remains of the Day*
- K Kieslowski: *Decalogue*
- C Ginzburg: *The Night Battles*
- R Rorty: *Contingency, Irony and Solidarity*
- R Mapplethorpe exhibition opens in Washington, DC
- B Beresford: *Driving Miss Daisy*
- † H von Karajan, Director of the Austrian Symphony Orchestra
- Nobel Prize for Literature awarded to CJ Cela
- Pink Floyd present their 'A Momentary Lapse of Reason' Tour

### Historical events

- experiments in cold nuclear fusion
- Germany: fall of the Berlin Wall
- democracy comes to Czechoslovakia, Romania, Hungary and Bulgaria
- Soviet troops pull out of Afghanistan
- China: protests in Tiananmen Square in Beijing
- Ayatollah Khomeini announces a fatwa against Salman Rushdie, the author of *The Satanic Verses*

## 1990

### Buildings completed

- Z Hadid, Monsoon Restaurant, Sapporo, Japan, 1989–90
- S Calatrava, Stadelhofen Train Station, Zurich, Switzerland, 1983–90
- R Piano, Institut de Recherche et Coordination Acoustique/Musique (IRCAM), Paris, France, 1987–90
- C de Portzamparc, Cité de la Musique, Paris, France, 1984–90

### Architecture: other important events

- Pritzker Prize awarded to A Rossi
- † L Mumford, American urban planner
- † G Michelucci, Italian architect

- an exhibition is held in Amsterdam to mark the 100th anniversary of Van Gogh's death
- C Paglia: *Sexual Personae*
- D Walcott: 'Omeros'
- L Lippard: *Mixed Blessings: New Art in a Multicultural America*
- K Costner: *Dances with Wolves*
- † K Haring, American artist
- J-M Jarre presents a concert-performance set against the evocative backdrop of La Défense in Paris
- Nobel Prize for Literature awarded to O Paz
- L Ronconi presents a production of K Kraus's *The Last Days of Humanity*
- beginning of the Human Genome Project to map the genetic make-up of the human species

### Historical events

- Poland: Lech Wałesa wins elections
- Soviet Union: Mikhail Gorbachev begins the process of democratic renewal
- East Germany holds its first democratic elections in 57 years
- South Africa: Nelson Mandela is freed, marking the end of apartheid
- Saddam Hussein invades Kuwait
- Germany: reunification takes place
- UK: Margaret Thatcher resigns as Prime Minister

# 1991

### Buildings completed

- FO Gehry, Chiat/Day Building, Los Angeles, California, USA, 1986–91
- R Koolhaas, Villa Dall'Ava, Paris, France, 1985–91
- P Eisenman, Rebstock Park, Frankfurt, Germany, development plan: 1990–1
- N Foster, Sackler Galleries, Royal Academy of Arts, London, UK, 1989–91
- Venturi, Scott Brown & Associates, Sainsbury Wing, National Gallery, London, UK, 1986–91

### Architecture: other important events

- Pritzker Prize awarded to R Venturi
- T Ito, contribution to 'Visions of Japan' exhibition, London

### The arts, literature, criticism, science, fashion and trends

- A Carter: *Wise Children*
- 'Dislocations' exhibition opens at the MoMA, New York
- J Demme: *The Silence Of the Lambs*
- Nobel Prize for Literature awarded to N Gordimer
- † Miles Davis, American jazz musician

### Historical events

- Iraq: Gulf War
- Gorbachev resigns
- creation of the European Union in Maastricht
- UK: two IRA bombs devastate Victoria and Paddington Stations in London

# 1992

### Buildings completed

- R Koolhaas, Kunsthal, Rotterdam, The Netherlands, 1987–92
- S Holl, Stretto House, Dallas, Texas, USA, 1990–2
- T Fretton, Lisson Galleries, London, UK, 1992
- † Ando, Contemporary Art Museum, Naoshima, Japan, 1988–92
- S Calatrava, Alamillo Bridge, Seville, Spain, 1987–92
- R Moneo, Atocha Train Station, Madrid, Spain, 1984–92

### Architecture: other important events

- 'House with No Style' competition, promoted by *Japan Architect*
- Pritzker Prize awarded to A Siza
- Zaha Hadid designs the exhibition entitled 'The Great Utopia: The Russian and Soviet Avant-Garde'
- † J Stirling, British architect

### The arts, literature, criticism, science, fashion and trends

- J Barnes: *The Porcupine*
- D Jarman: '*Wittgenstein* and *Blue* – Double Take' opens at The South Bank Centre in London
- opening of the 'Post Human' exhibition in Turin, Lausanne, Athens and Hamburg
- M Augé: *Non-lieux*
- Nobel Prize for Literature awarded to D Walcott
- inauguration of the Museo Nacional Centro de Arte Reina Sofía in Madrid
- † J Cage, American composer
- U2 begin their 'Zoo TV' Tour

### Historical events

- signing of the Maastricht Treaty, calling for the monetary union of Europe by 1999
- Italy: beginning of the *Mani Pulite* investigations
- USA: Bill Clinton elected President

# 1993

### Buildings completed

- FO Gehry, American Center, Paris, France, 1988–93
- M Fuksas, Musée des Graffiti, Niaux, France, 1988–93
- N Foster, Carré d'Art, Nîmes, France, 1987–93
- Herzog & de Meuron, Ricola Europe SA Factory, Mulhouse-Brunnstadt, France, 1992–93
- N Grimshaw, Waterloo International Terminal, London, UK, 1988–93

### Architecture: other important events

- Pritzker Prize awarded to F Maki
- AD issue 'Folding in Architecture' edited by Greg Lynn
- M Wigley: *The Architecture of Deconstruction*

### The arts, literature, criticism, science, fashion and trends

- J Demme: *Philadelphia*
- N Bobbio: *Destra e sinistra*

- A Tabucchi: *Sostiene Pereira*
- S Spielberg: *Schindler's List*
- Nobel Prize for Literature awarded to T Morrison
- † F Fellini, Italian film director
- Depeche Mode begin their 'Devotional' Tour

- George HW Bush and Boris Yeltsin sign the START II nuclear disarmament treaty
- birth of the Czech and Slovak Republics
- Bosnia: Serbian war crimes against Muslims
- USA: Rudolph Giuliani is elected Mayor of New York City

# 1994

## Buildings completed

- Z Hadid, Vitra Fire Station, Weil am Rhein, Germany, 1989–94
- G Behnish, Geschwister-Scholl-Schule, Römerstadt, Germany, 1992–4
- J Nouvel, Fondation Cartier, Paris, France, 1991–4
- A Siza, University Library, Aveiro, Portugal, 1988–94
- T Ando, Museum of Wood, Mikata-gun, Hyogo, Japan, 1991–4
- W Alsop, Hôtel du Département des Bouches-du-Rhône, Marseilles, France, 1990–4
- S Calatrava, TGV Station, Lyon, France, 1989–94
- R Piano, Kansai International Airport Terminal, Osaka, Japan 1988–94
- A Mendini, M De Lucchi, P Starck, Coop Himmelb(l)au, Groninger Museum, Groningen, The Netherlands, 1986–94

## Architecture: other important events

- Pritzker Prize awarded to C de Portzamparc
- B Zevi: *Architettura: concetti di una controstoria* and *Architettura della modernità*
- C Rowe: *The Architecture of Good Intentions*
- FL Wright exhibition opens at the MoMA in New York
- Bernard Tschumi introduces the Paperless Design Studios at Columbia University

## The arts, literature, criticism, science, fashion and trends

- P Auster: *Mr Vertigo*
- S Tamaro: *Va' dove ti porta il cuore*
- Q Tarantino, *Pulp Fiction*
- R Zemeckis: *Forrest Gump*
- The Rolling Stones begin their 'Voodoo Lounge' Tour
- Peter Gabriel begins his *Secret World* Tour
- Nobel Prize for Literature awarded to K Oe
- † C Bukowski, American poet
- † K Popper, Austrian philosopher

## Historical events

- Italy: the DC Political Party splits into two new parties; the Alleanza Nazionale rises from the ashes of the MSI Party; creation of the Forza Italia Party
- identification of the Top Quark Particle
- Israel and Jordan sign a Peace Treaty

- Nobel Peace Prize awarded to Yasser Arafat, Shimon Peres and Yitzhak Rabin

# 1995

## Buildings completed

- D Perrault, Bibliothèque Nationale de France, Paris, France, 1989–95
- G Domenig, GIG Headquarters, Völkermarkt, Carinthia, Austria, 1994–5
- Herzog & de Meuron, Signal Box 4, Auf dem Wolf, Basel, Switzerland, 1992–5
- M Fuksas, Maison des Arts, Bordeaux, France, 1992–5
- Mecanoo, Faculty of Economics and Management, Utrecht, The Netherlands, 1991–5
- E Ambasz, ACROS Building, Fukuoka, Japan, 1990–5

## Architecture: other important events

- 'Light Construction' exhibition opens at the MoMA in New York
- R Koolhaas, OMA, B Mau: *S,M,L,XL*
- C Jencks: *The Architecture of the Jumping Universe*
- K Frampton: *Studies in Tectonic Culture*
- Pritzker Prize awarded to T Ando

## The arts, literature, criticism, science, fashion and trends

- Christo wraps the Reichstag in Berlin
- D de Kerckhove: *The Skin of Culture*
- E Kusturica: *Underground*
- M Gibson: *Braveheart*
- signing of the Dogme95 film directors' manifesto in Copenhagen
- Nobel Prize for Literature awarded to S Heaney
- † E Cioran, Romanian philosopher
- † H Roth, American novelist

## Historical events

- implementation of the Schengen Treaties
- the USA imposes a Peace Treaty between Bosnia, Croatia and Serbia
- Internet connections exceed 3 million
- Israel: Yitzhak Rabin is assassinated in Jerusalem
- Japan: fanatical members of the 'Sublime Truth' sect release nerve gas in the Tokyo subway system

# 1996

## Buildings completed

- P Eisenman, Aronoff Center for Design and Art, Cincinnati, Ohio, 1991–6
- EO Moss, Samitaur Complex 1, Culver City, California, 1989–96
- R Koolhaas/OMA, Euralille, Lille, France, 1989–96
- P Zumthor, Thermal Bath Complex, Vals, Switzerland, 1994–6
- T Herzog, Exhibition Hall, Hanover, Germany, 1995–6
- R Viñoly, Tokyo International Forum, Japan, 1989–96

- B van Berkel & C Bos (UNStudio), Rijksmuseum Twenthe extension and renovation, Enschede, The Netherlands, 1992–6

Architecture: other important events

- B Tschumi: *Architecture and Disjunction*
- R Venturi: *Iconography and Electronics Upon a Generic Architecture*
- D Ghirardo: *Architecture after Modernism*
- Pritzker Prize awarded to R Moneo
- Venice Architecture Biennale curated by H Hollein
- 'Radical Architecture' exhibition presented at the Venice Biennale
- creation of the Stirling Prize, the first of which is awarded to S Hodder for his Centenary Building at the University of Salford, UK

The arts, literature, criticism, science, fashion and trends

- D Boyle: *Trainspotting*
- A Minghella: *The English Patient*
- † LJ Prieto, Argentinian linguist
- † M Mastroianni, Italian Actor
- Nobel Prize for Literature awarded to W Szymborska
- the hole in the ozone layer is estimated at 10 million square metres

Historical events

- the Russian Federation is admitted to the European Council
- UK: beginning of the Mad Cow Disease epidemic
- Italy: Romano Prodi is elected Prime Minister
- Palestine holds its first ever legislative and presidential elections
- Russia: Boris Yeltsin wins the presidential elections
- USA: Bill Clinton wins his second mandate
- Fidel Castro visits the Vatican
- Kofi Annan, born in Ghana, is elected Secretary General of the United Nations
- † François Mitterand, French politician

........................................................

# 1997

Buildings completed

- B Tschumi, Le Fresnoy art school, Tourcoing, France, 1992–7
- FO Gehry, 'Ginger & Fred', Prague, 1992–7
- T Mayne, Sun Tower, Seoul, Korea, 1994–7
- SANAA, N-Museum, Wakayama, Japan, 1995–7
- S Holl, Chapel of St Ignatius, Seattle, Washington, 1995–7
- R Piano, Fondation Beyeler, Basel, Switzerland, 1991–7
- MVRDV, WOZOCO Housing for the Elderly, Amsterdam, The Netherlands, 1994–7
- Neutelings Riedijk, Minnaert Building, Utrecht, The Netherlands, 1994–7
- R Koolhaas/OMA, Educatorium, Utrecht, The Netherlands, 1993–7
- FO Gehry, Guggenheim Museum, Bilbao, Spain, 1991–7
- Herzog & de Meuron, Dominus Winery, Yountville, California, 1995–7

Architecture: other important events

- D Libeskind: *Radix-Matrix*
- Pritzker Prize award to S Fehn
- M Wilford wins the Stirling Prize for his Music School in Stuttgart, Germany
- C Slessor: *Eco-Tech*

The arts, literature, criticism, science, fashion and trends

- A Yehoshua: *A Journey to the End of the Millennium*
- J Cameron: *Titanic*
- Andrew Wiles solves Fermat's Last Theorem
- Nobel Prize for Literature awarded to D Fo
- The Rolling Stones begin their 'Bridges to Babylon' Tour
- U2 begin their 'PopMart' Tour

Historical events

- Albania: political crisis
- UK: Tony Blair elected Prime Minister – Labour Party wins the elections after 18 years of Conservative government
- the *Pathfinder* lands on Mars
- The English return Hong Kong to the Chinese
- Iran: a moderate government wins elections in Iran
- USA: Madeleine Albright becomes the first woman to hold the position of Secretary of State
- Princess Diana is killed in a car accident in Paris
- Hong Kong: over one billion chickens are destroyed to avoid a potentially lethal epidemic of avian flu

........................................................

# 1998

Buildings completed

- R Koolhaas/OMA, House in Floriac, France, 1994–8
- B van Berkel & C Bos (UNStudio), Möbius House, Het Gooi, The Netherlands, 1993–8
- S Holl, Kiasma Museum, Helsinki, Finland, 1993–8
- R Piano, Jean-Marie Tjibaou Cultural Center, Noumea, New Caledonia, 1991–8
- A Siza, Portuguese Pavilion for Expo '98, Lisbon, Portugal
- Mecanoo, Delft Polytechnic Library, Delft, The Netherlands, 1993–8

Architecture: other important events

- H Ibelings: *Supermodernism*
- Pritzker Prize awarded to R Piano
- Foster and Partners win the Stirling Prize for their American Air Museum at the Imperial War Museum in Duxford, UK

The arts, literature, criticism, science, fashion and trends

- † Octavio Paz, Mexican writer
- J Madden: *Shakespeare In Love*
- Nobel Prize for Literature awarded to J Saramago

Historical events

- USA: beginning of impeachment procedures against President Bill Clinton
- Ireland is awarded the right to self-determination
- Germany: the Social Democrats win the elections

- Italy: Massimo D'Alema elected Prime Minister
- Pope John Paul II travels to Cuba
- first transplant of a human hand completed in France

..........................................................

# 1999

### Buildings completed

- J Pawson, Pawson House, London, UK, 1999
- D Libeskind, Jewish Museum, Berlin, Germany, 1988–99
- G Lynn, D Garofalo, M Mcinturf, Presbyterian Church, New York, USA, 1995–9
- Z Hadid, Landesgartenschau, Weil am Rhein, Germany, 1999
- N Foster, Reichstag, Berlin, Germany 1992–9
- M Hopkins, Dynamic Earth, Edinburgh, UK, 1990–9
- R Moneo, Kursaal Auditorium, San Sebastian, Spain 1990–9

### Architecture: other important events

- N Leach: *The Anaesthetics of Architecture*
- 'The Un-Private House' opens at the MoMA in New York
- Pritzker Prize awarded to N Foster
- Future Systems and Buro Happold win the Stirling Prize for their Lord's Media Centre, London
- re-opening of the renovated Reichstag in Berlin
- T Ito, *Blurring Architecture*
- EO Moss: *Gnostic Architecture*

### The arts, literature, criticism, science, fashion and trends

- S Mendes: *American Beauty*
- Nobel Prize for Literature awarded to G Grass
- P Almodóvar is named Best Director at the Cannes Film Festival for his *All About My Mother*

### Historical events

- introduction of the Euro (single European currency)
- Yugoslavia: beginning of NATO bombings (Allied Force Operation) to end the repression of the Albanian minority in Kosovo directed by the Serbian Nationalist Slobodan Milošević
- USA: significant demonstrations in Seattle against the World Trade Organisation
- Italy: birth of the No-Global Movement, also known as The People of Seattle
- Russia: President Boris Yeltsin resigns and is succeeded by Vladimir Putin

..........................................................

# 2000

### Buildings completed

- J Nouvel, KKL (Culture and Convention Centre), Lucerne, Switzerland, 1989–2000
- West 8, Borneo Sporenburg, Amsterdam, The Netherlands, 1996–2000
- MVRDV, Dutch Pavilion, Expo 2000, Hanover, Germany, 2000
- S Holl, Sarphatistraat Offices, Amsterdam, The Netherlands, 1996–2000
- R Rogers, Millennium Dome, London, UK, 1996–2000
- Herzog & de Meuron, Tate Modern, London, UK, 1994–2000

- FO Gehry, Experience Music Project, Seattle, Washington, USA, 1995–2000
- Alsop & Störmer, Peckham Library, London, UK, 1995–2000

### Architecture: other important events

- Hanover Expo
- Venice Architecture Biennale curated by M Fuksas
- H Ibelings, *The Artificial Landscape*
- Pritzker Prize awarded to R Koolhaas
- † E Miralles, Spanish architect
- † B Zevi, Italian critic
- Alsop & Störmer win the Stirling Prize for the Peckham Library, London

### The arts, literature, criticism, science, fashion and trends

- opening of the show to celebrate the new millennium and London's Millennium Dome designed by R Rogers on 1 January
- J-M Jarre presents his show to celebrate the new millennium at the Great Pyramids of Giza
- R Scott: *Gladiator*
- Nobel Prize for Literature awarded to G Xingjian
- Apple introduces the first version of the iPod
- the UK House of Lords authorises the cloning of human embryos for therapeutic purposes

### Historical events

- Spain: José María Aznar's Partido Popular wins political elections
- Israel and the PLO return to Camp David, USA for Peace Talks
- USA: the Republican George W Bush Jr narrowly wins presidential election

..........................................................

# 2001

### Buildings completed

- T Ito, Sendai Mediatheque, Japan, 1995–2001
- N Grimshaw, Eden Project, Cornwall, England, 1995–2001
- FO Gehry, DZ Bank Building, Berlin, Germany, 1995–2001

### Architecture: other important events

- Pritzker Prize awarded to Herzog & de Meuron
- Wilkinson Eyre, Buro Happold win the Stirling Prize for their Magna Centre in Rotherham, England

### The arts, literature, criticism, science, fashion and trends

- R Howard: *A Beautiful Mind*
- a legal sentence in the USA establishes that Napster, a program for downloading music from the Internet, is illegal and must be shut down
- at the World Climate Conference in Bonn, a secondary agreement saves the Kyoto Protocol. The United States reiterates its unwillingness to sign
- Nobel Prize for Literature awarded to VS Naipaul
- The Netherlands: the first civil marriage between homosexuals, for three gay and one lesbian couple, takes place in Amsterdam

- Greece adopts the Euro
- technology shares lose 111.41 points on Wall Street; it is the lowest point reached by NASDAQ since October 1998
- UK: Tony Blair's Labour Party is re-elected
- USA: Islamic terrorists hijack four commercial American aeroplanes to attack an equal number of targets, hitting three: the Pentagon in Washington and the Twin Towers in New York
- Nobel Peace Prize awarded to Kofi Annan

# 2002

## Buildings completed

- Foreign Office Architects, International Port Terminal, Yokohama, Japan, 1995–2002
- K van Velsen, Media Authority Building, Hilversum, The Netherlands, 2002
- Diller + Scofidio, Blur Building, Swiss Expo, Yverdon-les-Bains, Switzerland, 2002
- J Nouvel, The Monolith, Swiss Expo, Biel, Switzerland, 2002
- N Foster, City Hall, London, UK, 1998–2002
- SeARCH, Theehuis Pavilion, Veluwezoom National Park, Rheden, The Netherlands, 1998–2002

## Architecture: other important events

- Swiss Expo
- Pritzker Prize awarded to G Murcutt
- Venice Architecture Biennale curated by D Sudjic
- † A Castiglioni, Italian designer
- Wilkinson Eyre, Gifford win the Stirling Prize for their Gateshead Millennium Bridge, England

## The arts, literature, criticism, science, fashion and trends

- R Marshall: *Chicago*
- Nobel Prize for Literature awarded to I Kertész
- China inaugurates its first high-speed rail line (30km)

## Historical events

- Argentina defaults on its credits: bonds are declared bankrupt
- France: Jacques Chirac is re-elected President of the Republic
- Vladimir Putin and George W Bush sign a Strategic Nuclear Arms Reduction Treaty

# 2003

## Buildings completed

- FO Gehry, Walt Disney Concert Hall, Los Angeles, California, 1988–2003
- J Nouvel, Agbar Tower, Barcelona, Spain, 2000–5
- M Fuksas, Ferrari Headquarters, Maranello, Italy, 2000–3
- Herzog & de Meuron, Laban Dance Centre, Deptford, London, 1997–2003
- NL Architects, Basket Bar, Utrecht, The Netherlands, 2002–3

- P Cook and C Fournier (Spacelab), New Kunsthaus, Graz, Austria 2000–3
- Future System, Selfridges, Birmingham, UK, 1999–2003

## Architecture: other important events

- Pritzker Prize awarded to J Utzon
- Herzog & de Meuron: win the Stirling Prize for their Laban Dance Centre in Deptford, London
- Y Michaud: *L'art à l'état gazeux*

## The arts, literature, criticism, science, fashion and trends

- P Jackson: *The Lord of the Rings: The Return of the King*
- † Ilya Prigogine
- birth of the Mozilla Foundation
- Nobel Prize for Literature awarded to JM Coetzee
- Cape Town's Green Point Stadium hosts the '46664' humanitarian rock festival, sponsored by Nelson Mandela to sensitise the population to the devastating effects of AIDS; it is the largest musical event ever organised in South Africa

## Historical events

- the US invades Iraq
- Serbia and Montenegro separate
- China: SARS spreads across the country
- Poland: referendum on whether to join the European Union
- Cuba: the regime arrests 75 political dissidents

# 2004

## Buildings completed

- N Foster, Swiss Re Office Tower, London, UK, 1997–2004
- R Koolhaas/OMA, Seattle Central Library, Seattle, Washington, USA, 1999–2004
- T Mayne/Morphosis, Caltrans Offices, Los Angeles, USA, 2002–4
- T Ito, Tod's Omotesando Building, Tokyo, Japan, 2002–4
- Miralles Tagliabue, Scottish Parliament, Edinburgh, UK, 1998–2004
- W Alsop, Sharp Centre, Ontario College of Art & Design, Toronto, Canada, 2000–4
- SANAA (K Sejima + R Nishizawa), 21st Century Museum of Contemporary Art, Kanazawa, Japan, 1999–2004

## Architecture: other important events

- AMO/OMA, R Koolhaas: *Content*
- Pritzker Prize awarded to Z Hadid
- Venice Architecture Biennale curated by K Forster
- Foster and Partners and Arup win the Stirling Prize for the Swiss Re Building, London ('The Gherkin')
- D Libeskind, *Breaking Ground*

## The arts, literature, criticism, science, fashion and trends

- C Eastwood: *Million Dollar Baby*
- P Haggis: *Crash*
- † Susan Sontag, American writer
- Nobel Prize for Literature awarded to E Jelinek

- Russia: President Vladimir Putin signs the Kyoto Protocol on Global Warming; the protocol is thus effective as of 2005

- † Yasser Arafat in Palestine
- † Ronald Reagan, former President of the United States
- 10 new countries enter the European Union: Poland, Slovenia, Hungary, Malta, Cyprus, Latvia, Lithuania, Estonia, and the Czech and Slovak Republics
- USA: George W Bush obtains his second mandate

# 2005

### Buildings completed

- R Koolhaas/OMA, Casa da Música, Porto, Portugal, 1999–2005
- R Piano, High Museum of Art, Atlanta, Georgia, USA, 1999–2005
- R Piano, Zentrum Paul Klee, Bern, Switzerland, 1999–2005
- M Fuksas, Milan Trade Fair, Milan Italy, 2002–5
- Herzog & de Meuron, Allianz Arena, Munich, Germany, 2000–5
- Miralles Tagliabue, Santa Caterina Market, Barcelona, Spain, 1997–2005
- T Ito, Green Green, I-Project, Fukuoka, Japan, 2002–5

### Architecture: other important events

- Pritzker Prize awarded to T Mayne
- † K Tange
- Miralles Tagliabue win the Stirling Prize for the Scottish Parliament Building, Edinburgh
- R Moneo: *Theoretical Anxiety and Design Strategies in the Work of Eight Contemporary Architects*
- S Pollack: *Sketches of Frank Gehry*

### The arts, literature, criticism, science, fashion and trends

- Nobel Prize for Literature awarded to H Pinter
- 2005 Academy Awards: 5 Oscars for Martin Scorsese's *The Aviator* and 4 for *Million Dollar Baby* by Clint Eastwood
- Spain: homosexual marriages are recognised by law
- U2 present the 'Vertigo' Tour
- 'Live 8' benefit concerts

### Historical events

- † Pope John Paul II. J Ratzinger named Pope Benedict XVI
- UK: Prince Charles weds Camilla Parker Bowles
- USA: Hurricane Katrina devastates New Orleans
- † Prince Rainier III of Monaco
- UK: 4 terrorist attacks rock London, causing 55 deaths and leaving 700 wounded

# 2006

### Buildings completed

- Z Hadid, Phaeno Science Centre, Wolfsburg, Germany, 2000–6
- R Rogers, Terminal 4, Madrid Barajas Airport, Spain, 1997–2006
- S Holl, School of Art and Art History, Iowa City, Iowa, USA, 2000–6
- UNStudio, Mercedes-Benz Museum, Stuttgart, Germany, 2001–6
- Diller Scofidio + Renfro, Institute of Contemporary Art, Boston, Massachusetts, USA, 2000–6
- Neutelings Riedijk, Mediacentre, Hilversum, The Netherlands, 1999–2006
- Shigeru Ban, Travelling Museum, 2006

### Architecture: other important events

- Pritzker Prize awarded to P Mendes da Rocha
- Venice Architecture Biennale curated by R Burdett
- R Rogers wins the Stirling Prize for his Terminal 4 at the Barajas Airport in Madrid

### The arts, literature, criticism, science, fashion and trends

- M Scorsese: *The Departed*
- Nobel Prize for Literature awarded to O Pamuk
- 40th anniversary of 'Star Trek'

### Historical events

- Iraq: execution of Saddam Hussein
- † Augusto Pinochet, former dictator of Chile
- England: plot to hijack aeroplanes directed to the US uncovered in London

# 2007

### Buildings completed

- FO Gehry, IAC/InterActiveCorp Building, New York, USA, 2007
- J Nouvel, Musée du Quai Branly, Paris, France, 1999–2007
- R Piano, New York Times Building, New York, 2000–7
- T Ito, Mikimoto, Ginza 2, Tokyo 2004–7

### Architecture: other important events

- Pritzker Prize awarded to R Rogers

### The arts, literature, criticism, science, fashion and trends

- † M Antonioni, Italian film director
- † I Bergman, Swedish film director
- † L Pavarotti, Italian tenor
- Nobel Prize for Literature awarded to D Lessing

### Historical events

- Slovenia adopts the Euro
- the South Korean Ban Ki-moon replaces the Ghanaian Kofi Annan as Secretary General of the United Nations
- Northern Ireland holds elections for its Assembly

# 50 books, 10 of which are must-haves

## General Texts

Francisco Asensio, *New Architecture: An International Atlas*, Abrams (New York), 2007

A book for those seeking information on recent events. Beautiful photographs, accompanied by brief texts.

Francis Rambert, *Architecture Tomorrow*, Terrail (Paris), 2005

A general description, in four chapters, of recent architectural trends. For English readers, the author's French prose may be excessively literary. Optimum illustrations.

Aaron Betsky and Erik Adigard, *Architecture Must Burn: Manifestoes for the Future of Architecture*, Thames and Hudson (London), 2000

The book presents 27 manifestoes that investigate the poetics which animate contemporary architectural debate.

★ ★ ★ Charles Jencks and Karl Kropf (editors), *Theories and Manifestoes of Contemporary Architecture*, Academy Editions (London), 1997

An extremely well-organised collection of texts that deal with important architectural issues, from 1955 onwards.

Kate Nesbitt (editor), *Theorizing a New Agenda for Architecture: An Anthology of Architectural Theory 1965–1995*, Princeton Architectural Press (New York), 1996

For those who wish to know more and from various authors, after reading the books listed above.

....................................................

## Deconstructivism

Jacques Derrida and Peter Eisenman, *Choral Works*, edited by Jeffrey Kipnis and Thomas Leeser, The Monacelli Press (New York), 1997

A reconstruction of the (failed) collaboration between an architect interested in theoretical questions and the philosopher who invented Deconstruction.

Daniel Libeskind, *Radix-Matrix*, Prestel (Munich and New York), 1997

A hermetic and obscure Libeskind presents his own writings and Deconstructivist projects. It makes for interesting reading, even simply as an understanding of the intellectual quirks of the late 1990s.

Mark Wigley, *The Architecture of Deconstruction: Derrida's Haunt*, The MIT Press (Cambridge, MA), 1993

A difficult text. Recommended to those who enjoyed the texts listed above and wish to know more.

★ ★ ★ Bernard Tschumi, *Architecture and Disjunction*, The MIT Press (Cambridge, MA), 1996

A collection of writings that, even while dealing with relevant theoretical questions, can also be appreciated by readers without a significant understanding of philosophical arguments. It is very good at explaining the connections between theory and design.

Jeffrey Kipnis, 'Forms of Irrationality', in John Whiteman, Jeffrey Kipnis and Richard Burdett (editors), *Strategies in Architectural Thinking*, The MIT Press (Cambridge, MA), 1992

How can we move beyond rationality? This is the interesting question that the author, a theoretician involved in contemporary architectural discussion, has tried to answer.

....................................................

## The Metropolis and its Contradictions

Rem Koolhaas (editor), *Content: Perverted Architecture*, Taschen (Cologne, London, Madrid, New York, Paris and Tokyo), 2004

What design approach is to be taken in the contemporary metropolis that refuses any idea of order? A eulogy to kitsch that continues where Venturi, Scott Brown and Izenour left off in their famous homage to the fascination of Las Vegas (*Learning from Las Vegas*, 1972).

Rem Koolhaas, Stefano Boeri, Sanford Kwinter, Daniela Fabricius, Hans Ulrich Obrist and Nadia Tazi, *Mutations*, Actar and Arc en rêve centre d'architecture (Barcelona), 2000

An investigation, in some instances photographic, of the mutations of the contemporary city over the last 10 years.

Nan Ellin (editor), *Architecture of Fear*, Princeton Architectural Press (New York), 1997

A collection of writings by various authors that describes the state of the art in terms of changes to the form of the city, caused by fear and a growing desire for security: against theft, violence and attacks.

★ ★ ★ William J Mitchell, *City of Bits: Space, Place, and the Infobahn*, The MIT Press (Cambridge, MA and London), 1995

For those looking to understand how the digital revolution is changing the city, this is the book to read.

Marc Augé, *Non-Places: Introduction to an Anthropology of Supermodernity* (Verso, London, 1995), translated by John Howe from *Non-lieux: Introduction à une anthropologie de la surmodernité*, Seuil (Paris), 1992

Non-places are those spaces around the world that are repeated and continually the same: hotels, shopping centres, railway stations and airports. This is the first book that seeks to understand the changes faced by society through an analysis of these non-places.

......................................................

## Blob and Digital Architecture

★ ★ ★ *Architectural Design*, 'Folding in Architecture', guest-edited by Greg Lynn, 1993; revised edition, 2003

A historic issue, recently re-edited by *AD* magazine, which takes us to the origins of blob architecture, as described by a few of its protagonists.

John K Waters, *Blobitecture: Waveform Architecture and Digital Design*, Rockport Publishers (Gloucester), 2003

A very useful and didactic text for understanding what blobs are and what produced them.

Christian Pongratz and Maria Rita Perbellini, *Nati con il computer: Giovani architetti americani* Testo&Immagine (Turin), 2000. Published in English as *Natural Born CAADesigners: Young American Architects*, Birkhäuser (Basel, Boston and Berlin), 2000

An analysis of the generation of architects for whom the computer has become more than a simple instrument that substitutes the traditional drafting table.

Robert Venturi, *Iconography and Electronics Upon a Generic Architecture: A View from the Drafting Room*, The MIT Press (Cambridge, MA and London), 1996

Electronic pixels will change architecture in exactly the same way that mosaic tiles change Byzantine architecture.

William J Mitchell, *e-topia: 'Urban Life, Jim – But Not As We Know It'*, The MIT Press (Cambridge, MA and London), 1999

For those who have read *City of Bits*, this sequel introduces us to some relevant architectural questions in the digital age.

......................................................

## Minimalism

★ ★ ★ Anatxu Zabalbeascoa and Javier Rodrígues Marcos, *Minimalisms*, Editorial Gustavo Gili (Barcelona), 2000

For the authors of this easy-to-read book, there exist many forms of Minimalism.

Francisco Asensio, *The Architecture of Minimalism*, Arco for Hearst Books (New York), 1997

An informative book, primarily due to the use of images.

Iñaki Ábalos and Juan Herreros, *Áreas de impunidad/Areas of Impunity*, Actar (Barcelona), 1997

A presentation of one of the most interesting couples from the contemporary Spanish panorama through a collection of their writings and projects. The result is a Minimalist approach reminiscent of Supermodernism.

Vittorio E Savi and Josep María Montaner, *Less Is More. Minimalisme en arquitectura i d'altres arts/Minimalism in Architecture and the Other Arts*, Col-legi d'Arquitectes de Catalunya and Actar (Barcelona), 1996

The two authors of this book see Minimalism as antithetical to the confusion of Deconstructivism. The book features an optimum bibliography of texts on Minimalism.

Rodolfo Machado and Rodolphe el-Khoury, *Monolithic Architecture*, Prestel (Munich and New York), 1995

This exhibition catalogue is one of the first to have relaunched Minimalism within architectural debate, at the time monopolised by discussions of complexity.

......................................................

## Supermodernism, Technology and Nature

William W Braham and Jonathan A Hale (editors), *Rethinking Technology: A Reader in Architectural Theory*, Routledge (London and New York), 2007

This is an anthological collection of writings by 19th-century authors interested in the relationship between architecture and technology.

★ ★ ★ Hans Ibelings, *Supermodernism: Architecture in the Age of Globalization*, NAi Publishers (Rotterdam), 1998

Supermodernism is the opposite of Deconstructivism, recovering the simplicity of the Modern Movement, and moving in the direction of Minimalism.

Bart Lootsma, *Superdutch: New Architecture in the Netherlands*, Thames and Hudson (London), 2000

For those who wish to know more about Dutch architecture in the late 1990s.

Catherine Slessor, *Eco-Tech, Sustainable Architecture and High Technology*, Thames and Hudson (London), 1997

In this well-illustrated book, Slessor analyses the Eco-Tech movement, the ecological evolution of High Tech.

Charles Jencks, *The Architecture of the Jumping Universe – A Polemic: How Complexity Science is Changing Architecture and Culture*, Academy Editions (London), 1995

Jencks investigates the relationship between the sciences of complexity that study the evolution of nature and the forms produced by the most creative architects of the late 1990s.

## Landscape, Ecology and Nature

Paola Gregory, *Territori della complessità: New Scapes*, Testo&Immagine (Turin), 2003. Published in English as *New Scapes: Territories of Complexity*, Birkhäuser (Basel, Boston and Berlin), 2003

What has changed in our conception of the landscape? Why does the majority of current architectural research deal, in more or less explicit terms, with this precise theme?

Hans Ibelings (editor), *The Artificial Landscape: Contemporary Architecture, Urbanism, and Landscape Architecture in the Netherlands*, NAi Publishers (Rotterdam), 2000

This book uses contributions from various critics to demonstrate how the Dutch, a people with very few natural landscapes, are progressively more oriented towards an architecture focused on the construction of the artificial landscape.

★ ★ ★ James Wines (author) and Philip Jodidio (editor), *Green Architecture*, Taschen (Cologne, London, Madrid, New York, Paris and Tokyo), 2000

This book uses a vast range of case studies to analyse the various ways in which the most interesting contemporary architects have inserted the theme of nature within their buildings.

Kenneth Yeang, *Bioclimatic Skyscrapers*, Artemis (London), 1994

The precursor of ecological skyscrapers, Yeang's theories anticipated much of what is now taking place in this field of design.

Sim van der Ryn and Stuart Cowan, *Ecological Design*, Island Press (Washington DC), 1996

For those who want to know more about the theme of ecological design and its origins in the writings of the scientist and philosopher Gregory Bateson.

## The Skin, the Envelope and Perception

★ ★ ★ Steven Holl, Juhani Pallasmaa and Alberto Pérez-Gómez, *Questions of Perception: Phenomenology of Architecture*, William Stout Publishers (San Francisco), 2006

A book that sets out the reasons why we must design not only to create visual pleasure, but to satisfy all five senses.

Toyo Ito, *Blurring Architecture*, Charta (Milan), 1999

In the world of digital media, the boundaries between the building and the world tend to disappear. This exhibition catalogue demonstrates how Toyo Ito confronts this issue in some of his most important projects, including the Sendai Mediatheque.

Charles Jencks, *Ecstatic Architecture*, Academy Editions (London), 1999

The special effects of much of contemporary architecture also refer to the more ancient traditions of ecstatic architecture.

Daniela Colafranceschi, *Sull'involucro in architettura. Herzog, Nouvel, Perrault, Piano, Prix, Suzuki, Venturi, Wines*, Edizioni Librerie Dedalo (Rome), 1996

Interviews with the protagonists of the movement investigating the theme of the skin and superficial effects that examine why this approach is now so important in architectural debate.

Daniela Colafranceschi, *Architettura in superficie. Materiali, figure e tecnologie delle nuove facciate urbane*, Gangemi Editore (Rome), 1995

One of the first investigations that analyses the reasons for the growing interest amongst architects for superficial effects.

## Philosophy, Art and Aesthetics

Yves Michaud, *L'art à l état gazeux: Essai sur le triomphe de l'esthétique*, Éditions Stock (Paris), 2003

Why does modern art progressively resemble advertising? Why is the world an increasingly more aestheticised place?

Jean Baudrillard and Jean Nouvel, *The Singular Objects of Architecture*, University of Minnesota Press (Minneapolis), 2002

A philosopher who has focused on the theme of the simulacrum speaks with an architect enchanted by the theme of transparency.

★ ★ ★ Derrick de Kerckhove, *L'architettura dell'intelligenza*, Testo&Immagine (Turin), 2001. Published in English as *The Architecture of Intelligence*, Birkhäuser (Basel, Boston and Berlin), 2003

Is it possible for an architecture of intelligence to exist in a digital culture? The answer is provided by this disciple of Marshall McLuhan, the most important contemporary media scholar.

Neil Leach (editor), *Rethinking Architecture: A Reader in Cultural Theory*, Routledge (London and New York), 1997

A good anthology of texts that deal with questions balanced between philosophy, the arts, science and architecture.

Paul Virilio, *The Aesthetics of Disappearance*, Semiotext(e) (New York), 1991

Does the contemporary aesthetic lead towards the dissolution of the object? If the answer is yes, what are the consequences for the body?

## The Star System

*Al Manakh*, a special issue of *Volume* (no 12) edited by Ole Bouman, Mitra Khoubrou and Rem Koolhaas on the occasion of the International Design Forum Dubai, 27 to 29 May 2007

In Dubai, where the Star System is now hard at work, our way of looking at and designing the city is changing. It would be a serious error, in the opinion of Rem Koolhaas, to under-evaluate these transformations.

Daniel Libeskind, *Breaking Ground: Adventures in Life and Architecture*, John Murray Publishers (London) and Riverhead Books (New York), 2004

Under the pretext of writing an autobiography, Libeskind tells the behind-the-scenes story of some of his projects, above all Ground Zero. The result is an unflattering portrayal of many of the exponents of the Star System.

★ ★ ★ Neil Leach, *The Anaesthetics of Architecture*, The MIT Press (Cambridge, MA and London), 1999

A tough and articulate accusation of an architecture focused exclusively on special effects.

Gabriella Lo Ricco and Silvia Micheli, *Lo spettacolo dell'architettura*, Bruno Mondadori (Milan), 2003

The first analysis of the formation of the Star System and its techniques of communication.

OMA, Rem Koolhaas and Bruce Mau, *S,M,L,XL*, The Monacelli Press (New York) and 010 Publishers (Rotterdam), 1995

This book became a cult object, even amongst those not directly involved in the profession, launching Koolhaas into the firmament of the Star System.

## Critical and Neo-Traditionalist Positions

★ ★ ★ Rafael Moneo, *Theoretical Anxiety and Design Strategies in the Work of Eight Contemporary Architects*, The MIT Press (Cambridge, MA), 2005. Also published simultaneously in Spanish (Actar) and Italian (Electa)

Through an examination of the work of eight contemporary architects or firms – Venturi, Scott Brown & Associates, James Stirling, Aldo Rossi, Peter Eisenman, Álvaro Siza, Frank O Gehry, Rem Koolhaas and Herzog & de Meuron – Moneo describes an eclectic framework that permits different architectural trends.

Ada Louise Huxtable, *The Unreal America: Architecture and Illusion*, The New Press (New York), 1997

This book is a clear declaration by one of the most influential American critics, against the architecture of images and spectacle.

Kenneth Frampton, *Studies in Tectonic Culture: The Poetics of Construction in Nineteenth and Twentieth Century Architecture*, The MIT Press (Cambridge, MA), 1995

The return to tectonics appears to Kenneth Frampton as one of the paths that may allow architecture to rediscover its concrete and material qualities.

Roger Scruton, *The Classical Vernacular: Architectural Principles in an Age of Nihilism*, Carcanet (Manchester), 1994

Praise for the historical methods of composition, in opposition to Modern architecture, the fruit of a culture of nihilism.

Charles, Prince of Wales, *A Vision of Britain: A Personal View on Architecture*, Doubleday (London and New York), 1989

Prince Charles, whose primary counsellor is the Post-Modernist Leon Krier, describes his desire for a harmonious architecture that does not sever its ties with the past.

# INDEX

Figures in italics indicate captions. Index does not include the footnotes.

Aalto, Alvar *88*, 109, 171
Ábalos & Herreros *215*
Acconci, Vito *212, 213*
Adriaan Geuze & West 8 104
Ahrends, Burton & Koralek 60
Aix-en-Provence, France:
  Centre Choréographique
  Nationale *216*
Alicante, Spain
  Centro de Gímnasia Ritmica
  y Deportiva 76, *77*
  University Rectorate 171
Alsop, Will *46, 56, 99, 100,*
  *102, 169*, 213-14, *214*
Alsop & Stormer *169*
Ambasz, Emilio 157-8, *158*,
  159, 211
Amersfoort, Netherlands:
  Villa Wilbrink 105
Ammar Eloueini Digit-all
  Studio (AEDS) *217*
AMO *192*, 197
Amsterdam
  Borneo Sporenburg *144*
  housing project (Koolhaas)
  125-6
  IJ Plein neighbourhood 15
  Sarphatistraat Offices *165*,
  166
  WOZOCO Housing for the
  Elderly *108*, 142
Ando, Tadao 54-5, *55, 69, 90,*
  170, 171-2, 201
Archigram 12, 14, 127, 153,
  213
Architectures Jean Nouvel 79
Archizoom Associati 125
Arets, Wiel 104, 112, 142
Asymptote 68, 167-8, *167*
Atlanta, Georgia: High
  Museum of Art *192*
Aveiro, Portugal: University
  Library *88*, 171

Baldeweg, Juan Navarro *91*
Ban, Shigeru 135, 138, 139,
  *217*, 218
Bangkok, Thailand: Octospider
  Cafeteria, Satin Textile Co.
  Ltd. *218*, 220, 222
Barcelona, Spain
  Agbar Tower *210, 211*
  Barcelona Pavilion 97
  Forum 2004 building 209
  Meteorological Centre in the
  Olympic Village *61*
  requalification of waterfronts
  188
  Santa Caterina Market 160,
  *160*
Basel, Switzerland
  Auf dem Wolf signal building
  50
  caricature museum, St Alban
  Vorstadt 85
  Fondation Beyeler 102-3, *103*
  Pharmaceutical Research
  Centre, Basel Hospital *156*,
  157, *157*
  Schützenmattstrasse
  apartments 50-51, 83
  Signal Box 4, Auf dem Wolf
  84, *85*
  signal tower 84, 86
  SUVA Apartment Building
  50, 83-4
Baumschlager & Eberle *150*
Behnisch, Günter *75*, 150-51
Beijing
  China Central Television
  (CCTV) Headquarters *203, 203*
  Olympic Stadium 201
  Sino Italian Ecological and
  Energy Efficient Building
  (SIEEB) *224*
Berlin
  City Edge 19, *19*
  DZ Bank Building *160*, 162-3

GSW Headquarters *110*
IBA complex 14-15
Jewish Museum 45, 64, 129-
  32, *131, 132*, 193
Kurfürstendamm office
  building 15
Potsdamer Platz 57, 103-4,
  154-5
Reichstag 56, 100, 152, *154*
Schültenstrasse block 61
Sony Centre 103
Virtual House 165
Bern, Switzerland: Zentrum
  Paul Klee *190*
Best supermarkets 18
Bezons, France 79
Biel, Switzerland
  The Monolith, Swiss Expo
  2002 185, 186-7, *187*
  steel towers, Arteplage,
  Swiss Expo 2002 185
Bilbao, Spain
  Guggenheim Museum 40, *41*,
  64, 68-9, *68*, 117-23, *118*,
  *119, 121, 123*, 129, 132, 162,
  187, 193, 211
  Ponte Bianco 159
Birmingham, England:
  Selfridges department store
  212, *213*
Bonn Parliament 150
Bordeaux, France: Maison des
  Arts *90*
Bos, Caroline 140
Boston, Massachusetts:
  Institute of Contemporary Art
  208, 209-10
Botta, Mario 61-2
Bowman, Obie 148
Boxtel Police Station,
  Netherlands 142
Breamlea, Victoria, Australia:
  Carter/Tucker House 148
Brentwood, California:

Schnabel Residence 39
Bruder, William 148, 149
Buckminster Fuller, Richard
  14, 34, 153, *154*, 185
Burgee, John 17
..................................
Calatrava, Santiago 48, 49, 55,
  56, *57, 59*, 98, 100, *100*, 105,
  129, 159
California: Stage Set Design
  for John Jasperse Company
  *217*
Cambridge: University of
  Cambridge Faculty of Law
  99, *99*
Candela, Felix 56
Carate, Brianza, Italy:
  sculpture garden 158
Carinthia, Austria: GTG
  Headquarters, Völkermarkt *73*
Cattani, Emmanuel 79
Chareau, Pierre 82, 128, 136
Chattanooga, Tennessee:
  park 158
Chatwin, Bruce (London
  apartment, renovation by
  Pawson) 51
Chipperfield, David 51, *87*,
  188, *218*
Chu, Karl S 168, *170*
Cincinnati, Ohio
  Aronoff Center for Design and
  Art *68*, 110
  Contemporary Arts Center 71
Cleveland, Ohio: Lewis House
  164
Columbus, Ohio: Wexner
  Center for the Arts 16
Connell, Amyas 136
Cook, Peter 213, *214*
Coop Himmelb(l)au 9, *9*, 10,
  12, 16, *18*, 19, 21, 44, 44, 72,
  78, *79*, 122-3, 185, 186, 187
Copenhagen, Denmark:

Maritime Youth House 220, 223
Cornette, Benoit 73
Cornwall, Connecticut: House VI 138
Cornwall, England: Eden Project 153, 154
Cranbrook, Bloomfield Hills, Michigan: Williams Natatorium 173
Cucinella, Mario 224
Culver City, California
Beehive/Annex 73
Box 73
Pittard Sullivan Building 73
Samitaur Complex 1 72, 73
Samitaur Complex 2 73
Wedgewood Holly Complex 73, 164
Cutler, James 148
. . . . . . . . . . . . . . . . . . . . . . . . . .
Dallas, Texas: Stretto House 47-8, 48
Dax, France: Les Thermes Hotel and Spa 52
De Hoge Veluwe Park, Netherlands 105
De Lucchi, Michele 78, 79
Decq, Odile 73
Delft, Netherlands: Polytechnic Library 142, 142, 143, 145
Derrida, Jacques 16, 20, 21, 65
Des Moines, Iowa: Public Library 218
Digital House, The (project for 'The Un-Private House' exhibition) 135, 136
Diller + Scofidio 67-8, 136, 185, 186, 187
Diller Scofidio + Renfro 208, 209-10
Doha, Qatar: Museum of Islamic Arts 158
Domenig, Günter 73, 75, 76
Don Benito, Spain: House of Culture 173
Dream Team 182, 183, 184
Dreams (Ito) 25
Duffy, Roger 182
Duisburg, Germany: Microelectronics Park 99
Dutch Parliament extension 13
Duthilleul, Jean-Marie 92
. . . . . . . . . . . . . . . . . . . . . . . . . .
Edinburgh
Dynamic Earth 154
Scottish Parliament 76, 159-60
Eichstätt, Germany: Catholic

University library 150
Eindhoven, Netherlands: OfftheRoad...5Speed, project for prefabricated housing 147
Eisenman, Peter 9, 9, 16, 17, 19, 20, 21, 38, 42-4, 45, 66, 68, 95, 96, 110, 138, 164, 165, 182, 184, 186, 194, 199
Elciego, Spain: Marqués de Riscal Winery 211
Eloueini, Ammar 168
Embryological House (Greg Lynn) 167, 167
Enschede, Netherlands: Rijksmuseum Twenthe extension 105
European Court of Human Rights (Strasbourg) 100
Exposure Architects 218, 220, 222
. . . . . . . . . . . . . . . . . . . . . . . . . .
Fairfield Corner, Connecticut: Raybould House 96
Familian house (Los Angeles) 19
Farnsworth House (Plano, Illinois) 86, 125, 137
Fernández-Galiano, Luis 109-10
Floriac, near Bordeaux, France: house by Koolhaas 124-8
Foreign Office Architects 139, 145, 145
Foster, Norman 57, 58, 59, 99, 99, 110, 129, 151, 152, 154
Foster & Partners 152, 182, 183
Fournier, Colin 213, 214
Frampton, Kenneth 109, 170, 187
Franchini, Gianfranco 102, 127
François, Edouard 158, 222
Frankfurt, Germany
Rebstock Park 45, 66
University of Frankfurt: Biocentre 16, 17, 19
Freear, Andrew 219
Fretton, Tony 51-2, 52
Frey, Konrad 75
Fuksas, Massimiliano 46-7, 47, 90, 129, 174-5, 205, 206-7, 206, 213
Fukuoka, Japan
ACROS Building 158, 158
apartments 48, 125
Grin Grin, I-Project 201-2, 201
Il Palazzo Hotel 61

Future Systems 153, 153, 212, 213
. . . . . . . . . . . . . . . . . . . . . . . . . .
Garofalo, Douglas 167, 168
Gastines, Jean de 218
Gaudí, Antoni 75
Gehry, Frank O 9, 9, 10, 15-16, 15, 19, 21, 37-40, 38, 39, 41, 64, 66, 67, 68-9, 68, 77, 83, 117-23, 118, 119, 121, 123, 129, 132, 160, 162-3, 162, 164, 194, 199, 204, 210-11, 210, 223
Geneva, Switzerland: United Nations Library 165
Genoa, Italy
Columbus International Exposition 57, 57
port 154
Gerngross, Heidulf 75
Geuze, Adriaan 105
Giencke, Volker 75
Gifu, Japan: Slither Housing 209
Gigon, Annette 85
Godi, Oliviero 218
Godsell, Sean 148
Graham, Dan 82
Grassi, Giorgio 103
Graz, Austria: New Kunsthaus 213, 214
Gregotti, Vittorio 61, 62
Grimshaw, Nicholas 57, 68, 99, 99, 153
Groningen, Netherlands
Glass Pavilion 54, 54
Groninger Museum 78-9, 79, 122-3
Music Video Pavilion 29
Guadalajara, Mexico: Children's Museum 164-5
Günter Behnisch & Partner 149-50
Guthrie + Buresh 135
Guyer, Mike 85
Gwathmey, Charles 182, 184
. . . . . . . . . . . . . . . . . . . . . . . . . .
Hadid, Zaha 9, 9, 11, 12-15, 19, 21, 28-31, 29, 30, 68-72, 69, 70, 71, 129, 160, 160, 188, 208-9, 208, 223
Hafner, Bernhard 75
Hague, The
City Hall and Central Library 62-3
dance theatre 15
Dutch Parliament extension 13
The Hague Villas 29, 30
Hamburg Skyline 19

Hanover, Germany
Dutch Pavilion for Expo 2000 145, 147
Exhibition Hall 96
Expodach for Expo 2000 149, 151
Japanese Pavilion, Expo 2000 218
Swiss Pavilion, Expo 2000 150
United States' Pavilion, Expo '98 158
Hara, Hiroshi 110
Hariri & Hariri 135, 135, 136, 136
Hasegawa, Itsuko 110
Hejduk, John 13, 131
Helsinki, Finland: Kiasma Museum 166, 166
Henley on Thames, Oxfordshire: River and Rowing Museum 87
Herne-Sodingen, Germany: Training Academy 151
Hérouville-Saint-Clair, France: Europe Tower 46
Herzog, Thomas 96, 149, 150, 151
Herzog & de Meuron (Jacques Herzog and Pierre de Meuron) 48-51, 49, 82-5, 83, 84, 85, 86, 88, 112, 115, 129, 135, 136, 156-7, 156, 189, 198, 199-200, 199, 200, 201, 201, 209
Het Gooi, Netherlands: Möbius House 105, 139, 142
Hilversum, Netherlands
Media Authority Building 143
Mediacentre 212-13, 213
Royal Dutch Paper Mills Headquarters 63
Villa VPRO 106, 142
Holl, Steven 47-8, 48, 87, 88, 88, 112, 135, 165, 166, 166, 182, 184, 205
Hollein, Hans 60
Hong Kong
Bank of China 62, 63
Hongkong and Shanghai Banking Corporation Headquarters 59
Hopkins, Michael 57, 99, 154
Houston, Texas
Menil Museum 56
Museum of Fine Arts 174
Huesca Sports Facility, Spain 76
. . . . . . . . . . . . . . . . . . . . . . . . . .
Ian Ritchie Architects 99
Igualada Cemetery, Spain 76

Iowa City, Iowa: School of Art and Art History 205
Isozaki, Arata 25, 61, 104
Ito, Toyo 23-8, *24*, *25*, 54, *55*, 96-8, 110, 111, 113, 115, *115*, 122, 139, 155-6, *155*, *156*, 157, 201-2, *201*, *202*
..............................

Jackson, Wyoming: Teton County Library 149
Jahn, Helmut 103
Jakob + MacFarlane 96, *96*
Jencks, Charles 94, 95
Johnson, Philip 9, 16-18, 20, 136, 164-5
Jourda, Françoise-Hélène 151
..............................

Kada, Klaus 75
Kahn, Louis 172
Kanazawa, Japan: 21st Century Museum of Contemporary Art 214-15, 218
Kansai International Airport, Japan: passenger terminal 57
Karlsruhe: Zentrum für Kunst und Medientechnologie 32-3, *33*
Kawagoe, Japan: the 'Naked House' 218
Kishy, Waro 139
Klagenfurt, Austria: Hypo Alpe Adria Centre 163, 164, 205
Klotz, Mathias 216
Kolatan/MacDonald 96, 168
Kollhoff, Hans 104
Koolhaas, Rem 9, *9*, 10, 13, *13*, 15, 19, 21, 29, 32-6, *32-7*, 38, 46, 55, 91-3, 104, 105, *106*, 112-13, 122, 124-9, 133, 135, 139, 143, 176, 189, 191, 192, 197, 199, 200, 202-3, *203*, 209, 212, 223
Koolhaas, Rem/OMA *66*, *92*, *93*, *104*, *113*, *125*, *126*, *127*, *202*, *203*
Kovatsch, Manfred 75
Kuma, Kengo 217
Kumamoto, Japan: Saishunkan Seiyaku Women's Dormitory 55, *55*
Kyoto, Japan: Miho Museum 63
..............................

La Jolla, California: Neurosciences Institute 90
Las Palmas de Gran Canaria: Multifunctional Building 215
Laufen, Switzerland: Ricola Warehouse 49-50, *49*
Le Corbusier 15, 35, *35*, 63,

*88*, 109
Libeskind, Daniel 9, *9*, 16, 19, *19*, 21, 38, 44-5, 64, 129-32, *129*, *131*, *132*, *180*, 181-4, *182*, 188
Lille, France
  Euralille 92-3, *92*, *93*, 200
  Congrexpo 92, 93, *93*
  Crédit Lyonnais tower 92
  Shopping Centre 80, 92, *92*
  TGV station 92, 93
  World Trade Centre 92
Maison Folie de Wazemmes 216
Lisbon: Portuguese Pavilion, Expo '98 171, *172*
London
  24 Cathcart Road apartment building 29
  Channel 4 Headquarters 59, *98*, 100
  City Hall *151*, 152, *152*
  Eco-House, Islington *218*, 219-20
  Habitable Bridge 71, *71*
  Jubilee Line extension 99
  Laban Dance Centre, Deptford 189, *198*, 199-200, *199*, *200*
  Lisson Galleries 51-2, *52*
  Millennium Dome *153*
  Pawson House *87*
  Peckham Library *169*
  Sackler Galleries, Royal Academy of Arts 57-8, *58*
  Sainsbury Wing, National Gallery 60, *60*
  Swiss Re Office Tower 152, *152*
  Tate Modern 157, *157*
  Victoria and Albert Museum: Boilerhouse Extension 71
  Waterloo International Terminal 99, *99*
Loos, Adolf 109
Los Angeles
  Caltrans Offices 204-5, *204*
  Cathedral of Our Lady of the Angels 174, 204
  Getty Center/Museum 120, 163
  Science Center School 205
  Walt Disney Concert Hall 40, *68*, 204, 211
Louviers, France: housing 222
Lubecca, Germany: Schleswig-Holstein Regional Insurance Centre 150
Lucas, Colin 136
Lucerne, Switzerland
  Culture and Convention Centre (KKL) 82, 133-4, *133*,

*134*
  Station Hall 56
Lupo, Frank 136
Lynn, Greg 45, 65, 66-7, 94, 95, 139, 165, 167, *167*, *168*, 175, 191-2
Lyon, France
  Opera House 79
  TGV station 100, *100*
..............................

Maastricht, Netherlands: Bonnefanten Museum 61
MacCormac Jamieson Prichard 99
Mcinturf, Michael 167, *168*
Madrid
  Atocha Train Station *60*
  Gregorio Marañón Hospital 174
  Regional Documentary Centre *215*
  Terminal 4, Madrid Barajas Airport *207*
Mahon, Spain: Mahon Courthouse *91*
Malmö, Sweden: Secret Garden 145
Mansilla+Tuñón Arquitectos *215*
Maranello, Italy: Ferrari Headquarters *206*
Marble, Scott 66-7
Marne-la-Vallée, France: École Supérieure d'Ingénieurs en Électronique et Électrotechnique (ESTEE) 52
Marseilles, France: Hôtel du Départment des Bouches-du-Rhône ('Le Grand Bleu') 100, *102*
Mason Bend, Alabama: Lucy's House 219
Matta-Clark, Gordon 18
Mayne, Thom 72, 73, 163-4, 204-5, *204*
Mecanoo *106*, *107*, 142, *142*, *143*
Meier, Richard 62-3, 120, 163, 182, *184*, 191-2, *192*
Melbourne, Australia: Kew House 148
Melun, France: Law Courts 151
Mendini, Alessandro 78-9, *79*
Mérida, Spain: National Museum of Roman Art 172-3
Metz, France: Pompidou Centre 218
Mies van der Rohe, Ludwig 15, 17, 35, *35*, 82, 85, 86, 91, 97, 124, 125, 128, 136, 137

Mikata-gun, Hyogo, Japan: Museum of Wood *90*
Milan
  Linate Airport extension 61
  Milan Trade Fair 205, 206-7, *206*
  Teatro Armani 172
Milwaukee, Wisconsin: Art Museum extension 159
Miralles, Enric 76, *77*, 159-60, *160*
Miralles Tagliabue 159, *160*
Mizrahi, Dorit 218
Mockbee, Samuel 219
Moneo, Rafael *60*, 61, 62, 104, 109, 117, *170*, 172-4, 189, 198-9, 204, *215*
Morphosis 72-3, *75*, 76, 163, *204*, 205
Moss, Eric Owen 72, 73, 75, 164
Motosu, Gifu Prefecture, Japan: Gifu Kitagata Apartment Building 216
Moussavi, Farshid 145
Mulhouse-Brunstatt, France: Ricola Europe factory 83, *83*, 84, *84*
Munich
  Allianz Arena 201, *201*
  Goetz Fallery 50
  Olympiapark 150
Murcia, Spain: City Hall 173-4
Murcutt, Glenn 148
MVRDV 104, 105, *106*, *108*, 135, 142, 143, 145, *147*
..............................

Nanterre, France: Highway Bridge and Control Centre *73*
Nantes, France: City of Justice 82
Naoshima, Japan: Contemporary Art Museum *55*, *75*
Neeltje Jans, Netherlands: Water Pavilion and Interactive Installation, Delta Expo 'Waterland' 96, 105, *108*
Neutelings Riedijk *106*, 142, 212-13, *213*
Nevada desert: Spring House 17
New Canaan, Connecticut: Glass House 17
New Haven, Connecticut: psychiatric centre 39
New Visions 182
New York
  42nd Street Hotel 70-71

Advanced Trading Floor Operations Center, New York Stock Exchange *167*
AT&T Tower 17
Brasserie Restaurant, Seagram Building 209
DE Shaw & Co Office and Trading Area 48
Dunescape Installation at PS1 *169*
Guggenheim Museum *34*, 117, 122
IAC/InterActiveCorp Building *210*, *211*
Jay Chiat Offices 77, *77*, *78*
MoMA extension 112-13, *113*, 115, *115*, 117, 122
MoMA gardens pavilion 218
New York Times Building *189*
Presbyterian Church 166-7, *168*
Project for Ground Zero *180*, 181-5, *182*, *183*, *184*
Seagram Building 17
Staten Island Institute of Arts 96
Statue of Liberty *180*, 181
Technology Culture Museum, Manhattan 167-8
Twin Towers 178, 181, 183, 224
West Side Masterplan *168*
New York 4 *see* Dream Team
Newbern, Alabama: Fire Station 219
Niaux, France: Musée des Graffiti 46-7, *47*
Niemeyer, Oscar 14
Nîmes, France: Carré d'Art *58*, 59, 99
Nishizawa, Ryue *86*, 214-15, 217, *218*
NL Architects 220, *222*
Noisey-le-Grand, France: Saint-Exupéry College 46
Nomad Restaurant (Roppongi, Japan) 110
Nomadic Museum (Shigeru Ban) 218-19
Noumea, New Caledonia: Jean-Marie Tjibaou Cultural Center 57, 103, 154, *155*
Nouvel, Jean 22, 23, *23*, 46, 52, 79-80, *80*, 86, 92, *92*, 129, 133-4, *133*, *134*, 185, 186-7, *187*, *210*, 211-12, *211*, *212*
Novak, Marcos 67
NOX 96, 104, 105, *108*, *147*, 216

OCEAN NORTH 169
Okawabata River City, Tokyo: *Egg of Winds* 25
Old Chatham, New York: Torus House *137*
Oldenburg, Claes 15, *15*
OMA *106*, 192, 197
*see also* Koolhaas, Rem/OMA
Oporto School of Architecture, Portugal *91*
Orlando, Florida
Disney Building 61
Walt Disney Headquarters 61
Osaka, Japan: Kansai International Airport Terminal *101*, 102
Otto, Frei 150, 218

Pallasmaa, Juhani 87-8
*Pao I* installation (Ito) 24
*Pao II: Dwelling for Tokyo Nomad Woman* installation (Ito) 24
Paris
American Center 16, 39, *39*
Bibliothèque Nationale de France 32, *32*, 52, 54, 202
Canal+ Headquarters 63, *63*
Centre Pompidou *59*, 101, 117, 127, 202
Cité de la Musique 61, *62*
Fondation Cartier 52, 80-82, *80*, 86, 133, 187
Hôtel Industriel Jean-Baptiste Berlier 52, *52*, 54
îlot Candie Saint-Bernard 46
Institut de Recherche et Coordination Acoustique/ Musique (IRCAM) 56-7
Institut du Monde Arabe 22, 23, *23*, 187
Jussieu Library *66*, 202
Louvre expansion 122
Louvre pyramid 63
Maison de Verre 128
Melun-Sénart museum 16
Musée du Quai Branly 211-12, *211*, *212*
Parc de la Villette 10, 12, *12*, *13*, 16, 19, 20, 41, 46
Restaurant Georges, Centre Pompidou 96, *96*
Tour Sans Fin, La Défense 52
University Library 27-8
Villa Dall'Ava 15, 35, *35*, 125
Pawson, John 51, *87*
Peak, The, Hong Kong 10, *11*, 12, 19, 29
Pei, IM 62, *62*, 63, 122
Pembrokeshire, Wales: house

(Future Systems) 153, *153*
Perraudin, Gilles 151
Perrault, Dominique 52, *52*, 54, 112, 189
Perrella, Stephen 139
Pesce, Gaetano 77, *77*, *78*
Peterson/Littenberg Architecture 182
Phoenix, Arizona: Central Library 149
Piano, Renzo 56-7, *57*, *59*, 101-4, *101*, *103*, 127, 129, 154-5, *155*, 160, 189, *189*, *190*, 191-2, *192*
Pikionis, Dimitris 109
Pinós, Carme 76, *77*
Piranesi, Giovanni Battista 172
PLOT 220, *223*
Poissy, France: Villa Savoye 35
Pomona, California: Diamond Ranch High School 163-4
Porto, Portugal
Casa da Música *202*, 203
Santa Maria Church 171
Serralves Foundation 171
Portzamparc, Christian de 61, *62*, 92, *92*
Potsdam, Germany: Riehl House 124
Prague: Dutch National Bank headquarters ('Fred & Ginger') 39, *67*, 211
Preston Scott Cohen 135, *137*, 168
Price, Cedric 14, 100

Rashid, Hani 66-7, 175
Reiser + Umemoto 168, *168*
Renfro, Charles *208*, 209-10
Rezé, France: Culture Centre and Media Library 46
Rheden, Netherlands: Theehuis Pavilion, Veluwezoom National Park 220, *220*
Ricciotti, Rudy *216*
Richter, Helmut 75
Riehen, Switzerland: Koechlin house 85
Ripoll, Spain: Devesa 56
Ritchie, Alan 164
Roche, François 158
Rogers, Richard 57, 59, *59*, 98, 100, 102, 104, 110, 127, 129, *153*, 191-2, 207, *207*
Rome
Contemporary Arts Centre 160
Parca della Musica

Auditorium 154, 155, 160
Römerstadt, Germany: Geschwister-Scholl-Schule *75*, 150
Ronchamp, France: Notre Dame du Haut 88
Rossi, Aldo 61, 131, 194, 199
Rotondi, Michael 72
Rotterdam
Apartment Building and Observation Tower 19
Erasmus Bridge 105
housing project 125
KPN Telecom Tower 189
Kunsthal 36-7, *36*, *37*
Megabioscoop 106
patio houses 15
Schouwburgplein 105, *105*, 106
Rowen, Daniel 136

Saarinen, Eero 56
Saee, Michele 164
St Louis, France: Pfaffenholz Sports Centre 50, *50*, 51, 83, 84
St Petersburg, Russia: Mariinsky Cultural Centre 164, 189
St Veit/Glan, Austria: Funder 3 factory 44
Salerno, Italy
judicial buildings 188
maritime station 188
Salford, Lancashire: Trinity bridge 100
Salford Quays, near Manchester
Imperial War Museum North 188
The Lowry 188
San Francisco
De Young Museum 201
US Federal Building 205
San Giovanni Rotondo, Italy: church of Padre Pio 57
San Sebastian, Spain
Auditorium and Conference Centre *170*, 174
Kursaal 189
SANAA (Kazuyo Sejima + Ryue Nishizawa) *86*, 218
Santa Barbara, California: Blades Residence 73
Santa Monica, California
Edgemar Development 39
Gehry's home 9, *10*, 19, 38
house addition (Frank O Gehry) 223
Santiago, Chile: Faculty of

Economy, Diego Portales University 216
Santiago de Compostela, Spain
City of Culture of Galicia 164, 165
Faculty of Science and Information 171
Sapporo, Japan: Monsoon Restaurant 28-9, 30, 69
Sarah Wigglesworth Architects 218
Sarajevo, Bosnia-Hercegovina: Concert Hall 159, 169
Sauerbruch Hutton 110
Scofidio, Ricardo 185
Scogin, Mack 137
Scott, Sir Giles Gilbert 157
Scott Brown, Denise 60
Scottsdale, Arizona: Museum of Contemporary Art 149
Sea Ranch, California: Brunsell Residence 148
SeARCH 220, 220
Seattle, Washington
Central Library 202-3, 203
Chapel of St Ignatius 88, 88
Experience Music Project 162, 162
Sejima, Kazuyo 55, 55, 86, 110, 139, 214-17, 218, 220
Sendai Mediatheque, Japan 26, 98, 155-6, 155, 156
Seoul, South Korea
Seoul Performing Arts Centre 212, 213
Sun Tower 72-3, 75, 205
Seville, Spain
Alamillo Bridge 56, 59
Arabian Pavilion, Expo 1992 158
Kuwait Pavilion for Expo '92 56
Shanghai: Z58 Offices and Showroom 217
Shinohara, Kazuo 110
SHoP 169
SITE 18
Siza, Álvaro 61-2, 61, 69, 88, 91, 170-71, 172, 172, 199
Skidmore, Owings & Merrill (SOM) 181, 182, 184
Smithson, Alison 12
Smithson, Peter 12
Spacelab 214
Stanstead, Essex: London Stanstead Airport 58, 59
Starck, Philippe 78, 79
Steidle, Otto 46
Stimmann, Hans 162
Stirling, James 110, 194, 199,

200
Stockholm: Moderna Museet (Museum for Modern Art) 174
Strasbourg, France: Human Rights Tribunal 59
Stuttgart, Germany: Mercedes-Benz Museum 223, 224
Superstudio 125
Sydney, Australia: Aurora Place Office and Residential Buildings 154, 155
Szyszkowitz-Kowalski 75

Tagliabue, Benedetta 76, 159, 160
Tange, Kenzo 110
Taniguchi, Yoshio 112, 115, 115
Tatlin, Vladimir 31
Taut, Bruno 12
THINK group 182, 183, 183, 184
Tokyo
Century Tower 59
City Hall 110
House in a Plum Grove 215
Imperial Hotel 110
Kabuki-cho Tower 59
LVMH Headquarters, Omotesando 217
Mikimoto, Ginza 2 201, 202
Prada Aoyama Epicentre 200, 201
Tod's Omotesando Building 201, 202
Tokyo Forum 59, 59
Tokyo International Forum 100-101, 100
Toronto
BCE Place Gallery 100
Sharp Centre, Ontario College of Art & Design 213-14, 214
Tourcoing, France: Le Fresnoy art school 41, 42, 43
Tours: Congress Centre 79-80
Travelling Museum (Ban) 217
Treviso, Italy: Benetton Research Centre 172
Tschumi, Bernard 9, 9, 10, 12, 12, 13, 16, 19, 20, 38, 41, 42, 43, 43, 46, 54, 66, 112, 113, 113, 115, 122, 135, 139
Tsien, Billie 90, 112, 173
Tsuna-gun, Hyogo, Japan: Awaji-Yumebutai International Conference Center 172
Tugendhat House (Brno, Czech Republic) 128

U House (Tokyo) 110
UFO 159, 169
United Architects 182-3
UNStudio 104, 105, 105, 135, 139-43, 139, 140, 141, 223, 224
Utrecht, Netherlands
Basket Bar 220, 222
Educatorium 104
Faculty of Economics and Management 106, 107
Minnaert Building 106, 142
Utzon, Jørn 56

Valencia, Spain: City of the Arts and Sciences 159
Vals, Switzerland: Thermal Bath Complex 88, 88, 90
van Berkel, Ben 140
van Berkel & Bos (UNStudio) 104, 105
Vasconi, Claude 92, 92
Velsen, Koen van 104, 105-6, 143
Venhoeven, Ton (Venhoeven CS) 104, 106
Venice, California: Chiat/Day Building 15, 15, 77, 162
Venturi, Robert 60
Venturi, Scott Brown & Associates 60, 60, 199
Vesima, Italy: UNESCO Research Laboratories 57
Vienna
Apartment Building 19
apartment complex (Vienna2) 10
Falkestrasse: rooftop remodelling 6 19, 44, 44, 187
Haas Haus 60
residential building 18
Ronacher Theatre 16
Villa Mairea (Noormarkku, Finland) 109
Villeret, Switzerland: Cartier factory 52
Viñoly, Rafael 100-101, 100, 112, 182, 183, 184
Virtual Guggenheim Project 167

Wageningen, Netherlands: IBN Institute for Forestry and nature Research 150-51
Wakayama, Japan: N-Museum 86
Wang, Nonchi 168
Ward, Basil 136
Washington DC: Pentagon 178
Wayzata, Minnesota: Winton

Guest House 38-9, 38
Weil am Rhein
Landesgartenschau 160, 160, 208
Vitra Design Museum 15-16, 37-8, 41, 66, 211
Vitra factory 15-16
Vitra Fire Station 29, 68-70, 69, 70, 208
West 8 105, 105, 144, 145
West Cambewarra, New South Wales, Australia: Arthur & Yvonne Boyd Education Centre 148
Wigglesworth, Sarah 218, 219-20
Wilford, Michael 188
Williams, Tod 90, 112, 173
Wines, James 157-8, 159
Winterthur, Switzerland: extension to Art Museum 85
Wolfsburg, Germany: Phaeno Science Centre 208-9
Wolfurt (Innsbruck), Austria: Bank of Tyrol and Vorarlberg 150
Wright, Frank Lloyd 34, 110, 117, 122, 123, 137

X...Phylox project (Karl S Chu) 170

Yamagata, Japan: Asahi Shimbun Yamagata Building 220
Yamamoto, Riken 111
Yokohama, Japan
house designed by Shinohara 110
International Port Terminal 145, 145, 147
Tower of the Winds 23-4, 24
Yountville, California: Dominus Winery 157, 157
Yverdon-les-Bains, Switzerland: Blur Building, Swiss Expo 2002 185, 187, 209

Zaera Polo, Alejandro 145
Zeebrugge, Belgium: Sea Trade Centre 33, 34
Zumthor, Peter 49, 88, 88, 90, 150
Zurich, Switzerland: Stadelhofen Station 56, 57